MAMMOTH CAVE SALTPETER WORKS

By

Angelo I. George

H.M.I. Press
2005

Mammoth Cave Saltpeter Works

H.M.I. Press
P. O. Box 5426
Louisville, Kentucky 40255

ISBN 0-9713038-2-7

Printed in the United States of America

Cover: Vestibule of Mammoth Cave and the Rotunda Saltpeter processing center. Diana Emerson George photograph.

DEDICATION

James Warren Davis (1922-2004), M.D., was a well-known Louisville neurologist, poet laureate, inspirational role model, and life long family friend. He fostered a deeper desire to conduct research; and always lent a knowing ear to my latest discoveries associated with Kentucky's pioneer medical men.

Following in the footsteps of Arne Saknussemm, cavers push into the unknown. Wood engraving from Jules Verne's *Voyage au Centre de la Terre*, Edouard Riou illustrated edition (1863).

Engraving of Gothic Avenue in Mammoth Cave. *Supplement to the London News*, October 7, 1876.

Table of Contents

CHRONOLOGY

AGE OF GUNPOWDER, CHINA 605 A.D.

DECLARATION OF INDEPENDENCE, USA 1776

FORMATION COMMONWEALTH OF KENTUCKY 1792

1798 - Discovery of Mammoth, Great Saltpetre and Wyandotte caves.

September 14, 1798 - Valentine Simons purchased 200 acres by contract (not deed) containing two known saltpeter caves on Green River. Mammoth Cave and Dixon Cave known as saltpeter caves.

SALTPETER REPROCESSING FACTORIES OF E. I. Du PONT AND GEORGE HUNTER 1802

c. 1802 - Simons sells by contract (not deed) to John Flatt the 200 acres of land with the saltpeter caves. Mammoth Cave was then called Big Cave, changed to Flatt's Cave.

1804-1807 SALTPETER PRICE INCREASES

Price increases related to war in Europe, dependence on imported saltpeter, few domestic saltpeter factories and powder mills.

FIRST GUNPOWDER FROM E. I. Du PONT 1804

1806 - Discovery of Big Bone Cave, Tennessee.

Pre 1808 - George, Leonard and John McLean purchases by contract (not deed) Flatt's Cave and a small saltpeter cave later called Dixon Cave within the original 200 acres.

1808 - Charles Wilkins brokers saltpeter.

1808 - Archibald Miller, Sr., resident Mammoth Cave worker and possible saltpeter maker.

January 22, 1808 - Charles S. Morton purchases by contract (not deed) 44 acres containing the small saltpeter cave from the McLean brothers for $600.00. Morton subcontracts the mining to John and Henry Dixon. The cave is now known as Dixon Cave.

EMBARGO ACT 1807

DOMESTIC SALTPETER PRICE INCREASE 1808-1814

NON-INTERCOURSE ACT 1809

January 1, 1810 - Fleming Gatewood, Sr. and Charles Wilkins purchase 156 acres containing Flatt's Cave and change its name to Mammoth Cave. Gatewood is manager and saltpeter maker. Miller is saltpeter maker. Miller's brother-in-law John Holten is overseer in the cave.

1811 - DuFour style vats in Mammoth Cave.

NEW MADRID EARTHQUAKES 1811-1812

Mammoth and Great Saltpetre caves' industrial machinery damaged by earthquakes. Saltpeter production disrupted throughout the region.

April 13, 1812 - Fleming Gatewood, Sr., sells his share in cave to Hyman Gratz.

DECLARATION OF WAR WITH ENGLAND 1812

NAPOLEON RULES MOST OF EUROPE

1816-1816 - Archibald Miller, Sr., superintendent and saltpeter maker.

April 20, 1813 - Charles S. Morton sells Dixon Cave by contract (not deed) to Gratz and Wilkins.

Late 1813 - Gratz stages hostile take over of Wilkins' share in Mammoth Cave.

End 1813 - Mammoth Cave closes its door as a major producer.

1814 - Charles Wilkins purchases Gatewood's Salt Petre Cave.

INTERRUPTION OF EXPORT OF SALT & SALTPETER FROM INDIA 1814-1817

RATIFICATION OF TREATY OF GHENT February 16, 1815

END OF THE WAR OF 1812 February 17, 1815

Peacetime, economic recession and depression 1815-1829.

1816 - End of saltpeter mining and start of tourist era in Mammoth Cave.

1816-1827(?) - Archibald Miller, Sr., caretaker and manager of tourist cave.

September 1827 - Death of Charles Wilkins.

June 28, 1828 - Hyman Gratz purchases Wilkins half interest in the cave from heirs. Miller and family move off the property.

mid 1828 - Fleming Gatewood, Sr., and family move to cave as manager, guide and caretaker of tourist cave.

1829 - Free Frank's (possibly Burton or Kelley) Saltpeter Cave, Pulaski County, is last known cave in Kentucky commercially mined for saltpeter.

October 1835 - Gatewood and family move away as new management takes control of the estate.

1836-1837 - Robinson Shackleford and Archibald Miller, Jr., lease cave. Archibald Miller Sr., part of the family unit and one of the guides.

April 17, 1838 - Franklin Gorin and A. A. Harvey purchase the cave. Gorin installs Stephen Bishop as guide. Miller, Jr. retained as manager along with family members as guides. Mat and Nick Bransford, bondsmen from Glasgow, Kentucky, are rented from Thomas Bransford.

October 8, 1839 - John Croghan purchases the cave.

MEXICAN WAR 1844-1848

1848 - Miller, Jr., retires because of ill health and dies the following year.

CHRISTIAN F. SCHÖENBEIN INVENTS GUN COTTON 1848

January 11, 1849 - John Croghan dies of Tuberculosis. Cave placed in trust for Croghan heirs.

LAMMOT Du PONT INVENTS SODA POWDER 1857

AMERICAN CIVIL WAR 1861-1865

Caves mined by Southern Confederacy, none in Kentucky.

ALFRED NOBEL INVENTS DYNAMITE 1866

J. F. E. SCHULTZE INVENTS SMOKELESS POWDER 1867

FRANCIS G. AND PIERRE S. Du PONT REINVENT SMOKELESS POWDER 1893

WRIGHT BROTHERS *FLYER III* AIRPLANE 1905

BIRTH OF MODERN AIR AGE

WORLD WAR I 1914-1917

1914 - DuPont diversifies into synthetic chemicals, ultimately becomes one of the largest multinational corporations.

BIRTH OF ROCKET AGE 1926

WORLD WAR II 1939-1945

BIRTH OF ATOMIC AGE

July 1, 1941 - Formation of the Mammoth Cave National Park under the guidance of the National Park Service.

September 18, 1946 - Dedication of Mammoth Cave National Park.

SPUTNIK LAUNCED INTO SPACE 1957

FIRST MAN ON THE MOON 1969

Sources:

Harold Meloy, 1973, Introduction to the Reprint Edition of *Rambles in the Mammoth Cave*, Johnson Reprint, Corp. Oliver Shackleford, n.d. An Account of the History of Mammoth Cave During the Middle Nineteenth Century by Oliver Shackleford, One of the Guides. Typewritten copy in Mammoth Cave Office Library. Samuel W. Thomas, E. H. Conner and Harold Meloy 1970. A history of Mammoth Cave, emphasizing tourist development and medical experimentation under Dr. John Croghan. *The Register of the Ky. Hist. Soc.*, 68 (4): 319-340.

PREFACE

Mammoth Cave Saltpeter Works came together as a desire to tell the story of the last six years (1810-1816) of the pioneer mining and business history of Mammoth Cave. Against the historical tapestry of Mammoth Cave are overlain geological discussions interwoven with engineering detail of artifacts in the cave. Hundreds of articles have been written about Mammoth Cave with enough redundancy to draw inferences from those early times. Newspaper and travelogue writers preserved oral traditions carried on by the early cave guides. These secondary sources are used with some caution in the absence of primary documentation (hand-written documents) composed near the time of an event. Primary and secondary documentation from the first twenty years in the pioneer life of the cave is rare. One always wants more information about the cave. Even though an extensive bibliography was assembled to write this book, there are significant gaps in our knowledge of the cave's history requiring conjecture, inference, and comparison with other industries with similar working conditions and methodologies.

Owners of Mammoth Cave before tourist-cave promoter John Croghan are best characterized as mystery men. These people seem to exist without a past except for brief references in scattered court documents and land transfers. The person we know the least about is Fleming Gatewood, Sr. He appears on the scene as a master saltpeter maker from Louisville, Kentucky. Where he learned his trade is unknown. Immediately south of the town was the earliest known industry in the state, the salt brine operations at Mann's and Bullitt's Lick that extended south to Shepherdsville along Salt River. Making saltpeter is not much different than making salt from brine, with the addition of a chemical exchange step. As operations manager at Mammoth Cave, Gatewood used the most advanced French technology to purify saltpeter to military grade. Nothing is known of Gatewood's correspondence, and letters written by his partner Charles Wilkins rarely mention Mammoth Cave. This is a major disappointment, because Wilkins had a multifaceted personality, a true savant when it came to making money. Wilkins was only in the saltpeter business seven years (1808-1815), although his salt brine investments spanned a longer time period and generated greater capital.

To paint a picture of what it was like to live and work in the Mammoth Cave saltpeter works, I have made comparisons with the similar salt brine industry. By my estimation, in 1813 more than 120 people were employed in the Mammoth Cave saltpeter operation, working two shifts of 12 hours each. By Kentucky standards, the equivalent of a large town existed around and in the cave. The cave was one of the largest nitrate mines in America, in the same league as Great Saltpetre Cave, Rockcastle County, Kentucky, and Big Bone Cave in east central Tennessee. Pioneer mining of Mammoth Cave area saltpeter caves was big business at a time when a workman's wages were only $12-15 a month. The $50,000 invested in the Mammoth Cave saltpeter works might seem small until factored in today's dollars as $704,000. There is not enough information to provide an estimate of the profit returned on this investment, but certainly Mammoth Cave was a wealth generator for its owners. Like many new business ventures, the Mammoth Cave mine works suffered its share of operational problems, including manufacturing and management difficulties, labor strikes, shipping delays, resource depletion, and natural disasters.

The work in Chapter Five on Dixon Cave was originally published in the *Journal of Spelean History*. Significant refinements and additions have been made, fleshing out certain ideas associated with the transfer of saltpeter technology from France. The writing of the manuscript was a learning process; as the story unfolded it soon became clear that events at Dixon Cave were critical to the saltpeter mining history of Mammoth Cave.

As part of my research, I visited a number of French saltpeter mining sites during the 1980s. One of these is in a remarkable village west of Paris called La Roche Guyon. This is a very special place, with an enchanting atmosphere that attracted Impressionist artists Braque, Pissarro and Picasso, as well as Monet before he moved on to Giverny just down the road. The place is full of underground chalk quarries, which in the past were mined for saltpeter and sometimes used today as troglodyte homes. Only two weeks after my return to the states in 1989, I came across, to my astonishment, the story of "Rosalie" and her lover William Short. Rosalie's husband, the Duc de La Rochefoucauld, conducted saltpeter experiments in these quarries on regenerative nitrification, which, through William, led to a connection with Mammoth Cave, Dixon Cave and Short Cave manufacturing. Short Cave is named for William's brother Peyton, its owner and operator of the mine works there. This "French connection" is also an important part of the Mammoth Cave story.

Mammoth Cave Saltpeter Works was sidetracked until a baseline of historical continuity could be produced with the publication of *Saltpeter Empires of Great Saltpetre Cave and Mammoth Cave* along with *Outer Door to the Auger Hole ... and Beyond, the Exploration of Wyandotte Cave*. Great Saltpetre Cave is the engineering prototype of a modern saltpeter factory used years later in Mammoth Cave. By comparison, Wyandotte Cave was a smaller operation whose owners had close family ties to Charles Wilkins and Fredrick Ridgely. *Mammoth Cave Saltpeter Works* is the third part of a trilogy covering the development of the pioneer saltpeter industry in Kentucky, Indiana, and to a lesser extent, Tennessee.

ACKNOWLEDGMENT

Kind appreciation is extended to Mr. Richard E. Hand for comments and field assistance in the cave over the years. Mammoth Cave National Park gave permission to study pre-1816 saltpeter industrial technology in Mammoth Cave, and I am grateful to the Cave Research Foundation for field support. My mentor, the late Mr. Robert E. McDowell, editor of *The Filson Club History Quarterly*, introduced me to Kentucky's salt brine industry and the wonders of history research.

I thank my caving companions who helped with the on-site Dixon Cave investigation, especially: Mrs. Diana Emerson George, Mr. Laurence McCarty, Mr. James Patrick Stephens, the late Mr. Frank Reid, Mr. Alex Hicks and Mrs. Jenny Bramstedt Hicks. Dr. Carol Hill and Mr. Marion O. Smith read early drafts of the Dixon Cave chapter and offered technical suggestions for its improvement.

The American Philosophical Society provided assistance in securing historical manuscripts and maps of Mammoth Cave and gave permission to quote and reprint their Mammoth Cave map. The Hagley Museum and Library has always been helpful in locating saltpeter related manuscripts and maps of Mammoth Cave, and gave permission to publish their copy of the Mammoth Cave map. The Wisconsin Historical Society gave permission to publish the Daniel Drake map of Mammoth Cave. The National Cave Museum at Diamond Caverns, Kentucky, gave permission to reprint photographs of early Mammoth Cave guides. The Filson Club; University of Louisville Medical Library; Department of Library Special Collections, Manuscripts, Western Kentucky University, Bowling Green, Kentucky; Louisville Free Public Library; and the National Ground Water Association Library provided invaluable assistance over many years on the saltpeter mining history in Kentucky and Indiana.

Mr. William S. Liebman is an engineering geologist, specializing in earthquake remediation of buildings and homes in California. He offered ideas as to how strong earthquakes affect wood structures. This helped to better identify New Madrid earthquake damage in Mammoth Cave on pioneer artifacts.

Mrs. Suzanne Perkins Allen translated French text appearing in the encyclopedias of Buffon and Diderot covering saltpeter regeneration experiments conducted by Louis-Alexandre Duc de La Rochefoucauld. She also secured documents central to the interpretation of the French connection in Chapter Six.

Mr. Gordon Smith is owner of Marengo Cave, part owner of Diamond Caverns and exhibitor of Wyandotte Cave, three of the oldest commercial caves in America. To him I owe sincere appreciation for allowing me access to his Mammoth Cave speleological collection. He saved me hundreds of travel miles and thousands of hours searching out obscure documentation used in this work.

My life long friend, Dr. Gary A. O'Dell, Assistant Professor of Geography, Department of Geography, Government, and History, Morehead State University, offered suggestions, rewrote sections for clarification and creatively edited the manuscript. He was instrumental in so many different ways during the course of this investigation and writing; I am forever grateful for all his work in making the book a cornerstone in spelean history research on Mammoth Cave.

Dr. Amanda M. Hunt, Assistant Professor of Geology, University of Cincinnati, offered comments on Chapter Three.

Mr. Laurence McCarty, part owner of Diamond Caverns, Kentucky, one of my best caving companions, was instrumental in taking me to most of the saltpeter caves in Kentucky, significant examples in Indiana, and a few in Tennessee. He also proofread the manuscript and offered suggestions for its improvement.

My wife, Diana Emerson George, produced photo documentation of saltpeter artifacts, accompanied me in the field, and provided assistance in immeasurable ways. She gave editorial guidance and orchestrated the publication of this book.

Figure 1-1. Woodcut engraving of Gorin's Dome by landscape artist and early French balloonist Albert Tissandier. He explored Mammoth Cave in 1885. *Six Mois aux États-Unis*, G. Masson, Paris, (1886).

CHAPTER ONE

MAKING SALTPETER IN MAMMOTH CAVE

"The Mammoth Cave is the most extraordinary and stupendous vault in the known world."
Nahum Ward, 1816

From about 1798 into 1816, Mammoth Cave was used as a saltpeter mine. Visitors to the Historic Section in Mammoth Cave are able to view a cross section of pioneer engineering and industrial chemical ingenuity. Relics from the saltpeter mining industry are visible in Houchin's Narrows, Rotunda, Methodist Church and Booth's Amphitheatre (Figure 1-2). As ownership and circumstances changed, so did the method of saltpeter extraction. In early 1810 there was a major alteration in saltpeter leaching construction from simple V-vats to the introduction of large nearly square hoppers (Figure 2-1). These state-of-the-art hoppers were augmented with hand bored hollow log pipelines to convey fresh water to leaching vats processing areas, and a hydraulic pumping system transported leachate called beer or liquor through a second pipeline to evaporation furnaces located on the surface. Merchant and part owner Charles Wilkins of Lexington, Kentucky, is considered the visionary responsible for engineering the saltpeter technology seen today in the cave. Ironically, the cave ceased to be a major producer at the close of 1813, just as the War of 1812 was heating up.

Gunpowder is made from a mixture of sulfur, charcoal and saltpeter. Saltpeter (potassium nitrate) is the oxidizing agent that puts the *bang* in gunpowder. Limestone caves were the principal source of calcium nitrate that had to be chemically converted with wood ash (potash) to yield saltpeter. Sandstone rockshelters contained pure potas-

1

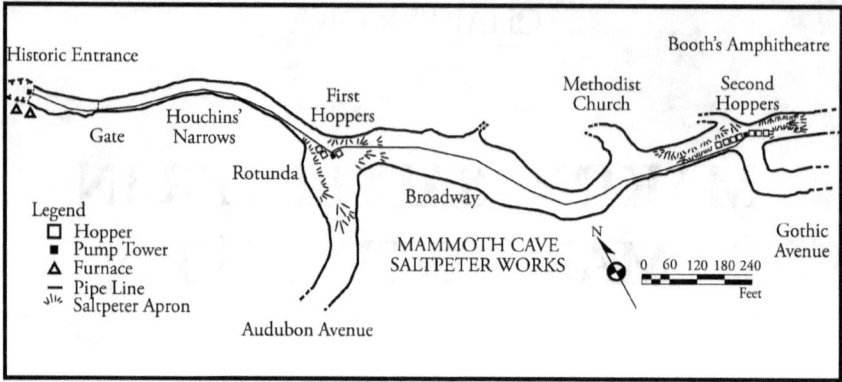

Figure 1-2. Location of saltpeter machinery in the Historic Section of Mammoth Cave.

sium nitrate from native sandstone and did not need to be chemically converted. Saltpeter is an all-encompassing term used interchangeably in this book for the raw product before and after processing. From approximately 605 AD up to 1848, black gunpowder was the strongest and most powerful explosive known.

Black powder was an indispensable commodity in America, with the best quality imported from France and England. Availability and manufacture of gunpowder and saltpeter were governed by political events that affected international trade. When trade was normal, America did not need to manufacture saltpeter, because this material could be cheaply imported from India and later South America. Production of domestic saltpeter became a significant American industry only during the Revolution, War of 1812 and breakaway Southern Confederacy during the Civil War. Over a twenty five-year period (1790-1815) America became more self-sufficient as saltpeter and gunpowder production became strategic industries.

On the Kentucky frontier far inland from east coast markets, pioneer settlers, backwoodsmen and explorers made do from what the land could provide. Two indispensable commodities needed on the western frontier were salt and gunpowder. Stockades and settlements sprang up along game trails near intersections with salt licks and springs. Caves and sandstone rockshelters were excavated and processed for saltpeter, first for personal use. By 1802, saltpeter and gunpowder manufactur-

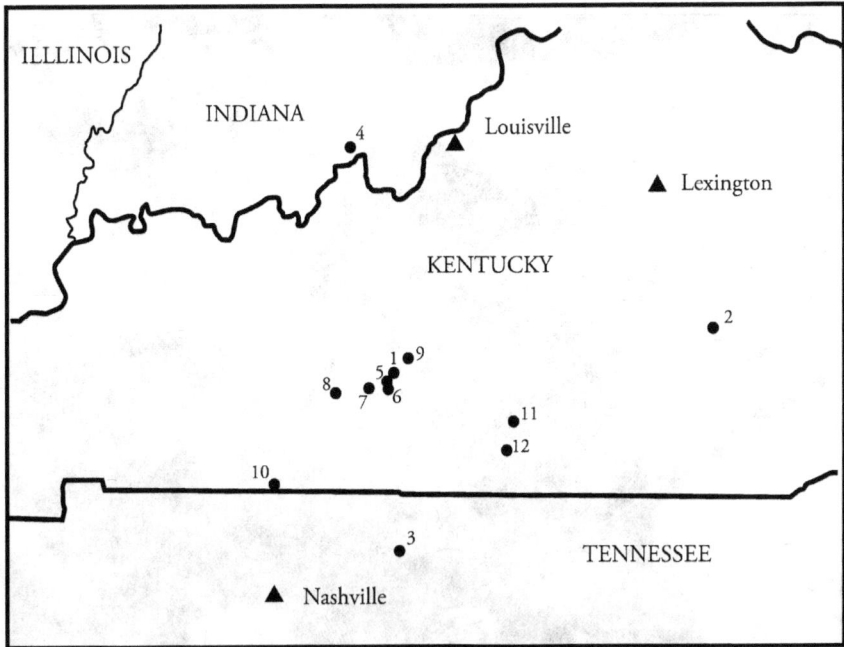

Figure 1-3. Sketch map showing the distribution of Midwest saltpeter caves mentioned in this book: (1) Mammoth Cave and Dixon Cave, (2) Great Saltpetre Cave, (3) Big Bone Cave, (4) Wyandotte Cave and Saltpeter Cave, (5) Longs Cave and Short Cave, (6) Coach Cave (Gatewood's Cave is also known as Hundred Dome Cave), (7) Beckner Saltpeter Cave, (8) Pruett's Saltpeter Cave, (9) Forestville Saltpeter Cave, (10) Savage Cave, (11) Breeding Saltpeter Cave, and (12) Dutch Creek Cave.

ing were fairly well established industries in Kentucky and neighboring states. The most significant sites were Mammoth Cave and Great Saltpetre Cave in Kentucky, Wyandotte Cave in Indiana and Big Bone Cave in Tennessee (Figure 1-3). Collectively, the historic artifacts and documents associated with these caves present a coherent picture of life and working conditions in saltpeter mines.

At first only a few people on the frontier knew the secrets of saltpeter and gunpowder manufacturing. Backwoods icon Daniel Boone and his contemporary, an African-American, Monk Estill (Figures 1-4 and 1-5) are the first on record to have made gunpowder in Kentucky. As the region became more settled and industry developed, individuals such as John James DuFour, Fleming Gatewood, Sr., Levi Brashear, Archibald Miller, Sr. and African-American "Free" Frank McWorter

3

Figure 1-4. Frontier explorer and Indian fighter Daniel Boone dressed "in the costume of a Western Hunter." Only later did artists and writers mythologize Boone wearing a coonskin hat. Wood engraving from *The Family Magazine*, 1842.

made saltpeter in commercial quantities. At the height of the industry, there were hundreds of these "strolling chemists" as they were termed in 1809 by Lexington entrepreneur Samuel Brown, M.D.

Charles Wilkins of Lexington and Fleming Gatewood, Sr., of Louisville, Kentucky, purchased Mammoth Cave for $3000 ($42,300 today) from the McLean brothers on January 1, 1810. Mammoth Cave contained a fabulous treasure trove of mineral wealth with "seven miles" of passage in the biggest cave then known (Anon., 1810). Only two other caves were in the same league, Big Bone in Tennessee and Wyandotte in Indiana. The estimated saltpeter deposits amounted to a gold mine in perceived wealth. Long after the Mammoth Cave factory closed, Mat Bransford, one of the most outstanding early African-American tourist guides, estimated a value of $50,000.00 ($704,000.00 today) was invested into building the Wilkins underground factory (Anon., 1853, p. 3). He had been a guide at the cave since 1838 (Meloy, 1985, p. 4). Much of Mat's guide training and tourist recitations relied heavily on what he learned from Gatewood and Miller, resident saltpeter makers at Mammoth Cave during the mining era (Figure 1-6).

Saltpeter was not the only mineral deposit of value in Mammoth Cave. The cave possessed an abundant supply of the sulfate minerals gypsum (calcium sulfate), Epsom salts (magnesium sulfate), and Glauber salts (sodium sulfate). Crystalline deposits of these minerals grew on cave walls and ceilings as white efflorescence and massive crystal clusters. Epsom and Glauber salts had therapeutic values and were sold in pharmacies as medicines; gypsum was used as an additive to paint or to make plaster of Paris. Crystals could be scraped from the rock surface and fractionally separated in the evaporation furnace. In saltpeter

---

WHAT'S IN A NAME?

After purchasing the cave, the next important business decision consisted of what to call their investment. Neither "Flatt's Cave," as it had been known since 1802, nor "Green River Cave" seemed to send the solid image Wilkins and Gatewood wanted to portray in their advertising. A "catchy" name that conveys a positive message can be a significant business asset. "Big Cave" was also used in 1802, but since this was a secondary name for Great Saltpetre Cave in present day Rockcastle County, they didn't want to create confusion. Sometime before January 21, 1810, the identifying name of Mammoth Cave was selected (Anon., 1810). Adoption was not based on the discovery of giant bones or vast rooms in the cave but simply because "Mammoth" had recently been added to the popular lexicon as synonymous with great size. This was the image Wilkins and Gatewood wished to place before potential investors.

Mammoth is a Russian name employed by the Tungus tribes of Siberia for giant beasts they found buried in the permafrost. In 1692, Nicolaus Cornelius Witzen (Dutch ambassador to Moscow) popularized the term *mammut* or *mammoth* in his book on the subject (Wendt, 1968, pp. 24-25). These animals were thought to be perennial subterranean creatures similar to gigantic moles. By the beginning of the 19th Century the scientific perception of a mammoth had evolved to represent a fierce carnivorous beast. It took the French anatomist Georges Cuvier to adduce their vegetarian nature as an extinct fossil having an affinity with modern elephants.

Following the excavation of two mammoths by Charles Willson Peale from a bog in Newburgh, New York, in 1801 and subsequent exhibition in his Philadelphia museum, the word mammoth became popular in America. Fossil exhibits in Peale's Museum created instant public recognition. People were astonished by the immensity and marveled at the possibility that such creatures might be still alive beyond the boundaries of civilization or at least west of the Mississippi River. Thomas Jefferson believed this, and it was one of his motivations in launching the Lewis and Clark expedition up the Missouri River and points west in 1804. Part of Lewis and Clark's job was to collect sighting reports, find and dispatch one and bring it back to Washington City. As late as 1818, people reported sightings of mammoths in the west (Anon., 1818, p. 2).

During the early 19th Century it was a common business practice for banks and many other establishments to incorporate the word "Mammoth" as part of an identifying signature. With this appendage the name gave the impression of something far greater than reality might suggest. The resources of a Mammoth Cave would therefore, likely be inexhaustible.

Figure 1-5. Kentucky's first saltpeter maker was Monk Estill. Only he and Daniel Boone knew the secret process of manufacturing saltpeter and gunpowder in the early settlement of Fort Boonesborough. Monk used his manufacturing skill and heroism during Indian battles to win his freedom. The wood engraving of Monk is a character representation of an African American dressed in Civil War attire and probably not a true likeness. He died about 1835, long before the depicted clothing, insignia and rifle came into vogue. Z. F. Smith, *The History of Kentucky*, The Prentice Press, Louisville, KY, (1895). Years later another African-American, "Free" Frank McWorter (Walker, 1983), manufactured commercial quantities of saltpeter from about 1810 to May 1829, in a cave that might be Burton (Kelley Saltpeter) Cave on Fishing Creek, Pulaski County, Kentucky.

Figure 1-6. Early photograph of brothers Mat (on the left) and Nick (on the right) Bransford. Adin F. Styles stereo view c. 1869. Several early Mammoth Cave guides were internationally celebrated. Mat Bransford distinguished himself as a cave explorer, discoverer of major passages in Mammoth Cave through courage and determination. Next to Stephen Bishop he was the most famous and accorded consideration and hospitalities normally reserved for European mountain climbers such as Michel Gabriel Paccard (*Mont Blanc*) and Edward Whymper (*Matterhorn*) or Nile River explorers John Speke and Richard Burton. Photograph courtesy of the National Cave Museum at Diamond Caverns, Park City, Kentucky.

caves, such minerals, if present, were usually mined first and hauled away by the barrel (Blane, 1824, p. 271) before any effort was made to process saltpeter. Saltpeter was a more labor-intensive operation; the end product was sold to gunpowder manufacturers and the meat packing industry as a preservative.

Of all the natural resources produced at Mammoth Cave, saltpeter possessed the most monetary value. Its worth increased weekly as the inflated price created an investment bubble in the years leading up to and through the War of 1812. The bubble burst with news of the signing of the Treat of Ghent in February 1815. Immediately after the War of 1812 there was a glut of the commodity on the market. Saltpeter prices tumbled to prewar and pre-speculation levels. Most of the cave mine operations shut down, although some held out hoping, in vain, that the price of saltpeter would go back up. Mammoth and Wyandotte caves continued to mine saltpeter briefly after the war, because there was still some demand. Some shipments of saltpeter made it to

8

MANUFACTURING BEFORE
AMERICA'S INDUSTRIAL REVOLUTION

There was little large scale manufacturing before America's Industrial Revolution. The majority of factories were small craft oriented enterprises. Events leading up to and through the War of 1812 laid the groundwork needed to streamline manufacturing in America. Europeans considered the Americas a source for raw materials and as a market for finished goods. American merchants and the common man considered this advantageous in a land of few skilled artisans. There was a limited manufacturing sector of so-called cottage industries, which consisted of individual households. They produced products on a limited scale needed to satisfy their own needs with any surplus taken to market and sold. This does not seem too effective until one considers most of the population was rural agrarian and as a whole supplied thousands of products of variable quality. A farmer might mine saltpeter and manufacture a small quantity of gunpowder for his own use with the remainder taken to market. The same could be said of textiles, ceramics, furniture, jellies, etc. Multiplied many fold, there was enough to satisfy most basic needs.

Few integrated factories existed during Colonial and Pioneer times. There was considerable resistance to the idea of building factories using the European Industrial Revolution model to produce one or two products. Americans were of the mindset that their small cottage industries could fill any gap or supply needs; and believed there would always be imports for quality merchandise and goods beyond their technical expertise. There was no need to build factories, after all, who would build them, finance them, supply a skilled labor force, let along produce finished quality goods? The best goods could be imported from England, France, and Germany. It was just easier to place a European order and wait four to six months until it arrived on our shores, followed by another six to eight weeks to be transported into frontier Kentucky. People accepted this time delay as a normal business practice.

Hostilities with England precipitated the Embargo Act (1807) and the Non-Intercourse Act (1809) as a prelude to the

War of 1812. National economic hardships resulting from these two pieces of legislation produced a wake up call to fledging American manufacturers. With commodities embargoed from Europe, everything that once was imported had to be manufactured here. America's Industrial Revolution did not happen overnight. Rather it was gradual and would not make great strides until after 1820.

European expatriates were responsible for introducing large scale manufacturing factories in America along with skilled emigrant mechanics and artisans. These people possessed the necessary expertise and were familiar with the advanced technology needed to manufacture iron, make castings, weave textiles and fabricate finished apparel, make wine, orchestrate shipbuilding, and make gunpowder. Against great financial obstacles but aided by good political connections, one of the first really large factories was the Du Pont Powder Works in Wilmington, Delaware, established in 1802. As war clouds gathered, Americans learned self-sufficiency, and international events changed people's perceived notions about building homeland-manufacturing plants.

For Colonial and Pioneer times, the first big industry employing a large labor pool of skilled and unskilled workers was the salt brine industry. New York, West Virginia, Kentucky, and Illinois were primary suppliers of this commodity at various times. By 1808, the developing saltpeter and gunpowder industries helped to change the fabric of American manufacturing. This industry needed investment capital, business methodology, skilled personnel, a distribution infrastructure of end user clients, and a cash economy. Cash replaced barter and became the standard for business after 1820.

Source: Lawrence A. Peskin, *Manufacturing Revolution, the Intellectual Origins of Early American Industry*; The John Hopkins University Press, 2003.

America in 1815 from other ports of call. It would, however, be a number of years before shipments to America from British Crown Colony India were resumed. The British monopolistic salt and connected saltpeter trade was interrupted globally from 1814 into 1817 as a result of labor problems and open armed insurrection by locals connected with the industry (Kurlansky, 2002, pp. 357-358). In Kentucky, the saltpeter industry never resumed, the caves remained vacant, and by the late 1840s, "their location [was] fading from distinct remembrance," according to Thomas Kite during his 1847 visit to Mammoth.

SALTPETER WORKING CONDITIONS

Comparisons made between the saltpeter industry and the salt brine industry are useful, because both used similar manufacturing processes resulting in an essential commodity. Much has been written about the salt brine industry, and many primary and secondary references are available. In contrast, pre-Civil War saltpeter references are sparse and understanding the industry is facilitated by comparisons to the salt brine industries that operated at the same time as the saltpeter mines.

The mining of saltpeter was an environmental disaster wherever it took place on a large scale, producing a dreary eroded moonscape devoid of trees for miles. This *was* the typical landscape of the Industrial Revolution – considered a *good thing* and equaled progress. Accounts of the contemporary salt brine industry, which used similar processes and resources, give us a good idea of the impact of saltpeter operations. Anne Royall (1826, pp. 46-47) visited West Virginia's Kanawha salt works and describes a "dismal" picture with "the sameness of the long low sheds; smoking boilers; men, the roughest that can be seen, half naked ...; horses and oxen, ill-used and beat by their drivers; the mournful screaking of machinery, day and night." This vivid portrait could equally apply to the above ground activities of the Mammoth Cave works or any other large saltpeter-mining establishment.

Logging crews would harvest all the standing timber to make potash, which was needed to convert calcium nitrate into the desired form, potassium nitrate. This was not seen as an undesirable effect, because cleared land was worth more than timbered. Other crews specialized in chopping wood only to fuel the evaporation furnaces or for barrel making. The skies were dark and overcast from smoke generated by fires

11

Figure 1-7. Charcoal makers repair a fire breakout along the side of a furnace. Known as "the blackest job in America," charcoal makers stayed with their task 24-hours a day for a month until their job was complete. They slept there on the job next to their furnace in little houses or in log and sod tee-pee like structures that resembled their furnaces. Wood engraving from *Frank Leslie's Popular Monthly*, May 1877.

of charcoal makers and saltpeter evaporation furnaces (Figure 1-7). At night from dozens of sites an eerie glow lit the horizon. Only a small amount of wood went into actual construction of living quarters and machines inside the caves. A clue to the amount of fuel needed for the Mammoth Cave furnaces might be the requirements of iron furnaces of the era. An iron furnace in Salisbury, Connecticut, in 1840 used "five thousand cords of wood a year in the manufacture of iron. This amount is hardly more than a mathematical figure, but if you visualize it in the form of one pile of wood in cord-width (4' X 4'), such a wood-pile would be over seven miles long" (Sloane, 1986a, p. 339).

Much of the specialized work conducted in the saltpeter and similar salt brine industries was subcontracted. Ebenezer Meriam (1844) was contracted to supply $20,000 ($238,000.00 today) worth of potash in 1814 to Mammoth Cave. He had a crew of men whose sole function was to cut and process trees. Other cave owners in the region probably retained his services as well. Charcoal burners (Figure 1-7) employed to make potash had rough-hewn personalities (Joy, 1877, p. 633), employed in the "blackest job in America" (Sloane, 1986b, p, 284). They "often lived like solitary animals in sod-huts similar to their charcoal mounds" (Sloane, 1986a, p. 341). Pipeline manufacturers bored out logs and shaped them into pipe segments. Other skilled work may have been subcontracted, especially evaporation furnace construction and fabrication of pump towers. The Rotunda pump tower was prefabricated and assembled in the cave, using a pattern much like a modern Erector Set™. A land surveyor might prepare a map of the cave with a station of vertical levels relative to the entrance (pioneer era transit surveys of Mammoth Cave are not known to exist). Such maps were needed by a hydraulic engineer to design pipeline elevations and pumping lift stations in the cave. Pump manufacturing and finished carpentry were also most likely contracted out. Some slaves may have been artisans capable of skilled work. Large saltpeter mines had to be self-sufficient, utilizing a staff of hunters for game, wranglers, teamsters, farmers and cooks who prepared meals for a hundred or more persons. People working the mines shared one common bond -- they were frontiersmen!

Workers in the saltpeter mines and salt brine industry were the roughest of sorts, generally illiterate, and often dishonest, cut from the same cloth as the rough and tumble brawler and heartbreaker of folklore, Mike Fink. The legendary Salt River keelboat captain called himself "half horse, half alligator" and was every bit as fearsome when it came to a fight. Fink was a real person who became a folk hero in his lifetime. The Kanawha salt brine industry again provides a basis for comparison: Anne Royall (1826, p. 47) described brine workers as men who "gloried in a total disregard of shame, honor and justice, and an open avowal of their superlative skill in petty fraud."

The unreliable and lawless nature of many of the itinerant backwoods saltpeter producers is reflected by observations of Charles Wilkins (1809), future owner of Mammoth Cave and saltpeter broker in Lexington. Contracted to supply the Du Pont Powder Works of Delaware with saltpeter, Wilkins was called to task for allegedly mixing sand and gravel in his shipments. Not so, he wrote in response, this was the fault of some dishonest suppliers, "generally living in caves and mountains on our frontiers," so numerous that he was unlikely to recognize any individual swindler. Wilkins obviously held these frontier miners in disdain, because their lack of honesty reflected upon his business integrity. He promised to inspect and repack every barrel of saltpeter that came into his shop, to assure Du Pont of its purity.

Wilkins was an aristocrat in the modern and refined "Athens of the West," Lexington. His friends and business partners were well educated, lived a fine genteel existence, yet were not afraid to get their hands dirty, or ride horseback for days along trails barely called roads. These were necessary characteristics for a successful entrepreneur on the western frontier.

During the mining era, visitors often compared going into these caves as a visit to Hell, full of demonic workers seen fitfully through smoky torchlight, accompanied by loud sounds of heavy machinery that deafened ones' senses. D. T. Maddox, writing in 1813 of the Big Bone Cave saltpeter works near McMinnville, Van Buren County, Tennessee, paints a frightening picture of what it was like to enter an operation as large as Mammoth Cave's.

> The sun was declining in the west, and his rays bore in a direct line against the mouth of the cavern, intermixing light and darkness with such hideous perplexity, as to leave the mind in doubt, which of the two to adopt. At the same time that there is issued from its mouth a column of smoke, occasioned by the burning of torches within, which gave to the whole an appearance that seemed to realize the most exaggerated picture of the infernal regions! While a smutty crew, in tatters, resembling nothing but devils incarnate, bore in black sacks, the nitre and bitumen which seemed to constitute the horrors of the place.
>
> We now had proceeded beyond the atmosphere of smoke, occasioned by the burning of torches employed to light the workmen. The cautious wanderer hearing nothing but the indistinct echoes of hammers and pick-axes, dying upon the ears, with most appalling sounds, and seeing at intervals, the flames of torches, followed by men in the shape of devils, was easily impressed with the belief, that the place was inhabited by a thousand fabled Cyclops, occupied with their bellows and forges in fabricating thunder! (p. 175)

The atmosphere in Mammoth Cave had to be thick with smoke from torches and tapers burning lard in open pan iron frog lamps.

Figure 1-8. Half naked salt diggers in the Wieliczka mine Poland. Supervisors (the one holding the lamp) were better clothed than common workers. Woodcut from Thomas W. Knox, *The Underground World: a Mirror of Life Below the Surface*, Australian Publishing Co., Sydney and Melbourne, (1879).

After the mining era ended, smoky passages were a problem for John Croghan, M.D., who purchased and developed the cave as a modern tourist attraction. The natural ventilation of the cave slowed when the outside air temperature became equalized with the temperature in the cave (Meriam, 1844, p. 328). Smoke from tourist lights and pyrotechnic displays collected in the rooms and passages to a troublesome degree. A small door built during saltpeter times in the entrance to Houchin's Narrows only exasperated the problem during winter months when it was closed.

Working conditions inside the saltpeter mines were horrible. Poor lighting combined with fine dust churned up from the mining operation reduced visibility greatly, similar to lighting ones way at night through fog. Even though the average cave temperature was 58 degrees Fahrenheit and close to 90-100% relative humidity, the usual mining costume of the slaves was shirtless (Bird, 1837, p. 529). Descriptions of the attire of early coalminers, salt miners and tunnel diggers indicates a similar state of partial clothing for many (Figure 1-8), while others were completely naked (Cobden, 1859, p. 42).

At Mammoth Cave, some of the saltpeter miners were actually required to live inside the cave, in the Rotunda. In "the same room, separated from the hoppers by an artificial wall.... are still found the remains of tents, stables, etc. for at one time there were upwards of fifty persons employed here, with wagons, cattle, etc" wrote John S. Wood in 1841 (p. 89). His visit was during the time when John Croghan, M.D., was building huts in Audubon Avenue and deeper into the cave for experimental treatment of tuberculosis patients (Wood, 1841, p. 184). Possibly this reference to "tents" in the Rotunda could be one of the TB huts because the wood and stone huts were finished off with a canvas roof.

Poor clothing contributed to harsh working conditions in a factory housing its workers underground. When poorly clothed workers are housed in a cool damp underground environment 24-hours a day, everyday, one might expect their health to deteriorate. Quite the contrary, "there was no case of sickness among the numerous workers. They all enjoyed excellent health," wrote eyewitness Ebenezer Meriam (1844, p. 319). Although this claim may have been an apocryphal public relations gimmick, such reports and feelings of invigoration experienced by tourists suggested that caves were healthy environments. This prompted Dr. Croghan to experiment with cave residences to find a possible cure for the fatal disease called Consumption (Tuberculosis). The experiment offered great expectations to willing participants with terminal TB, desperate for any cure, who ended up in an environment that ironically only accelerated their death. The intended cure was an example of medical practice using strong measures for strong foes. In 1842, a number of people set up residence in the cave. Their condition worsened underground, resulting in death in the cave or soon after being extracted. Croghan died of Tuberculosis in 1849 without finding a remedy.

During the winter, freezing cold air flowed into the cave from the entrance and could be uncomfortably felt as far as the Rotunda. Lower temperatures coupled with wind chill could freeze the pipes; dissolving or "leaching" saltpeter from cave soils with super cooled water was difficult. A small door built in Houchin's Narrows acted as an air lock and

Figure 1-9. Example of chevron style mattock marks in a soil profile in Gratz Avenue of Mammoth Cave. Diana Emerson George photograph.

solved part of the problem. This stabilized air temperature in the cave and made for better working and living conditions, although increasing the smoke problem somewhat.

Saltpeter workers toiled with small iron-bladed hand mattocks and wooden shovels as they filled bags and buckets with earth. Mattock excavations form distinct chevron cut marks in cave soils (Figure 1-9). A tallyman kept track of the number of loads by inscribing a vertical mark on the wall of the cave (Figure 1-10). Presence of tally marks in numerous saltpeter mines suggest the owners employed a task system based on the number of bags excavated each day. One vertical mark is assumed to represent one bag of earth.

Earth was carried out of the excavation bays and loaded onto a cart pulled by oxen. An early report describes these carts with small wheels. These oxcarts were a pioneer conveyance called a caravel. Oxen carting earth from Gothic Avenue were stabled on the other side of the Second Hoppers just beyond Booth's Amphitheatre (Figure 1-2). A natural rock loop was used as a rope hitch for the oxen. It is positioned along the left wall and is still visible today along with an ox footprint on the floor. According to early accounts there used to be a large quan-

Figure 1-10. Tally marks and lamp seat soot marks in Beckner Saltpeter Cave. Diana Emerson George photograph.

tity of corncobs and straw and myriads of oxen footprints in this part of the cave.

Other specialized scratch marks were inscribed on the cave walls near tallies in the form of an asterisk made with four straight intersecting lines. This is a religious archetypal "cosmogram" image used by slaves from West Africa, surviving today in the Congo region of southwestern Zaire (Adams, 1993, p. 8). They are seen in the historic area of Mammoth Cave, Longs Cave and Forestville Saltpeter Cave up river from Mammoth Cave. This symbol implies the slaves may have practiced religious beliefs from their country of origin.

Excavation sites are relatively close to leaching stations in the cave. The furthest transit was Blue Spring Branch, two and a half miles from the Second Hoppers (Figure 1-11). Because of the distance and travel time that locality was not as intensely mined as, for example the area along Gratz Avenue, closer to the Second Hoppers. A plank bridge was built up from the Second Hoppers to reach Gothic Avenue (Ward, 1816; Farnham, 1820, p. 358). This enabled oxen to make the trip almost as far as the Cataracts in a passage then called the Haunted Chamber. By the time Anonymous (1816, p. 1) visited the cave, the

18

bridge had been replaced with a ladder, suggesting this area was no longer being mined.

Large salt brine works were in operation around the clock, because of the time and effort required to build the fires and bring the kettles to the boiling point. The furnaces were never allowed to go out. We don't really know how many hours individual workers labored in the cave; conceivably, work shifts may have been twelve hours on and twelve hours off. This is justifiable, because at the time people generally worked from dawn to dusk in this largely agricultural nation. Charles Dickens observed textile mill working conditions during his American visit in 1842. "Their working day varied with the length of sunlight, from eleven hours and twenty-four minutes in December to twelve hours and thirty-one minutes in other months" (Groner, 1972, pp. 101, 135). Working hours didn't start to decline until mid century with the introduction of the ten-hour day.

In 1813, Big Bone Cave produced 300-500 pounds of saltpeter per day utilizing 100 men (Maddox, 1813, p. 176). Mammoth Cave in 1811, with less workers (20-30 slaves) was able to produce the same amount of saltpeter. Management was able to accomplish this using modern leaching equipment based upon the Great Saltpetre Cave model factory. Mammoth Cave increased its labor force in 1813 with the addition of 70 slaves. Listed below is a refined estimation of the actual number of workmen needed for various key functions about the mine in this vertically integrated factory, and whether these were skilled or unskilled positions. These job functions will be explained in detail later.

These estimates do not take into consideration the need for farmers, hunters, surface teamsters, or woodchoppers not directly associated with the works. About 22 persons, or about one-fifth the total work force, were skilled or supervisory positions and ran the operation, while the rest of the workers were semiskilled to unskilled. Whites filled most of the supervisory or skilled positions while the company probably owned skilled African-Americans outright. Unskilled laborers were generally slave workers most likely rented from their owners. About forty percent of all workers (46 persons) were employed at the works in tasks on the surface rather than underground. The surface component might seem disproportionately high until one compares

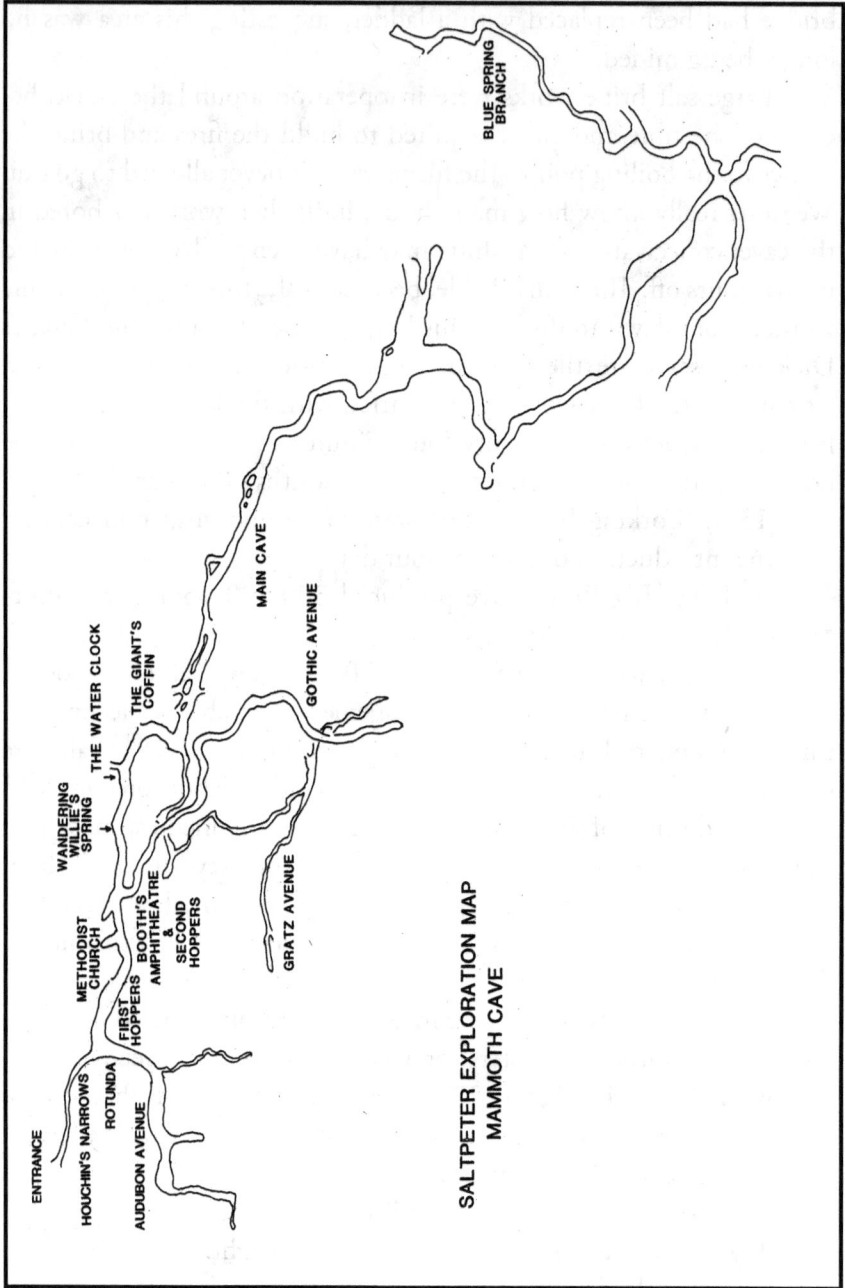

BLUE SPRING BRANCH

MAIN CAVE

GOTHIC AVENUE

THE GIANT'S COFFIN

THE WATER CLOCK

WANDERING WILLIE'S SPRING

METHODIST CHURCH

BOOTH'S AMPHITHEATRE & SECOND HOPPERS

FIRST HOPPERS

GRATZ AVENUE

ENTRANCE

HOUCHIN'S NARROWS

ROTUNDA

AUDUBON AVENUE

SALTPETER EXPLORATION MAP MAMMOTH CAVE

Figure 1-11. Partial map of Mammoth Cave showing key passages explored by miners in search of saltpeter. Modified from the great Max Kemper's *Map of the Mammoth Cave Kentucky* (1908).

this operation to salt brine operations. One of the Kanawha salt manufacturing plants employed 66 workers to tend two furnaces (Stealey, 1993, p. 134).

Estimated Workers Job Functions about the Mammoth Cave Works in 1813			
Job Title	Number per shift	Total Number.	Skilled Labor
Experienced saltpeter maker	1	2	2
Underground cave overseer	1	2	2
Pump operator	5	10	
Teamsters in cave	2	4	
Vat supervisor	2	4	4
Box vat men (3/vat)	9	18	
V-vat men	10	20	
Saltpeter diggers	10	20	
Evaporation Furnaces:			
Supervisor (boss kettle tender)	1	2	2
Kettle tender	3	6	6
"Cat-hole cleaner" (ash removal)	2	4	
Furnace & fire pit stoker	2	4	
Saltpeter lifters	2	4	
Calcining Furnace:			
Supervisor	1	1	1
Rock stuffer	2	4	
"Cat-hole cleaner"	1	2	
Unskilled floaters and packers	4	8	
Blacksmith	1	1	1
Cook	1	1	1
Coopers	3	3	3
Total	62	120	22

Supervisory personnel consisted of a manager (overseer), saltpeter maker, boss kettle tender and underground cave manager. Resident part owner Fleming Gatewood, Sr., would be considered the general superintendent and chief saltpeter maker. He saw to it that production goals were met, supervised the building and repair of machinery and made sure everything ran smoothly. Archibald Miller, Sr., was subordinate to Gatewood and manager of the works. Next in the command hierarchy were the Boss Kettle Tenders. They required a high degree of evaporation and precipitation chemical knowledge to supervise the furnace complex. Fleming's brother Joseph Gatewood and Joseph's brother-in-law John Holten, Sr., also acted as managers and overseers underground.

MAKING SALTPETER

Saltpeter could be extracted from both cave soils and from crushed cave rocks and gravel impregnated with nitrates. Materials excavated from deep within the cave were brought to processing areas nearer to the entrance and dumped into large hoppers, on average nearly twelve feet square and three-feet high. Water was then added in copious quantities, and vat men climbed into the hoppers and constantly mixed the soil and rock, using small wooden paddles and treading with their feet. A hopper full of wet fluid mud weighed more than 17 tons, requiring sturdy construction.

Mammoth Cave crib hoppers contained about 230 bushels of soil compared to about 57 bushels in the V-vats commonly used elsewhere in the industry -- a clear four to one processing advantage (see Chapter Two for further details). Introduction of the box hoppers streamlined the operation to such an extent other nearby cave owners soon emulated the design. Beckner Saltpeter Cave utilized the imbricate log-in-log filter leaching system. Pruetts Saltpeter Cave had crib hoppers too, although most of the leaching was done in V-vats (Figure 1-3).

The water dissolved out the calcium nitrate and seeped through the vat into a collection trough, yielding a brown liquid called *beer* (Farnham, 1820, p. 357; Lee, 1835, p. 8) or *liquor* (Hovey, 1882, p. 57) and its modern analog *leachate*. Separating calcium nitrate and other soluble salts from the soils was called lixiviation. Recycling the leachate back through the mixture increased the nitrate concentration. Leaching took 1½-weeks to fully process one load before the hopper could be cleaned out and made ready for another charge. Cave soils yielded 3-5 pounds of saltpeter per bushel "and when left in the cave became reimpregnated in three years (Meriam, 1844, p. 319). This was similar to Wyandotte Cave yielding "four pounds of Salt to the bushel; and the best from twenty to twenty five pounds" (Adams, 1820, p. 436). Cave soils exhausted of their chemicals were removed from the hoppers and dumped on the ground as lixiviated soil mounds. Mammoth Cave was considered a bountiful resource and recycling was not practiced.

Figure 1-12. Elevated leachate pipe on A-frame supports in Booth's Amphitheatre. Woodcut illustration from Horace Martin, *Pictorial Guide to the Mammoth Cave, Kentucky*, Stringer & Townsend, New York, (1851).

Fresh water from a spring at the Historic Entrance was conveyed through a wooden pipeline to leaching stations in the cave. Simple suction pumps carried the leachate from the cave via a second pipeline to evaporation furnaces on the surface (discussed more thoroughly in Chapter Four). Initially, the water line from the spring at the entrance extended only as far as the V-vat complex between the Entrance Vestibule and Houchin's Narrows. The pipeline was later extended as far as the Rotunda where another V-vat processing station was built. Until Wilkins and Gatewood built the freshwater pipeline as far as Booth's Amphitheatre, two springs (Wandering Willie's and The Water Clock) in the cave probably supplied the V-vat leaching center via a 600-foot long pipeline (Figure 1-11). A rendering in Horace Martin's (1851, p. 20), Mammoth Cave guidebook depicts the leachate pipeline in standing position supported by A-frame logs in Booth's Amphitheatre (Figure 1-12).

FURNACES

The mines operated continuously 24 hours a day, 7 days a week. In salt brine operations, fires beneath the boiling furnaces were never allowed to die down, because restarting the fires and bringing the kettles up to boiling takes too long. Two wood fired furnaces (Figures 1-2

Figure 1-13. Out of context example of an 80-gallon cast iron kettle in Cumberland Caverns, McMinnville, Tennessee. The kettle was made by the Columbus Iron Works (1853-1965), Columbus, Georgia; and probably dates to early in the companies manufacturing life. Kettles of various sizes were used in the salt brine, saltpeter, gunpowder, and syrup industries.

and 4-9) with 20-foot high chimneys were constructed on sandstone foundations measuring twelve by five feet near the entrance of Mammoth Cave (Hill and De Paepe, 1979, p. 257). Each furnace had a long fire pit jutting out to support a long row of kettles. About fifty iron kettles were still present in the 1840s (Anon., in Meriam, 1844, p. 322). This translates to about 25 kettles of perhaps 15-20 gallons each sharing a common fire bed in each furnace used to evaporate leachate. These were hemispherical shaped cast iron kettles with shallow nesting rims of the standard type used in the salt brine industry (Figure 1-13). In addition to the hemispherical kettles were a set of three large odd-looking 900-pound kettles with flattened sides and a capacity of 190 gallons nestled next to the chimney (De Paepe, 1986, pp. 19-20). Taking advantage of the hottest part of the fire, they, "stood side by side in each chimney; the middle kettle had two flat beveled sides and the end kettles each had one beveled side, a design which provided for better heat conduction between the three kettles" (Hill and De Paepe, 1979, pp. 256-257). A kettle similar in nature to the middle one is found in

Figure 1-14. Ruins of two evaporation furnace sheds in front of Nicka-jack Cave near Chattanooga, Tennessee. Woodcut view is after Union forces sacked the saltpeter works during the Civil War. A tall wood pump tower once stood right of center in front of the cave entrance. *Harper's Weekly*, February 6, 1864.

the entrance to Wyandotte Cave (George, 2001b, p.171). Giant kettles of this nature were probably used to heat process water needed to leach cave soils and to make fresh water from ice during the winter. A low shed roof was probably built over the kettle work area, as in the salt brine industry, to protect the fire pit from inclement weather (Figure 1-14).

On the surface, several stages of leachate evaporation were required before first run saltpeter could be produced. Boiling in large kettles reduced the liquid level and concentrated the calcium nitrate in solution. The concentrate was poured through a V-vat filled with wood ashes, which contain a high proportion of potassium carbonate, or potash. A chemical reaction occurs with the replacement of calcium ions by potassium ions, to produce potassium nitrate. In the collection trough, as the altered leachate cooled, a white precipitate called "thick stuff" would form (Brown, 1809, p. 240), that was high in calcium and magnesium hydroxide. The waste product is toxic to animals, especially cattle and oxen that had a penchant for licking the residue and would succumb from internal bleeding. Great Saltpetre Cave and Wyandotte Cave experienced this problem to a troublesome extent. A clear nitrate rich liquor was separated from the "thick stuff," drained off into another boiling kettle for further evaporation and concentration, but not to the point of evaporating all the liquid, since this would create a combustion hazard. The concentrated liquor was placed in a log trough and as it cooled saltpeter crystallized out of the solution. First run saltpeter was scraped away and spread out on a prepared surface on the ground to dry before packing in bags or barrels for market. The remaining mother liquor was recycled through the ash hopper to exhaust as much of the remaining nitrate as possible in a final evaporation-concentration pass.

Work around the furnaces was the most dangerous occupation at Mammoth Cave. Kettle tenders had to be alert at all times as they dealt with boiling water. Extreme care needed to be exercised when transferring boiling liquid from one kettle to the next in order to increase the nitrate concentration. Saltpeter lifters carried buckets full of hot water to potash V-vats or hoppers for the chemical conversion process and the leachate from these would be returned to the kettles. Sometimes, over heated cast iron kettles would burst, splashing 15-20 gallons of scalding water around the work area. The next most dangerous job was that of the "cat-hole cleaners." These workers cleaned out the ash in the furnaces and along the fire pits, and scalding was always a possibility. Everyone employed near the kettles, whatever their job function, had to walk with care to avoid slipping into a boiling caldron positioned near ground surface. One misstep could result in major scalding and burns. This was not a place for careless workmen. Kettle tenders had to be skilled and attentive and were paid the most for their expertise (Stealey, 1993, p. 151).

Saltpeter manufactured at Mammoth Cave was renowned for its purity. To make military grade saltpeter required removing impurities utilizing the method invented in 1797 by J. J. H. Bottée and J. R. D. A. Riffault in France. This method saw continued use through the Civil War. Fleming Gatewood, Sr., wore two hats as part owner and chief "nitre-maker" (Bird, 1837, p. 435). Gatewood probably used the Bottée and Riffault three-step (tertiary) method of purification. In the first step, the mother liquor from the kettle was percolated through the ash hopper to convert calcium nitrate to potassium nitrate. This was followed by two stages of evaporation, potash ion exchange and cooling in a log trough for crystallization, which yielded nearly pure saltpeter from the remaining deposit. In this way, the calcium and magnesium hydroxide impurities were removed from the system. Second and third stage saltpeter crystals were dissolved in fresh water and concentrated in a kettle between crystallizations in a log trough. Only Mammoth Cave and Gatewood's Salt Petre Cave employed this method (George, 2001a, p. 21). All other sites shipped first run saltpeter of lesser purity to market, leaving the specialized purification process to reprocessing establishments such as George Hunter's in Philadelphia or end user powder factories. From his letter to du Pont, we know that periodically Charles Wilkins at his Lexington shop, in order to satisfy client requirements for military grade saltpeter would subcontract the job order to others.

Frederick Hall (1838) visited the cave in June 1837 and saw some of the surface structures built during the mining era that were then in "ruinous condition" with "iron kettles, pumps, leeching vessels, aqueduct pipes, [and] crystalizing troughs." Other tourist accounts describe large ash heaps outside the cave that one had to climb over to get to the entrance. In 1937, "a charcoal-ash bank... thirty feet high" was still present (Ellis Jones, personal communication, July 1974, in Hill and De Paepe, 1979, p. 257).

Potash (potassium carbonate) supplier Ebenezer Meriam (1844, p. 328) with little elaboration characterizes three kinds of furnaces at Mammoth Cave. In general there were plain "furnaces" along with "calcining and evaporation furnaces." Meriam was a highly skilled industrial technologist with wide knowledge in numerous industries. The calcining furnace is a piece of equipment with a very specialized function, used to heat limestone to a high temperature to break it down. This calcined limestone was then leached using the normal routine to obtain saltpeter (see Chapter Five). Meriam's "furnace" is enigmatic as to the role it played at Mammoth Cave. It may have been used in Gatewood's saltpeter tertiary purification steps or more probably the furnace housed the giant 900-pound kettles. Meriam is the only one to discuss the presence of three different kinds of furnaces at Mammoth Cave.

Farnham (1820, p. 357) reported the Mammoth Cave factory manufactured 300-500 pounds of saltpeter per day (109,500-182,500 pounds per year) which locally sold at $0.16 to $0.25 (equivalent to $2.29-$3.57 today) per pound generating maximum yearly sales of $45,625.00 ($651,000.00 today).[1] Estimated overhead costs amounted only to $0.04 ($0.57 today) per pound or $4380.00-$7300.00 ($62,500-$104,000.00 today) per year depending upon output. The Du Pont Company purchased Mammoth Cave saltpeter in 1811 at $0.30 ($4.29 today) per pound delivered to the gunpowder mills in Delaware.

Archibald Miller, Sr., who had been at the cave since 1808 (Blane, 1824, p. 276; Meloy, 1969, p. 54), became superintendent and chief saltpeter maker of the works after Gatewood sold his interest in April 1812. After the war, Gatewood and Miller were periodically involved in the cave when Mammoth was opened to the public as a tourist attraction, serving as managers and guides. Mammoth Cave has continuously operated as a tourist cave since 1816, longer than any other cave except for Grand Caverns, Virginia.

THE CAVE HOUSE

A log cabin built during the saltpeter mining era was located on the hill adjacent to the ravine leading to the cave. Oliver Shackleford (n.d., pp. 2-3), one of the early commercial cave guides, describes it as a dogtrot house consisting of:

> two log rooms 18 feet square with a ten feet hall and upper story and a log kitchen back of them with stone chimneys these houses were built about 1800 [sic.]. They were built for Archibald Miller Sr. to live in and manage the estate, during his stay there in 1811 and 12 the Saltpeter works were in operation, Mr. Miller being head overseer and John Holten Sr. overseer in the cave to gather the saltpeter dirt make it ready for market.

Godfrey T. Vigne, one of the many Englishmen who traveled in the west during the 19th Century, noted in 1833 (p. 121), "a small lonely log house tavern, built about a hundred yards from the mouth of the great cave." This building was apparently "used as sleeping quarters" (Atherton, 1831, p. 216). Another "Cave House" was present as a small one-story frame structure "much out of repair" and located "several rods" (thirty feet) opposite the cave entrance (Hall, 1838). This was built by John Croghan and occupied by Archibald Miller, Jr., and family, 1842-1845. After they moved away in 1845, the building was used to store cave costumes and lamps used by tourists. It burnt to the ground a few years later (Shackleford, n.d.).

SLAVERY IN MAMMOTH CAVE

Forty percent of Kentucky's population in 1810 consisted of slaves. They provided the workforce needed in agriculture and many industries. Kentucky industries that employed slaves included gunpowder mills, saltpeter mines, salt brine works, coalmines and dozens of other industries. Slaves were used because there were not enough free white males to fill positions. Given a choice, African-Americans preferred working in industry over stoop and pick farm work. Meriam (1844, p. 319) interviewed Mammoth Cave slaves in 1813-1814 and found they "preferred this employment to that of labor outside." This was true even though the work was hard, dirty, heavy, physically rigorous, and often dangerous, because they garnered similar wages as their white counterparts (Boles, 1984, p. 122). Few industries (other than plantations) owned outright a large slave workforce but instead employed bondsmen. Bondsmen were slaves who were never in total control of their activity, yet could go out and solicit work. They were, however, required to split part of their wages with their master. Typically agents from a mining company would solicit work directly from bondsmen or from their owners in various communities (Stealey, 1993, p. 133). Leasing slaves lowered overhead costs and improved flexibility in manpower placement in the mines. Purchasing slaves to work in the mines was expensive in a fixed investment such as a cave. Slaves involved in accidents or death caused great financial loss to the cave owner, but leasing slaves removed this burden from the cave owner.

The mining operation at Mammoth Cave utilized about 120 workers in the factory. The resident workforce associated with Big Bone Cave in Tennessee (Maddox, 1813, p. 176) numbered "about one hundred." Villages sprang up around major saltpeter sites to care, house and feed this many individuals. There were pioneer towns without this many residents. By 1830 only one building associated with the former saltpeter factory remained at Mammoth Cave.

Laborers were housed in the cave where they "remained for months in succession, without any other interchange with the inhabitants of the neighborhood than was absolutely necessary in the purchases of the necessary of life," wrote an anonymous medical practitioner (1845, p. 43). Mammoth Cave slaves were described as contented (unlikely in my opinion) and there were no public notices of runaways from the factory, or for that matter from any other saltpeter site in Kentucky. Perhaps the system of slavery at the saltpeter mines was tightly controlled with monetary rewards for good behavior. This was more likely, because saltpeter factory locations were far removed from population centers in a sparsely settled wilderness. Slaves used at mine sites lived in isolation on the western frontier, with nearly insurmountable geographic obstacles that discouraged escape to free states such as Ohio. Salt brine factories, on the other hand, located near waterway transportation routes, experienced frequent runaways from places even the owners detested living in (Stealey, 1993, pp. 145, 134). We can speculate that saltpeter works were similarly unappealing.

We learn a lot about the health of the laborers working in this mine from contemporary medical men. Robert Montgomery Bird, M.D. (1837, p. 526), explored the cave on June 17, 1833, and inscribed his name on the cave wall, (Meloy, 1969, pp. 5-6) and returned again in 1836. His guide at the time would have been Fleming Gatewood, Sr. His glowing account conceals what was possibly one of the most deplorable hiring practices during the saltpeter-mining era at Mammoth Cave, 1810-1816.

> The nitre diggers were a famously healthy set of men; it was a common and humane practice to employ labourers of enfeebled constitutions, who were soon restored to health and strength, though kept at constant labour; and more joyous, merry fellows were ever seen.

This description was pure propaganda to justify the practice. Hiring sick and infirm workers at a cheaper salary than the going slave rental rate of $80.00 per year ($1120.00 today) with $20.00 bonus for good behavior ($281.00 today) was considered a sound business practice. Healthy unskilled Caucasian laborers were paid the same as healthy slave rental. Overhead costs for the mine operator were reduced at the expense of human life and well-being, while the original owner did not have to nurse the slave back to good health. This provided a win-win situation for both parties.

Any large industrial operation employing a hundred or more individuals will experience sickness and injury. During the saltpeter era there were cave accidents and deaths in the mines (Bird, 1837, pp. 434-435). On an inspection tour to gauge the mining potential in Longs Cave south of Mammoth, a Mr. Wright lost his life by falling into a deep pit in the cave. No such events were reported for Mammoth Cave.

Exactly where the Mammoth Cave slaves came from and who owned them is not adequately known, so we can only speculate. Wilkins and Gatewood were not large slave owners (Mullin, 1986, p. 14). By law, Wilkins' salt brine business at the United States Great Saline, Illinois Territory, could only use freed African-Americans (Eskew, 1948, p. 99). Great Saltpetre Cave ran advertisements in *The Kentucky Gazette* for African-American bondsmen to work in the cave. No advertisements for Mammoth Cave workers appeared in *The Kentucky Gazette* or surrounding newspapers. Almost half the inhabitants of Lexington were slaves and represented a valuable labor pool. Alternately, the workforce could have come from foreclosed properties associated with the Peyton Short Versailles, Kentucky, plantation estates that possessed a large slave workforce (George, 1994, p. 61). Short was brother-in-law to Wilkins, and owed more money to him and associates then he could possibly pay back in a lifetime. Wilkins and family members were given power of attorney by Peyton to settle his accounts. Peyton's land holdings were liquidated along with a bountiful nearby saltpeter cave by the name of Short Cave in which miners had found mummified Indian burials. The mummy Fawn Hoof who was exhibited through the country would propel Mammoth Cave to worldwide recognition as the most famous cave in the world. With 360 miles of surveyed passage, Mammoth is truly the greatest cave in the world.

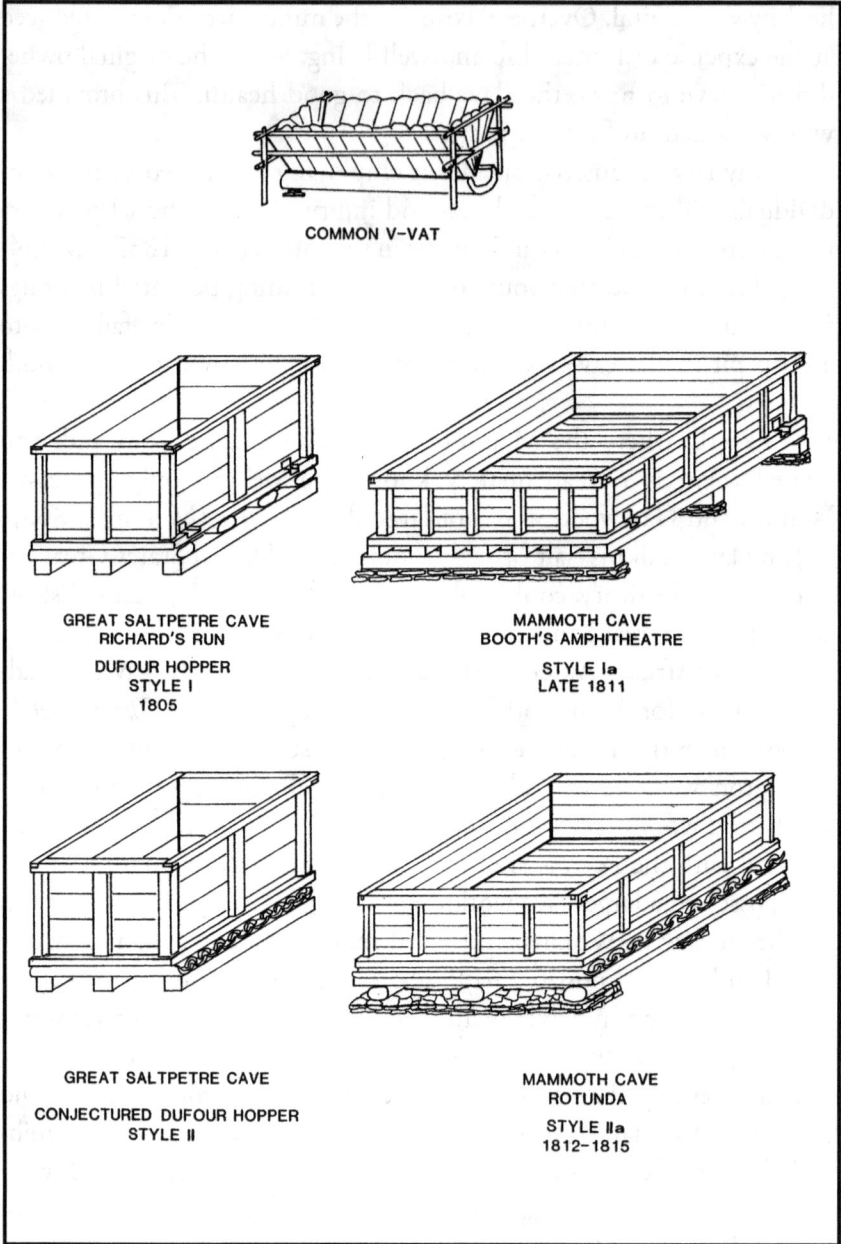

COMMON V–VAT

GREAT SALTPETRE CAVE
RICHARD'S RUN

DUFOUR HOPPER
STYLE I
1805

MAMMOTH CAVE
BOOTH'S AMPHITHEATRE

STYLE Ia
LATE 1811

GREAT SALTPETRE CAVE

CONJECTURED DUFOUR HOPPER
STYLE II

MAMMOTH CAVE
ROTUNDA

STYLE IIa
1812–1815

Figure 2-1. Exaggerated schematic of saltpeter hopper styles in Kentucky.

CHAPTER TWO

SALTPETER HOPPERS IN MAMMOTH CAVE

"Mammoth Cave ... the monarch of caves."
Robert Montgomery Bird, 1837

The mining artifacts present at Mammoth Cave represent several successive operational phases in the cave's history. Three different kinds of saltpeter hoppers are present in Mammoth Cave. The earliest variety was the simple V-vat (Figure 2-1). Nationally, V-vats were used for various purposes from the Colonial period to well into the late 19th Century. Besides leaching cave soils for saltpeter, and in making potash, they were used as corncribs for livestock feeding and as ash hoppers in the manufacture of soap. V-vat remnants are today found in many caves and rockshelters in Kentucky; five caves in the Mammoth Cave National Park still have examples: Dixon, Longs, Jim, Martin and Mammoth Cave (Figure 1-3). Separate bottom drain rails (channel logs) of these V-vats can be seen in Mammoth Cave near the entrance to Audubon Avenue on the south side of the Rotunda (De Paepe, 1975, p. 68; Mullin, 1986, p. 4). Mounds of lixiviated soil called ridge dumps (White, 1967) are found on the west side of the Rotunda and in Booth's Amphitheatre elevated above the Second Hoppers. These features are remnants of cave soils leached of their nitrate content and shoveled from V-vats to aid the structural integrity between hopper walls.

Although V-vats were the only style at Mammoth Cave during the earliest phase of mining, these were later supplemented by giant box hoppers constructed of wood that measured over twelve feet square (Figure 2-1). The ones in Mammoth Cave were introduced to the cave by Wilkins and were based upon smaller architectural examples in Great Saltpetre

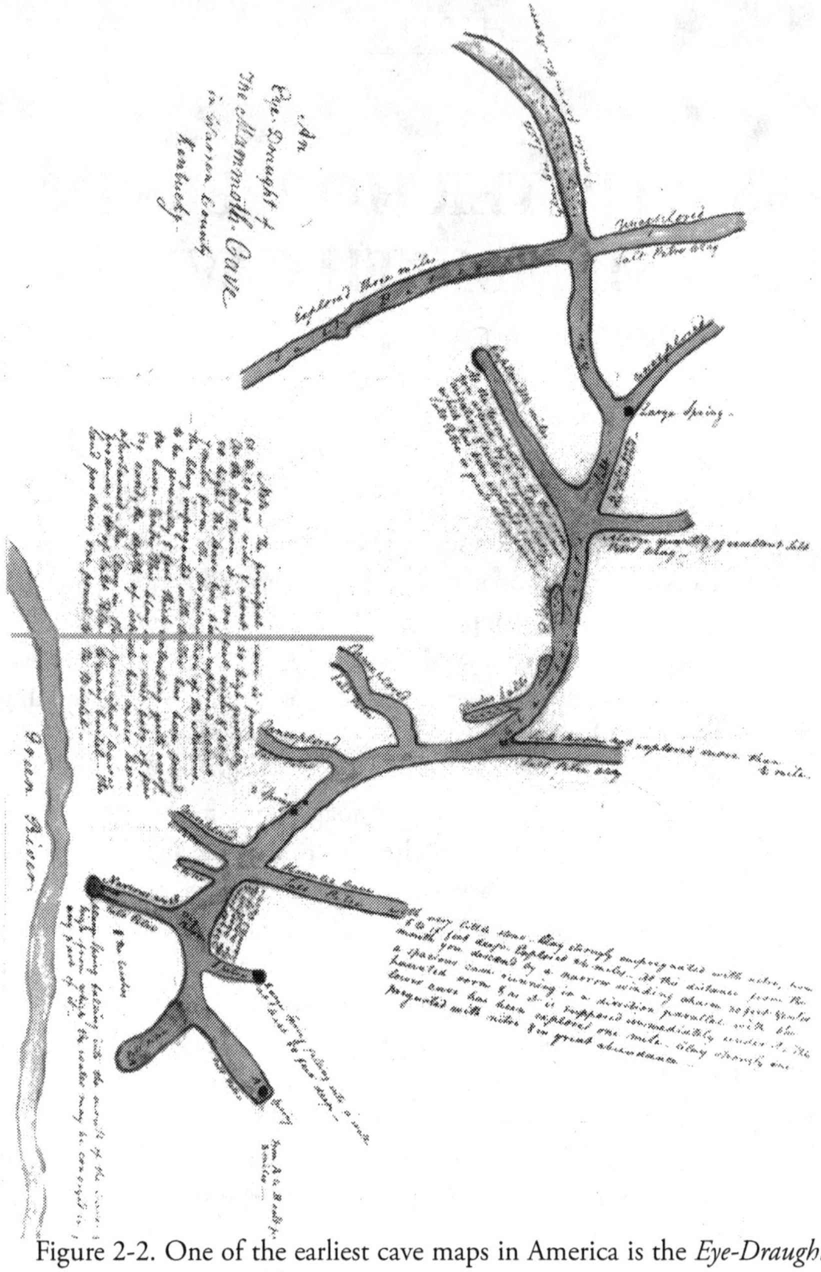

Figure 2-2. One of the earliest cave maps in America is the *Eye-Draught Map of The Mammoth Cave* given to Benjamin Rush, M.D., by Charles Wilkins' brother-in-law Frederick Ridgely, M.D., in 1811. The map shows the physical extent of the cave and saltpeter factory. Map probably dates to early 1810 at the time Wilkins and Fleming Gatewood purchased the cave. Courtesy of the American Philosophical Society.

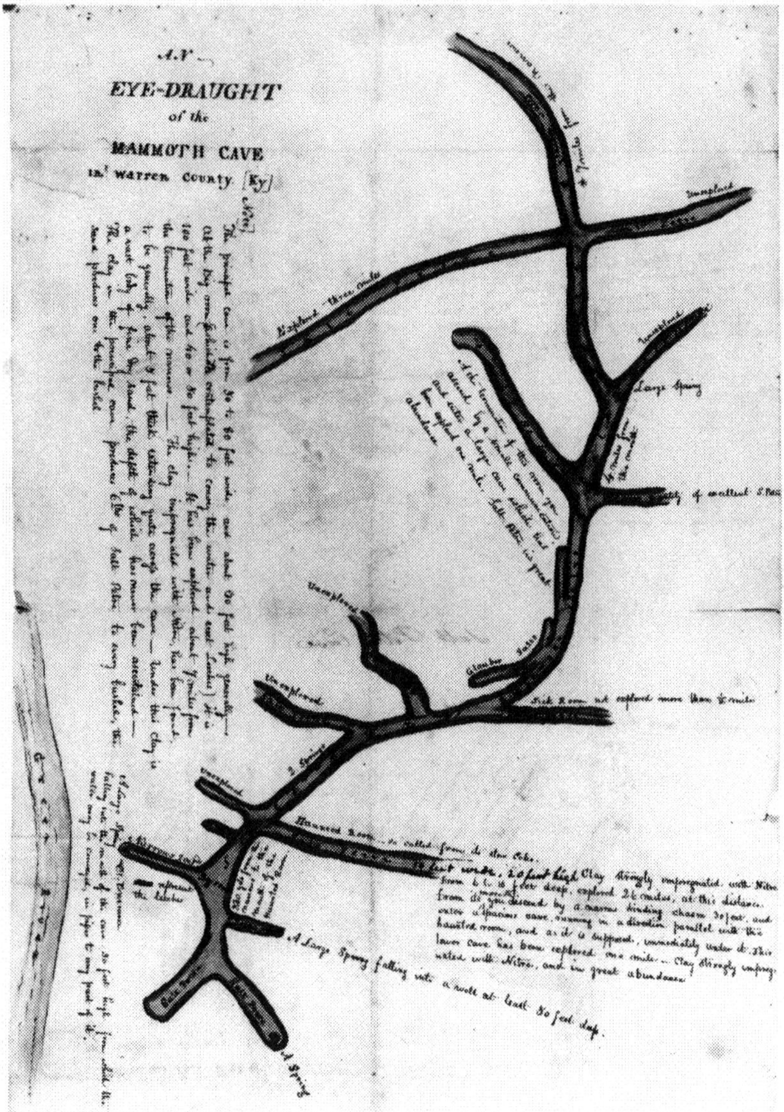

Figure 2-3. Another *Eye-Draught Map of The Mammoth Cave* was sent in mid-1811 to Archibald McCall, the saltpeter buyer for the E. I. du Pont Powder works. This is nearly identical to the first map with the exception of an expanded entrance hopper complex and additional text. Courtesy of the Hagley Museum and Library.

Plan of the Great Cave in Warren County, Kentucky.

For Description of which see Mon. Mag. April, 1816, p.266

EXPLANATIONS—by Mr. WARD.

A.—mouth of the Cave, 40 feet high, and 30 wide.
B.—Hoppers—where salt-petre is made by Wilkins & Gratz—the owners of the Cave—Oxen are worked 2 miles in.
C.—Pits 175 feet deep in many places in this chamber.
D.—This area contains upwards of eight acres, covered with one arch at least 150 feet high in the centre; called the main city.
E.—Contained about six acres—the walls around at least 80 feet perpendicular height—one arch.
F.—This chamber and avenue leading to it was never explored until I entered it—I went to the end.
G.—This is called the second city.
H.—The bed of this chamber, which is 1,800 feet in circumference, is 40 feet above the level of the passage leading to it. You go up a passage like that of a chimney for 40 feet perpendicular height.
I.—At this place I found a cedar pole 12 feet long, and which was perfectly sound.
O.—I went no farther than this—how much farther I might have gone I know not.
L.—From the side of the Cave issued a fine stream of water, which falls 60 feet.
R.—Green River passes over these branches of the cave.
S.—A long body of yellow ochre found here.
T.—A very beautiful dome, at least 40 feet diameter, and 60 feet high.
X.—Here are 6 or 9 large columns of spar, standing upwards of 60 feet perpendicular height—the base of which rest in elegant basins of water that is as clear as amber.—This is a beautiful sight.—Soda is found in great quantities in and by those columns of Spar.—I called the pool Clitorius.
Z.—Found no end.—N. ditto.   K.—The Mummy.
....—The dotted passages pass under the others.

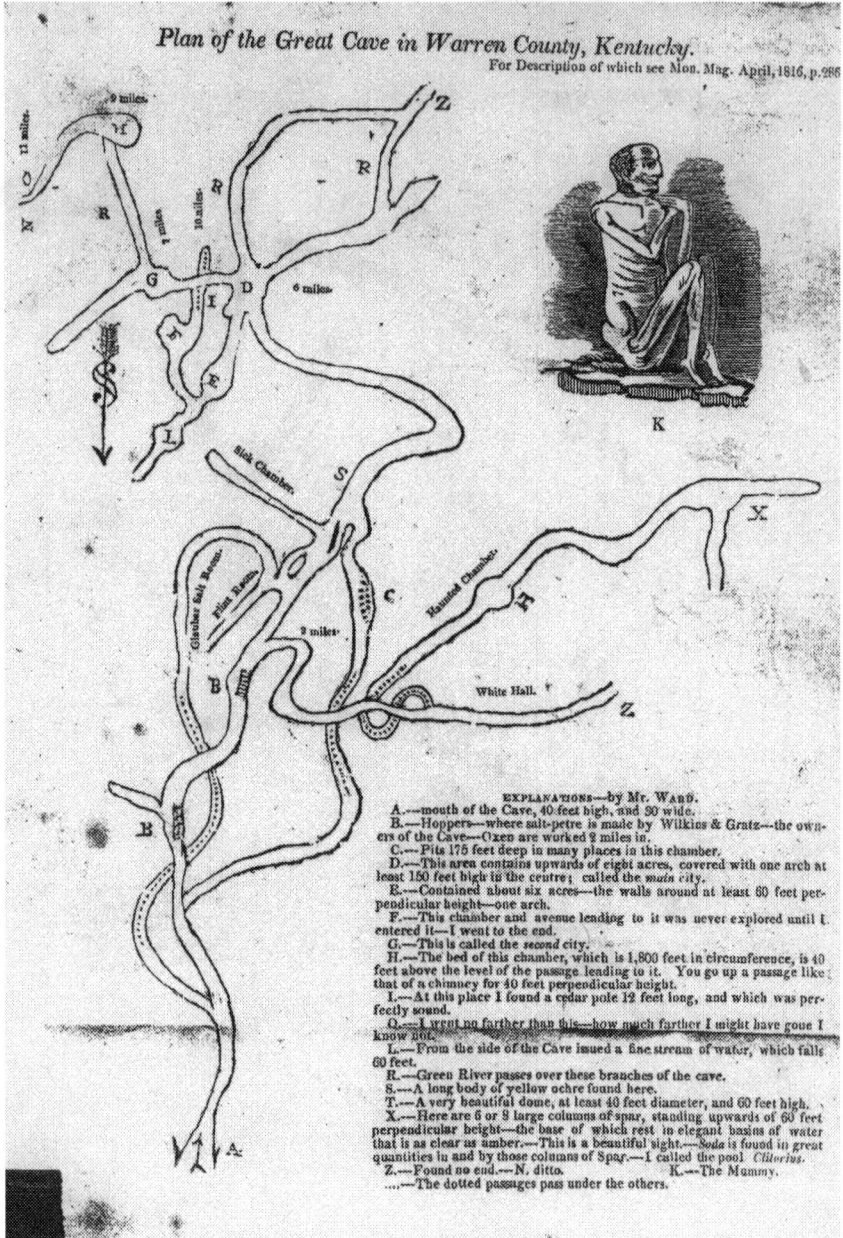

Figure 2-4. Woodcut engraving of Nahum Ward's 1816 map of Mammoth Cave. From *Worcester Spy*, reprinted in *The Monthly Magazine*, April 1816. Courtesy of the Gordon L. Smith collection.

Cave. The first group of hoppers was built in Booth's Amphitheatre in 1810 and a second set in the Rotunda somewhat later. Giant hoppers were able to process greater quantities of earth for saltpeter with less manpower than using V-vats. Only the largest factories such as Mammoth Cave and a handful of other caves used hoppers of this design.

Early descriptions of the various kinds of leaching hoppers often used the vernacular speech of the miners. Naturalist John H. Farnham (1820, p. 357) visited the cave in November 1811, witnessed the mining, and described the box hoppers as "square pits called hods." *The Oxford English Dictionary* (1971, p. 320) defines hod as "a kind of three square trough made up at one end and open at the other having a staff fixed to its bottom." This definition refers to a small box used to carry construction materials, such as bricks, supported over the shoulders. Hod is a holdover term used prior to the introduction of the box hoppers.

The simple V-vat was the dominant leaching apparatus in the cave used continuously from the earliest stages through the end of mining activity in 1816. Ebenezer Meriam (1844) frequently visited the cave in 1813-1814 and was the chief supplier in 1814 of fixed alkali (potash) used in the chemical conversion of calcium nitrate to potassium nitrate or saltpeter. He observed the current mode of construction of the saltpeter hoppers was "in the same manner as ash leeches are made, and the earth is lixiviated with water precisely in the same way that ashes are leached to make pot and pearl ash." His description clearly refers to V-vat construction, and indicates that the dominant leaching process had reverted back to V-vats by this time. The reasons for this technological decline are explained later in this chapter and in Chapter Three.

Burton Faust (1967) outlined how workers went about mining caves for saltpeter. Successful mining operations needed: (1) abundant water supply near the leaching center; (2) a forest in close proximity for lumber and making wood ash charcoal; (3) a bountiful supply of saltpeter in the dry cave soils and impregnating limestone cave walls; and (4) labor supply. A prototype-processing center was often built near the cave entrance to determine if the location was suitable for a greater investment of resources. The Mammoth Cave site was fortunate in possessing all the necessary characteristics and was nearly ideal, in fact, with a perennial spring just above the entrance. Child (1852, p. 19) described a mound of lixiviated earth opposite the entrance so high it obscured the cave opening from her vantage position. The presence of this feature is evidence that a proto-type processing center had been located above and in front of the entrance to Mammoth.

Workers at Mammoth, as at most cave mining operations, first mined out the entrance area before pushing deeper into the cave as the resource became progressively depleted. This initial foray prepared a flat wall-to-wall working area in the vestibule. The earliest Mammoth Cave map (Ridgley, 1811a) illustrates two gangs of V-vats built opposite one another next to the walls (Figure 2-2). This provided for ample working area in the center for a steady traffic of workers and oxcarts. Soils to be leached, mined deeper in the cave, were transported in small-wheeled carts called caravels pulled by oxen. Considerable effort went into improving the major transportation routes in the cave. Slabs of breakdown rock were collected from the passage and stacked into dry stone laid walls along Houchin's Narrows. Then cobbles and blocks of limestone were thrown behind the walls, clearing the trail and reinforcing the walls. Going into the cave, the stone wall extended as far as the Methodist Church along the left hand side of the passage. In time a wide flat oxcart road connected the entrance to Giant's Coffin, a distance of more than 2700 feet (Figure 1-11). Early guidebooks and correspondence compared the thoroughfare to a fine carriage road. One of the later owners (John Croghan, M.D.) envisioned building a troglodyte hotel deep in the cave (Thomas, et al., 1970, p. 326).

Beginning in January 1810, new owners Charles Wilkins and Fleming Gatewood, Sr., retooled the cave into a modern saltpeter manufactory utilizing advanced technology pioneered by Swiss immigrant John James DuFour at Great Saltpetre Cave (George, 2001). Under their direction, the double pipeline system, three elevated lift stations, numerous giant square hoppers and an expanded external furnace complex was built (Figure 3-3). The lift stations in the cave were fitted with suction pumps. The entrance lift station first used buckets to haul the leachate out of the cave and later suction pumps.

More than a year after Wilkins and Gatewood purchased the cave, Wilkins' brother-in-law Frederick Ridgely, M.D. (1811a), wrote of a "curiosity" to his Philadelphia colleague and mentor, Benjamin Rush,

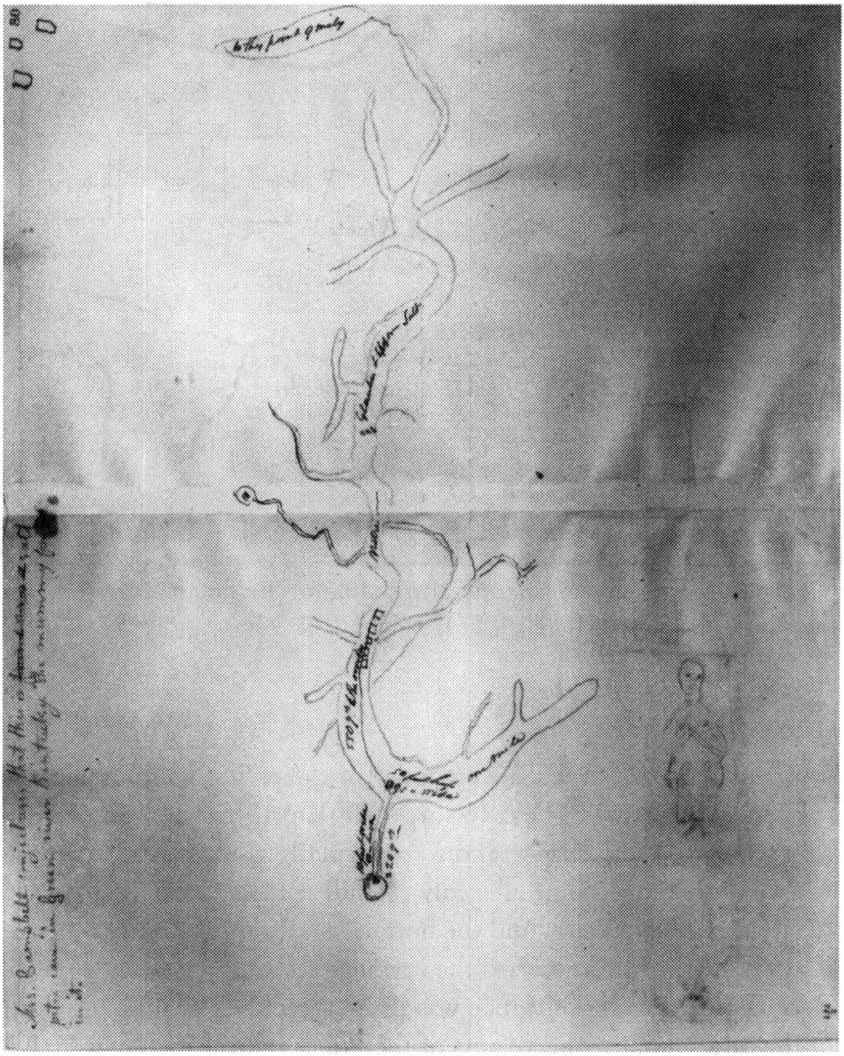

Figure 2-5. Daniel Drake's map of Mammoth Cave. The Daniel Drake Papers in the Draper Manuscripts, 2 O 80. Courtesy of the Wisconsin Historical Society.

M.D. The enclosed map featured a vast cavern depicted as a large format, hand colored sketch. It was called *The Mammoth Cave in Warren County Kentucky* (Figure 2-2). Rush was greatly excited by this map, and he brought it to the attention of the American Philosophical Society for their edification and judgment. Ridgely's claims of the mag-

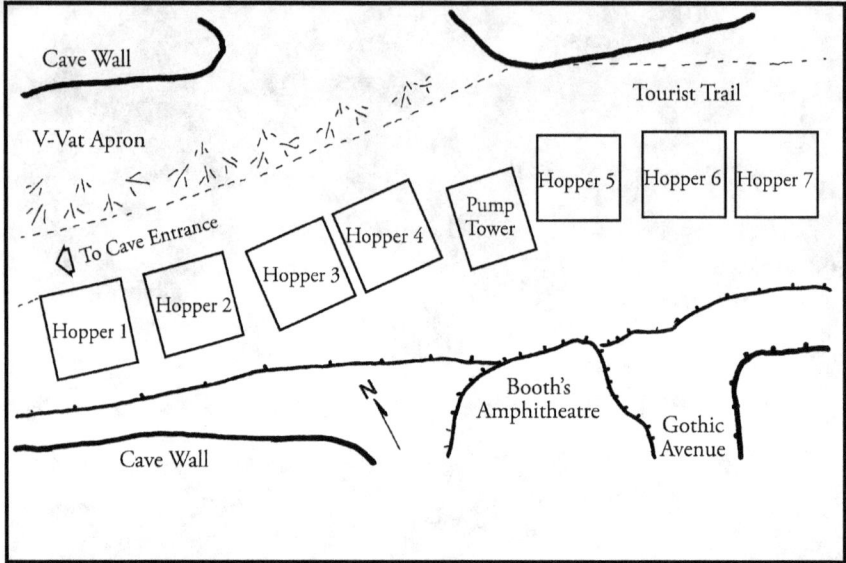

Figure 2-6. Map showing the distribution of the Booth's Amphitheatre saltpeter works (after Mullin, 1986).

nitude of this cave taxed the credulity of the review committee, who concluded that it was a hoax (George, 2001, p.13). They were sure the map abounded with exaggerations, particularly in regard to the reported miles of passage, some allegedly extending beneath Green River, its fabulous mineral wealth, and the notion of a stubborn compass needle that would only point toward the entrance.

The legitimacy of the map was also undermined by the anonymity of the cartographer. The savants of the Philosophical Society were unwilling to credit the existence of such a cave and questioned Ridgely's veracity, certain they were the butts of a wild traveler's tale in the fashion of Baron Münchausen. Although the Society committee rejected the authenticity of the map, they placed it in their archives where it resides today. This is the third oldest Kentucky cave map and ranks fourth oldest in the nation. It is the earliest known map of Mammoth Cave (Meloy, 1968, p. 56; 1975, p. 26).

Several such antique cartographic sketches, called *Eye-Draught Maps,* portray the evolution of vat construction and building architecture in the cave. Ridgely's (1811a) map copy shows the location of

14 V-vats called "leeches" built in the vestibule just before Houchin's Narrows (Figure 2-2). Gangs of seven V-vats flank the center entrance trail on both sides. By mid-1811, one of Ridgely's (1811b) associates produced a second map displaying an enlarged vestibule V-vat complex (Figure 2-3). Comparing the two maps, depiction of known passage remains the same but the second map provides more text. The later map contains an expanded note that refers to, "the Big room (to which it is contemplated to convey the water and erect Leeches)." The Big Room is today called the Rotunda (Meloy, 1975, p. 26). This map was sent to Archibald McCall on June 11, 1811. McCall was the purchasing agent for the E. I. Du Pont Powder Company, Wilmington, Delaware. The author of the map annotations is unknown, but comparison of the writing style to that of Ridgely and Wilkins suggest it is unlikely that they made these notes, so perhaps Gatewood or Miller were responsible. Today, there are few standing remnants of the V shaped wood leaching hoppers found anywhere in the cave. Field investigation reveals trace evidence of V-vats along the west wall of the Rotunda, indicated by the location of ridge dumps, and also above the Second Hoppers. These V-vats operated in tandem with the large hoppers in the Rotunda.

Researchers of Mammoth Cave history have presumed the reference to "erect Leeches" referred to the square hoppers built in the Rotunda. This assumption led Meloy (1969, p. 2) and Mullin (1986, p. 12) to suspect the Rotunda square hopper complex was built first. Their hypothesis was reinforced by Nahum Ward's (1816ab) account and map of Mammoth Cave (Figure 2-4). He locates the "First Hoppers" in the Rotunda and the "Second Hoppers" at the entrance to Gothic Avenue in a place known today as Booth's Amphitheatre. Ward visited the site during a period when very little mining and processing were going on in the cave. His lexicon of place names reflects designations given to these features after they were built. Determining the order in which hopper complexes and other elements of the mining operation were built requires some detective work. Analysis of antique maps of Mammoth Cave has helped resolve the historical puzzle.

Miners cleared breakdown out of the Rotunda to expose nitrate-impregnated soils and V-vats were built around the perimeter of the room. Some areas of Audubon Avenue were similarly prepared. Elsewhere (Figure 1-11), mining took place below Gothic Avenue along a passage called Gratz Avenue. In the Main Cave section, mining activity progressively moved deeper into the cave. We see evidence of major activity in the vicinity of Methodist Church, a Herculean example of pit bay mining through thick breakdown boulders. Wall rock and soils impregnated with saltpeter were excavated from this locality. The area behind the Giant's Coffin was also worked. Soils were also excavated beyond the TB Huts in the vicinity of the Side Cuts. Mining extended as far as Blue Spring Branch, more than three miles into the cave. Beyond this we find only faint traces of mining activity from the pioneer era, although prehistoric Native Americans mined some of the deepest recesses of Mammoth for medical sulfates.

BOOTH'S AMPHITHEATRE

Wilkins modernized the mining operation by installing a state-of-the-art saltpeter leaching system. The concept utilized specialized hopper designs borrowed from Great Saltpetre Cave, where they had been employed with great success since 1805. Swiss emigrant John James DuFour, pioneer vintner and merchant, was hired by the owners of Great Saltpetre Cave to set up a factory-style processing operation. DuFour invented a unique hopper design to process great quantities of saltpeter more efficiently than V-vats. He introduced large rectangular box hoppers of a design originally intended for the salt brine industry to leach salt laden soils. Drawing on his knowledge of processing grapes to make wine, DuFour's invention is architecturally similar to Spanish lagar vats (George, 2001, pp. 63-65) whose construction is exactly like the DuFour style hoppers in Great Saltpetre Cave. These hoppers were so large, the only way to process wet saturated earth was to churn or tread the mixture of soil and water using a team of men tramping around inside the tank. DuFour's machine revolutionized leaching cave earths for saltpeter. Aware of the success of inventions at Great Saltpetre Cave, Charles Wilkins borrowed the design concept and built an enlarged processing station with box hoppers below Gothic Avenue entrance, a locality already using V-vats. Process water was supplied from Wandering Willie's Spring and The Water Clock, a total distance of about 800 feet. This had to suffice until a 1700-foot long pipeline could be built from the cave entrance spring with a more copious supply.

The large box hoppers are built on top of a high saltpeter apron. The feature is so large that it could not have grown to its immense size during the short duration the giant box hoppers were in operation. It is unlikely that the box hoppers were there before Gatewood and Wilkins arrived on the scene.

The hoppers were built atop three parallel dry laid stone foundations (Figure 2-1). This created an air chamber beneath the hoppers that helped to prevent dry rot and to provide working space to make repairs. Removing the discharge water trough provided access to the air chambers.

An early (undated) eye draught map of Mammoth Cave in the Daniel Drake (n.d.) collection (George, 1990, pp. 74-75) provides details associated with Wilkins' engineering design (Figure 2-5). It is younger than the two Ridgely maps, because more detail is shown in areas vacant on the first two. The V-vat processing station in the entrance and the Rotunda are missing, suggesting all of the processing was concentrated at the entrance to Gothic Avenue, designated on later maps and descriptions as The Second Hoppers (Ward, 1816ab). The map shows symbols for four square hoppers positioned inside the cave below Booth's Amphitheatre, and a pipeline connected to three lift stations in the cave. The map presents the Rotunda and the Entrance lift stations using a box with a dot.

The Drake map shows an illustration of Fawn Hoof, the Indian mummy from nearby Short Cave, depicted in her sarcophagus (Figures 2-5, and 1-3). Its position is shown in approximately the same location as on an undated Nahum Ward manuscript map (Gordon Smith collection). Figure 2-4 shows Ward's published Mammoth Cave map and the character likeness of the Indian mummy. If the Drake (n.d.) map and the illustration are cartographically contemporaneous, then the map postdates her discovery in late September 1811 (George, 1994, p. 75) and cannot be younger than December 16, 1811, the day of the first New Madrid earthquakes.

Today the visible remains of the Booth's Amphitheatre leaching station consist of seven hoppers numbered 1 through 7 in ascending order away from the cave entrance (Figure 2-6). A large water tank is

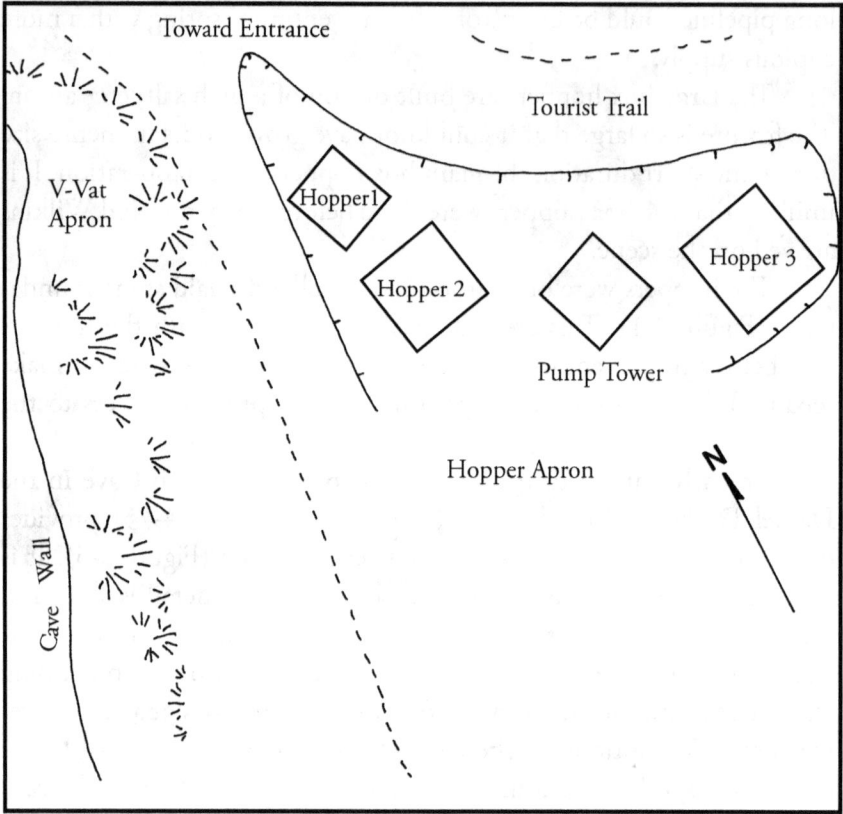

Figure 2-7. Map showing the distribution of the Rotunda saltpeter works (after Mullin, 1986).

positioned between Hopper Nos. 4 and 5. The Drake map shows Hoppers 3, 4, the water tank, 5 and 6 as being built first (Figure 2-5). A dot is used to denote the lift station south of the water tank near the wall leading up into Gothic Avenue. This is inaccurate, since the tower actually had to be over the water tank in order to operate. By December 16, 1811, Hoppers 1, 2 and presumably 7 were completed.

ROTUNDA V-VATS

Upon entering the Rotunda, one is confronted with three large nearly square saltpeter hoppers, a wooden tower, and hollow log pipelines. The whole complex is recessed into the floor of the cave, giving the appearance of a crater (Figure 2-7). According to tradition, lixiviated earth was taken from the hoppers and spread out in all directions, forming a saltpeter apron, which gradually raised the floor in this area of the cave. The apron stands at and above the level of the tourist trail in Main Cave. A larger saltpeter apron also exists at Booth's Amphitheatre.

Each box hopper complex and saltpeter apron has auxiliary features referred to as lixiviated soil mounds (Mullin, 1986, p. 3), or dumps of processed petre dirt (De Paepe, 1986, p. 17) taking on the appearance of miniature mountain chains (Hovey, 1897, p. 291). White (1967; and in manuscript) found similar features called ridge dumps in Great Saltpetre Cave. White (in manuscript) suggested the features formed when miners unhitched an oxcart full of leached soil cleared from the hoppers and tipped it backward, discharging its load onto the ground. This activity formed a line of hummocks. It was here along the west wall of the Rotunda the lixiviated earth was said to renitrify in three years time (Meriam, 1844, p. 319). The Rotunda-Audubon Avenue tourist trail is cut through the ridge dumps between the west wall and the hopper complex (Mullin, 1986, p. 4). De Paepe (1975, p. 68) observed V-vat channel logs in the Rotunda and theorized that these, "may represent smaller vats which were in the vestibule of the cave," at the time Wilkins and Gatewood purchased the cave. De Paepe thought they were not used during the War of 1812 in Mammoth Cave. There is some doubt these ridge dumps represent soils dumped from oxcarts, because excavation of ridge dumps in Great Saltpetre Cave reveal the presence of wooden V-vats in their interior.

Field evaluation of the ridge dumps reveals these features correlate to the intervening soil walls used to support a V-vat (George, 1989, pp. 74-76). The elevated position of the V-vats strengthens the concept that they operated in tandem with the Rotunda box hopper complex. Meriam (1844, pp. 318-319) observed that Rotunda "saltpetre

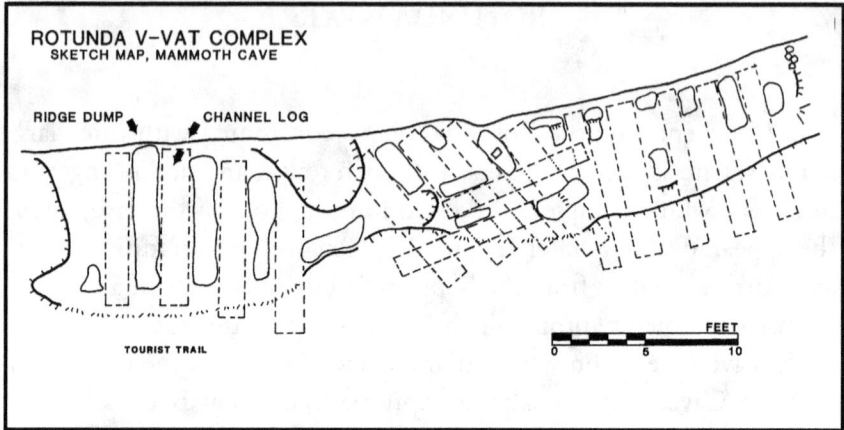

Figure 2-8. Sketch map of the Rotunda V-vat complex.

hoppers are constructed in the same manner as ash leaches are made," which implies V-vat construction. There is no documentation from the time period for box hoppers being used in the wood ash conversion of calcium nitrate leachate to saltpeter (potassium nitrate). Hunter's 1802 account of Great Saltpetre Cave describes what are obvious V-vats used in the wood-ash conversion process. Meriam makes no reference to box hoppers; rather his description is a direct reference to operational Rotunda V-vats in 1813. John Wood (1841, p. 89), with the same blind eye to the box hoppers, described the Rotunda processing center as dominated by "the remains of leaches in form of an inverted cone or like the *hopper* of a flower mill;" in other words, V-vats. They dominated the room, present in such numbers along the walls as to visually overpower the giant box hoppers in the middle of the room. After the war, V-vats gradually lost their preeminence, and were dismantled and damaged through vandalism and tourist traffic.

The location of the ridge dumps exhibits a symmetrical pattern. A sketch map (Figure 2-8) of surface topography along the west wall presents the basic layout of V-vat orientation. The topography consists of linear earth ridges, rarely over 3 feet high and usually spanning 2.5-5 feet measured between ridge crests. Lengths vary from 1.0-7.5 feet and approximately 1 foot wide at the crest. Cross-sections of ridge dumps are roughly triangular in shape with flat to rounded tops. Cavity floors average 1.3-1.8 feet wide. The majority of the ridges are perpendicular

46

Figure 2-9. Small V-vat channel log in place with lateral ridge dumps. Diana Emerson George photograph.

to the west wall of the cave. Nearest the tourist trail, 4 of them are parallel with the trail and oblique to the general orientation of 14 other ridges. Two additional V-vat ridges obliquely cross the 4 mentioned above. In their superposition, they represent a later generation of vat building. None of these features have in-situ channel logs (bottom drain rails of V-vats).

Near the south wall of the Rotunda are the remains of 7 channel logs. Channel logs are present in various lengths, although all are broken and some show charring on one end. These are massive logs measuring 1.35 feet or greater in diameter and from 2-7.7 feet long. A test fitting was made with one of the smallest channel logs. It was placed in several of the cavities between the ridge dumps with remarkably good fit (Figure 2-9).

The Rotunda V-vat processing center appears to have had an average channel log length of 8 feet, an internal hopper cavity 7.5 feet long with a wall height of about 3 feet. Based upon the author's field investigations, a plan of the hopper complex (dashed lines) may have looked similar to Figure 2-8. Positions for at least 15 hoppers with 8 feet long channel logs can be easily accommodated assuming ridge dumps were used as blocking wall structures. Site evidence indicates that 4 of the vats were later removed and 2 oblique ones built superimposed over the old removed hoppers.

From the pattern of spoil deposits and interpretation of the construction sequence, we can conclude that, as the level of discarded earth rose even higher, V-vats and hoppers were either abandoned or dismantled and reconstructed above their former level. Evidence for this practice is well preserved in Great Saltpetre Cave. The Mammoth Cave Rotunda group of V-vats is built on a higher saltpeter apron than the apron spread out from the box hoppers. Such a V-vat arrangement implies this apron grew at a faster pace than the box hopper apron. Furthermore, the V-vats may have operated in tandem with the box hoppers. These V-vats were left relatively empty at the end of the last mining season. Casual vandalism and tourist traffic, in the early years of operation as a tourist attraction, caused considerable harm to the mining artifacts. Bird (1837, pp. 431-433) and other antebellum writers witnessed the destruction of saltpeter artifacts by the cave guides. The guides broke apart and demolished many of the hoppers for bonfires used to illuminate the Rotunda. The large crib hoppers remaining today show damage, and Hopper No. 3 also displays considerable damage (Figure 2-7). All physical remnants of the V-vat structures have been removed from this area, most of the vat imprints on the cavity side of ridge dumps have been erased by foot traffic, and many of the ridge dumps leveled. Less damage to artifacts occurred at Booth's Amphitheatre. Ridge dumps flank both sides of the tourist trail, and good evidence for in-situ V-vats is present. Here, molds or casts of wood facing shingling and exterior supports in lixiviated earth remain intact.

The Great Comet of 1811 made its visual appearance on September 6th and continued until January 16, 1812. Brilliant by all accounts, the comet had a forked tail spanning more than 70 degrees above the horizon (Kronk, 1984, p. 27) and a visual head larger in appearance than our Sun (Sagan and Druyan, 1985, p. 137). Easily visible during the day, in the evening the comet provided a light show more spectacular than the aurora borealis. The comet cast shadows and generated a "peculiarly brilliant" light producing "twilight over the forest" (Penick, 1981, p. 118). To less educated people, the comet fed superstitions as a ill harbinger of things to come, the death of kings, Napoleon's rout from Moscow and devastating earthquakes. The New Madrid earthquakes discussed in detail in the following chapter completely changed the mining history of Mammoth Cave.

Figure 3-1. The "hard shock" earthquake of February 7, 1812, leveled the town of New Madrid. Henry Howe, *The Great West*, Cincinnati, (1851).

CHAPTER THREE

THE DAY THE EARTHQUAKE STRUCK THE SALTPETER WORKS

"... thunder is never heard in the Mammoth Cave, and a gentleman who was in it at the time a shock of an earthquake was experienced on the surface of the earth, did not perceive it."

Charles W. Wright, 1860

"The earthquake, the thunder of the nether world has here a solemn, a sublime, and awful echo. These walls tremble, and totter when the silence of its chambers are broken by the moaning of the earthquake's roar."

Ebenezer Meriam, 1844

Over a two-month time period, four devastating earthquakes originated from the vicinity of New Madrid, Missouri (Figures 3-1 and 3-2). The force of the disturbance was felt over a million square miles in eastern North America. The 1811-1812 temblors were the strongest earthquakes ever recorded in the contiguous United States during historic times. Hamilton and Johnston (1990, p. 3) tabulated the Moment Magnitude (M_w) for the strongest tremors. In rapid succession two devastating earthquakes struck on December 16, 1811 (M_w = 8.2, 7.8), followed by a massive shock on January 23, 1812 (M_w = 8.1), and the "hard shock" on February 7, 1812 (M_w = 8.3). Strong aftershocks continued to register from the locality during the next two years.

Physical evidence of earthquake wreckage was well documented in the vicinity of Louisville, Frankfort and Lexington, Kentucky.

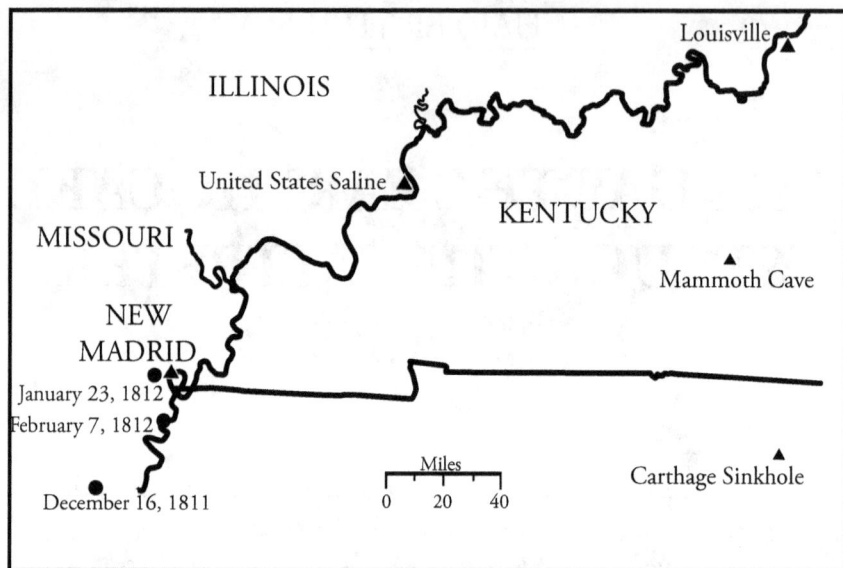

Figure 3-2. Sketch map showing the distribution of 1811-1812 New Madrid earthquake epicenters (solid circles) and geographic landmarks (solid triangles). Charles Wilkins leased much of the United States Saline, Illinois Territory, to manufacture salt from brine wells and was co-owner of Mammoth Cave. His Illinois operation experienced daily earthquakes for two years.

The extent of damage to industrial sites above and below ground has not been similarly described. Pioneer era Kentucky saltpeter factories in Mammoth Cave and Great Saltpetre Cave were severely affected (George and O'Dell, 1992; George, 2001a). The New Madrid earthquakes completely changed the mining history of Mammoth Cave.

Correspondence between purchasing agent Archibald McCall (1812) and his client Eleuthère Irénée du Pont is the earliest primary documentation describing damage to the Mammoth Cave works from the first two December earthquakes. Passing along information from his Kentucky saltpeter suppliers, he reported, "the earthquake on the 16th Dec'r had thrown down several of the hoppers & sunk the pump three feet." The Rotunda pump tower actually sank 4.7 feet into the ground. In Booth's Amphitheatre the Second Hoppers (named by Ward, 1816) were the only box hoppers that suffered damage. These hoppers are numbered 1 through 7 in ascending order away from the cave entrance (Figure 2-6). In the Rotunda area, box type First Hoppers (Ward, 1816) represent post earthquake construction (Figure 2-7).

There is no documentation to support the presence of box hoppers in this location prior to the earthquakes. The Rotunda is one of the areas in which soil liquefaction damaged engineered constructions during the December shock. The post-quake Rotunda hoppers are numbered 1 through 3 in ascending order counter clockwise away from the cave entrance (Figure 2-7). Figure 1-2 places the location of First and Second Hoppers, pipelines, pumping stations and the evaporation furnace complex in relation to the Mammoth Cave Historic Section.

DISRUPTION OF SALTPETER PRODUCTION

When the first temblor struck at 2:15 AM on December 16, 1811, workers and their supervisor Joseph Gatewood, brother to co-owner Fleming Gatewood, Sr., were in the cave making saltpeter at the Booth's Amphitheatre processing center. Terror stricken workers from Booth's Amphitheatre along with those bedded down in the Rotunda ran for the entrance as rocks fell in the cave (Ward, 1816). At 8:15 AM, another devastating earthquake hit the cave, almost as strong as the first one. "Large rocks sometimes became detached from the cliffs and tumble into the [Green] river with a tremendous noise, crushing every thing before them ... so many fell, as materially to impede the navigation of the river," wrote Edmund Lee (1835, p. 10). His source would have been Fleming Gatewood, Sr., tourist manager during Lee's engineers 1835 transit survey of Mammoth Cave. Evidently a close working association during Lee's survey of the cave prompted Gatewood to discuss his experiences during the earthquakes. This was something he rarely did and Lee's notes are cryptic at best. Hundreds and hundreds of strong aftershocks were felt for months and only slowly died out after a year of nearly constant vibration and shaking. Another year would pass until quiet returned to the countryside in the west. In between each of the major shocks, which occurred in December, January and February, workers gathered their courage as the earth gradually quieted and entered the cave to assess damage and make repairs, only to be driven out again by the next strong convulsion. Owner Charles Wilkins, resident in Lexington, was notified of damage to the works soon after the first quake.

Historically, the first inkling there was a problem in the manufacture of saltpeter at the cave is seen in the March 10, 1812 letter from Archibald McCall to Eleuthère Irénée du Pont, in which he passes

OVERVIEW OF EARTHQUAKE
TERMS AND CONCEPTS

Seismic activity in the vicinity of New Madrid is associated with a major fault rift zone analogous to the one in East Africa (McKeown, 1982, pp. 4, 9). Structurally it is a failed rift zone graben 44 miles wide and over 125 miles long, and is buried beneath a thick sequence of Quaternary sediments in a down warped structure called the Mississippian Embayment. The community of New Madrid is positioned over one of the bounding faults in a locality with a long geologic history for large and small earthquakes.

Modern earthquakes are recorded on seismographs. Richter Magnitude (R_m) indicates the size or strength of an earthquake with values ranging from 0-9.9 graphed on a logarithmic scale. The strength of Richter Magnitudes for the New Madrid temblors is significantly higher than other methods of determination, e.g., December 16, 1811, produced 8.6, January 23, 1812, generated an 8.4, and the "hard shock" of February 7, 1812, topped 8.7 (Penick, 1981, p. 141).

The size of the earthquake is determined by the largest surface wave recorded on a seismograph chart. Richter Magnitudes have been refined as Moment Magnitude (M_w) and these are often used interchangeably, although the two scales do not correspond exactly. Moment Magnitude values tend to better characterize strong earthquakes above Richter Magnitude 8. It is mathematically calculated from the Richter scale and is based on the amount of movement along a fault, amount of rupture, its depth and length, and the strength of the rock.

In the last two decades geologists have been able to measure this from faults in the vicinity of New Madrid and make extrapolations.

Before the advent of seismographs in the 1880s, the strength or destructive power of earthquakes relied on how people perceived the tremors based upon the amount of shaking felt and the amount of damage done to buildings or the landscape. This method was refined as the Modified Mercalli Scale (MM) with a range of I-XII. Most of what geologists know about 1811-1812 earthquake events has been converted to the Modified Mercalli Scale. Richter Magnitudes and Moment Magnitudes can be fitted to this chart of physical descriptions with a high degree of confidence.

Damage to man-made structures is caused by horizontal and vertical acceleration produced by the force of gravity during an earthquake. The shaking experienced during an earthquake is expressed as "g" or "g-force," and is equal to the weight of the object at a specific point. G-force acceleration establishes the force a structure experiences during an earthquake. Horizontal acceleration causes the back and forth movements during earthquakes, similar to the acceleration and sudden stopping of a car. Vertical acceleration adds to or subtracts the weight of an object due to gravity. Vertical acceleration is comparable to being in an elevator when it starts to move.

During strong earthquakes with magnitude (M_w) 5.5-7, saturated unconsolidated soils could be subjected to liquefaction (Rauch, 1997, p. 115). Liquefaction occurs during strong ground shaking causing soils to lose their cohesive strength to support solid objects on the surface. Objects may sink into the ground and, in some cases the earthquake may produce more dramatic features called catastrophic sinkholes. Unconsolidated sediments are redistributed in the ground, initiating general soil structural failure, which displays as an open hole in the ground.

Fuller (1912) discusses the occurrence and distribution of earthquake induced sinkholes in the New Madrid seismic disturbance locality. Objects built on landfill experience even greater ground motion during earthquakes by an amplitude factor of 5 to 10 (U. S. Geological Survey Staff, 1990), because seismic waves vibrate at a lower frequency through unconsolidated material and generate higher amplitudes (de Boer and Sanders, 2005, p. 15).

along information received from Charles Wilkins. Much of the saltpeter produced at Mammoth Cave was contracted to the Du Pont Powder Works. His communication from Wilkins described New Madrid earthquake damage to the saltpeter works and the reasons why there had been delays in shipments (McCall, 1812). This primary documentation is the earliest historic reference to difficulties with the manufacture of saltpeter as a result of the quakes. McCall's letter reveals that several of the hoppers were "thrown down" and the shaking had "sunk the pump three feet," all due to the December 16, 1811 earthquakes. This document becomes a significant benchmark from which new interpretations to Mammoth Cave history are made.

Wilkins had informed McCall that the operation was "under way" again, so presumably sufficient repairs had been made by late February 1812 to allow some saltpeter to be made. The operators hoped to soon bring the saltpeter works back up to speed, matching former production quotas of 3000 pounds of saltpeter per week. The damage was too extensive, however, and quantities produced were greatly reduced, little more than enough to cover expenses.

Wilkins notified McCall of shipment delays because his factory had suffered damage from the earthquakes. Unable to fill his contract obligation to Du Pont, Wilkins tried to cover shortfalls by obtaining saltpeter from other caves. To his misfortune, the earthquake had shut down all the producing caves in Kentucky. There was little saltpeter on the open market for Wilkins to purchase (McCall, 1812). News trickled in to east coast newspapers of the total destruction of New Madrid, Little Prairie, Big Prairie, and structural damage in Louisville. The lower Ohio River and Mississippi River in the epicenter area experienced channel blockage, creating new waterways, and islands appeared while others disappeared. Wreckage of numerous river crafts and tangles of tree snags obstructed the watercourses. As the early months of 1812 passed, attempts to restore normality to life and work at Mammoth Cave were disrupted by numerous daily aftershocks.

EARTHQUAKE DAMAGE

Borresen (1942) in his detailed archaeological survey of the Booth's Amphitheatre artifacts observed that vertical upright logs had been placed around the perimeter of the air chamber to reinforce several of the crib hoppers. This structural reinforcement helped support the hopper floor. All are nearly identical in construction with the exception of reinforcements in the first two. George (1990) identified Hopper Nos. 1 and 2 as the ones most likely to have been "thrown down" in McCall's letter (Figure 2-6). Recent fieldwork has confirmed that some repairs were made to the Second Hoppers after the December quake.

More great earthquakes occurred on January 23 and most serious of all, the "hard shock" on February 7, 1812. No documentation is known that describes damage to the saltpeter works from the last events. Separating the two later seismic events is not possible other than to suppose the February event would have produced the most destruction. We can postulate that damage to the processing stations similar to that produced by December quakes must have occurred during the January event followed by a more devastating effect on February 7. We are left to examine physical artifacts for clues needed to gauge the degree of damage.

The wood hoppers were constructed in such a way as to be taken apart and reassembled at a higher elevation to keep pace with a growing saltpeter apron. After the earthquakes it should have been a simple matter to take them apart, make repairs and reassemble the structures. This was not done. The destruction is thought to have been so complete it was easier to build gangs of new V-vats above the Second Hoppers (in what is today north of the tourist trail) and construct three new box hoppers of a new design in the Rotunda. These were augmented with gangs of new V-vats around the edge of the room (George, 1989). Repairs were presumably made to the Rotunda pump tower and pipeline.

SHOCKWAVE AND LIQUEFACTION DAMAGE

Shockwave damage and cave soil liquefaction during the 1811-1812 earthquakes may have generated the total destruction of the Second Hoppers processing station. To resolve this question, we must be able to identify and distinguish structural damage produced by an earthquake from expected deterioration consequent to a lapse of almost two hundred years. If what we see is earthquake damage, then each hopper represents a frozen moment from that time period. Using the water troughs located south of the tourist trail as a reference point, the spatial relationships among the Second Hopper grouping were inspected and assessed for potential earthquake damage (Figure 2-6).

Figure 3-3. Hopper No. 1 shows dry rot induced collapsed floors, sub-sided earth blocks, liquefaction soil induced wall bowing into the hopper cavity. View is toward the south from the tourist trail. Diana Emerson George photograph.

Hopper No. 1

The west wallboards of the hopper show considerable bowing toward the south in the vicinity of the water trough (Figure 3-3). Evidence includes broken nailing studs near the floorboards. Some of the nails are pulled through the wooden wallboards, leaving the nails still in the nailing stud. The wallboards along the east side are bowed into the hopper cavity below the top coaming frame rail. The coaming frame is made from hand hewn white oak beams 5 ½ X 3 ¾ inches, built around the top of the hopper to give it great structural support. The coaming rail is also bowed. Lixiviated earth along the east wall appears to be plumb even though wallboards are bowed into the cavity. The lixiviated earth next to the west wall has bowed toward the cavity of the hopper, breaking nailing studs and bending the wallboards. The south wallboards are bowed toward the south into the open cave passage. For this inward bulging to occur, the soils had to be in a wet, plastic condition at the time the hopper was in operation.

Figure 3-4. Aerial detail of Hopper No. 2 with skyward buckled floorboards. The wall on the right is bowed into the cavity. View is toward the south from the tourist trail. Diana Emerson George photograph.

Hopper No. 2

The hopper is mostly empty of earth (Figure 3-4). The east wallboards and top coaming frame are bowed into the cavity. The west wallboards have a slight bow into the cavity. South wallboards along the water trough are pushed outward toward the open cave passage and are about 2 ½ inches out of vertical alignment.

Half of the floorboards in the hopper have collapsed into the east air chamber (Figures 3-4). The center stone foundation wall in the air chamber supports the sloping floorboards in an upright position. East and west mortise stringers have been broken off in the tenons. Floorboards on the west side of the hopper were removed at some prior date.

Hopper No. 3

The east wallboards are bowed into the cavity along with the top coaming frame rail (Figure 3-5). The hopper has a broken top coaming frame rail along the west sidewall. The break continues down through the sidewall, forcing half the wall into the tank cavity. Bowing is pronounced toward the tourist trail (north). The west side third nailing

59

Figure 3-5. Hopper No. 3 illustrates dry rot collapse of the saltpeter earth and soil liquefaction breakage through the right (west) wall. View is toward the south from the tourist trail. Diana Emerson George photograph.

stud is broken and bent into the hopper cavity. The wall casts of lixiviated soil along the west side are bowed toward the cavity space.

Hopper No. 4

The east side wallboards appear forced into the hopper cavity, becoming more pronounced toward the tourist trail (north). The hopper wall has moved away from the coaming frame rail. The west wallboards are bowed into the cavity, although the vertical soil wall looks straight. South wallboards along the water trough are becoming detached but this does not appear to be related to the earthquakes.

Hopper No. 5

This structure was demolished during tourist trail construction to the Gothic Avenue staircase.

Hopper No. 6

This hopper does not exhibit any apparent bulge of the hopper wall. Most of the wood walls have been removed, and the remaining wall cast of lixiviated soil appears plumb.

Hopper No. 7

The east top coaming frame rail and wallboards display bowing inward into the cavity of the hopper. The wall cast of lixiviated soil appears plumb.

DISCUSSION

Mammoth Cave box hoppers are huge constructions when compared to the leaching V-vats and crib hoppers used at other saltpeter mining sites in the State. Average hopper dimensions in Booth's Amphitheatre measure 12 feet 11 ¾ inch by 12 feet 9 ¼ inch and 3 feet deep and are filled with 18 inches of dry cave soil having an estimated weight of 12.7 tons. Once water is added and mixed with the soil, the fluid mud contents of such hoppers would weigh in excess of 17.5 tons. This great weight placed considerable stress on the hoppers and required additional support. Structural reinforcement was usually provided along three sides of each hopper by placing spent soil around their perimeter, shoveled wet or dry from the hoppers as leaching was completed for each batch. The soil rose around the hoppers and kept the walls from bursting outward. Outward bowing is apparent in Hopper No. 1 in the Rotunda (Figure 2-7) along with the south walls of Hoppers Nos. 1 and 2 in Booth's Amphitheatre (Figure 2-6). Discarded wet lixiviated earth filled all the nooks and crannies around the outside of each hopper frame. In time this earth dried out and became as hard as adobe or cement (Borresen, 1942, p. 3). These deposits aided immensely in supporting the structural integrity of all the hoppers.

Wood floors in all the existing Second Hoppers have collapsed into their air chamber. This started to become apparent prior to 1837 (Bird, p. 438). Borresen (1942, p. 4) adduced the collapse occurred long after the mining era when the weight of "8-10" (12.7) tons of dry soil became "too much for the decayed material" to support. Even the floor in empty Hopper No. 2 collapsed into its air chamber (Figure 3-4).

On many of the hoppers the top coaming frame is bent. Wood will bend and break during a strong tremor, but it will not retain the bend once the force is removed. It will spring back to its original position. Bent coaming frames are probably related to the aging of the saltpeter hoppers.

Without doubt, all the saltpeter artifacts in Mammoth Cave have been subjected to dry rot, an organic decay of wood in contact with soils through the action of fungi. Certainly it must be considered as one of the agents responsible for the condition of the box vats today. Wood members in contact with cave soil are as light as balsawood and best described as fragile.

The physical character of the remnant soils in the hoppers supports dry rot. These soils were once a fluid to viscous mud combined with milled limestone gravel that had been mixed by hand and feet to uniform consistency. Hopper contents were all dry at the time of collapse into their air chambers (except Hopper No. 2). The collapse soils are characteristically broken into large joint blocks. The free face of each block represents a tension joint formed when the blocks pulled apart in sections and collapsed down through the wood floors into the bottom of the air chamber (Figures 3-3 and 3-5). If the soils were fluid to viscous at the time of collapse, blocks of hardened soil defined by joints would not have been the result. Instead, mudflow and mound structures would be present with in situ hopper deposits and on the broken hopper remains at the bottom of the air chambers. Wet, lixiviated soils manually dumped onto mounds east of the hopper complex during the mining era exhibit mudflow characteristics. The current site investigation agrees with Borresen (1942) in favor of dry rot. There remain however geologic features and certain damage to artifacts, that cannot be assigned to dry rot damage.

Shock waves from each of the New Madrid earthquakes struck the cave from the southwest. The main trunk passage in Mammoth Cave is oriented in such a fashion that the advancing earthquake hit the cavern broadside along its entire length. The seismic wave moved across the cave passage, whose shockwave amplitude was amplified by a factor of 5 to 10, magnified by spent saturated earth landfill (U. S. Geological Survey Staff, 1990) over thick unconsolidated alluvial deposits in Booth's Amphitheatre. The February 7 earthquake produced a shockwave ten to twenty times stronger than the December event. The proposed Modified Mercalli Intensity Scale (MM) for December was VIII intensity in Mammoth Cave (equivalent to Richter Magnitude of 6.9). The estimated Modified Mercalli intensity regional map supports this conclusion (Hamilton and Johnston, 1990, p. 7). The February "hard shock" would push the Mercalli Scale to an IX value (Richter

Magnitude of 7.0). This intensity would be ruinous for surface structures with partial or total destruction of some buildings along with pipeline breakage. One would expect similar damage to the structures and pipeline inside Mammoth Cave.

Nahum Ward (1816) described the effects of the New Madrid earthquakes in Mammoth Cave from notes written during his November 1815 exploration. He visited the site in the company of a slave guide who was at the Second Hoppers during the first temblors. According to the report he received, "...about five minutes before the shock, a heavy rumbling sound was heard coming out of the Cave like a mighty wind; that when that ceased, the rocks cracked, and all appeared to be going in a moment to final destruction – however, no one was injured, although large rocks fell in some parts of the Cave."

Three components of a seismogram can be partially constructed from the guide's description. The "heavy rumbling noise" heralded the arrival of the P-wave (Primary wave). "Five minutes" later (actually less than two minutes) the S-wave (Secondary wave) arrived followed by the surface compression or Rayleigh waves, which shook the ground strongly for 3½ to 4 minutes and registered considerable damage even beyond Louisville (Brooks, in McMurtrie, 1818, p. 233). Mammoth Cave is a hollow cavity located in the uppermost strata of the earth's crust. Surface rocks containing caves would be subjected to advancing wave front deformation normally visible at the earth's surface.

Surface compression wave effects were registered in the cave from descriptions made after the fact. Statements such as: the hoppers were "thrown down" (McCall, 1812); the cave "walls tremble, and totter" (Meriam, 1844, p. 324); "all appeared to be going in a moment to final destruction" (Ward, 1816); and "the tremulous motion of the earth filled the miners with alarm" (Binkerd, 1869, p. 17) can all be associated with surface compression waves. These statements correlate well with descriptions made by people who experienced ground shaking and witnessed structural damage in Louisville during the same time period (Brooks, in McMurtrie, 1818).

Evidence of structural damage to the saltpeter hoppers located in Booth's Amphitheatre can be interpreted as earthquake induced. Shockwaves propagated from the New Madrid February epicenter are used to recreate the direction and sequence of earthquake damage. At rest, the backfilling of dry lixiviated soils behaves as a rigid container around three sides of the embedded hopper enclosure. Liquefaction will not occur in dry unsaturated soils. Shockwave pulsations hit the hoppers at an oblique angle and applied a directional stress. The compression wave squeezed the east and west walls, flexing them toward the area of least resistance, the open hopper. During the earthquake, mud in the hoppers would slosh about generating compressive forces inside the hoppers on the walls and floor. The mud would have behaved much like water in a bathtub. Some of the wallboards were pushed right out of the nailing studs by the force, leaving the nails still in the stud (Hopper No. 1). Nailing studs and top coaming frames were broken toward the open cavity in the direction of the advancing earthquake wave front (Figure 3-5). Broken nailing studs near the floor suggest vertical motion (William Liebman, personal communication, January 8, 2005). Hoppers Nos. 1 thru 4 appear to have been damaged along a centerline through each hopper (Figure 2-6). Hopper No. 2 gives a better perspective to the earthquake damage (Figures 3-4). The floor of the hopper is buckled upward west of center over the north-south axis of the center stone foundation. This is the location of greatest structural support to the hopper floor. Three of the basal stringer supports are broken in a fashion that can only be produced by lateral up-arched compression. This visual evidence supports the concept of compression or Rayleigh wave damage to the hopper complex.

William Liebman (personal communication, January 8, 2005) offered suggestions based on his engineering geological experience with earthquake damaged frame houses and businesses in California. He thought the "hard shock" of February 7th was different than all the rest of the great earthquakes. Accounts from people located near the epicenter to places as far away as Louisville describe destruction and damage to physical structures far greater than the preceding earthquakes. Yet the Moment Magnitudes are closely comparable in strength. The February "hard shock" was different in how people perceived it and generated greater damage. Liebman offered reasons why the "hard shock" was different. Since the magnitudes are similar (much closer on a logarithmic scale), then "it has to be in the type of acceleration produced by the seismic waves." He offered:

If there is a difference in the type of motion in Feb than

previous then this could answer questions. A different motion could nullify a repair from different motion damage. Repairs to lateral motion would do nothing to protect from vertical motion. So a subsequent event could easily cause more problems. Vertical shocks tend to be "sharper" and louder and more snap than horizontal shaking. My impression is the February event was more vertical motion and the earlier events more lateral motion. The "hard shock" description also suggest this to me. A blown out container side or opposite side suggest horizontal acceleration forces at work. Bulged sides and a blown out bottom could suggest vertical motion.

Vertical acceleration is less likely to "throw the vats off their supports" than horizontal will. Vertical acceleration will blow out the lower portion of the sides, and bottom of the vat. Horizontal will take the sides apart evenly. Or a combination of this in oblique motion.

The one thing different about the New Madrid earthquake is the "rather remarkable vertical movements accompanied these tremors, which resulted in permanent changes in the landscape" (Brumbaugh, 1999, p. 150).

Field investigation for liquefaction indicates most of the soils around the exterior of the hoppers were dry at the time of the earthquakes. Hopper Nos. 1 and 3 provide the best evidence for the bowing of liquefied soils into their cavities (Figures 3-3 and 3-5). This damage can be observed only on the west side of each hopper (Figure 2-6). The lixiviated soils separating these two hoppers had to be wet at the time for wall damage associated with post December soil liquefaction to occur. This scenario is consistent with probable repairs made to Hoppers Nos. 1 and 2. Once made the excavation was backfilled with wet lixiviated earth around each of these hoppers. Hoppers Nos. 1, 2, and 3 show the greatest damage. They were nearest the point where the earthquake propagated through the cave and experienced the greatest force similar to being in the first few cars of a roller coaster. The abandonment of the Second Hoppers following the earthquakes is thought to have occurred under circumstances similar to those evident at Great Saltpetre Cave (George, 2001a). The watertight hoppers no longer functioned as designed. Broken structural members and floorboards, coupled with wallboard failure, promoted uncontrolled leakage to areas other than the saltpeter leachate collection troughs.

THE SUNKEN PUMP TOWER

Shockwave and liquefaction also affected the pump tower in the Rotunda. As situated today, it is actually 4.7 feet too low to allow gravity drainage to the entrance, when measured along the centerline from the pump spigot to the pipeline at the Cave Entrance Gate. The December New Madrid earthquakes evidently initiated liquefaction around the whole central area of the Rotunda. The soil around the tower subsided at least 3 feet along with the pump tower as Wilkins reported to McCall (McCall, 1812). Another 1.7 feet of subsequent liquefaction subsidence probably occurred during the January and February "hard shocks." Ideal circumstances for liquefaction were promoted by very wet and muddy conditions about the tower resulting from leaking pipes, tanks, priming overflow of the pump, and V-vats. Deposits in the Rotunda consisted of thick sands overlain with 5 feet of clay (Ridgely, 1811) and topped off with lixiviated landfill deposits. At the time of the earthquakes, the clay unit probably had already been mined away. Saturated landfill deposits were underlain by more than 82 feet of unconsolidated stream derived sand, gravel, and silt over cave breakdown boulders (George, 1990). Shaking like a bowl full of Jell-O™, the near surface saturated deposits lost their cohesive strength and turned to mud soup, along with differential compaction of sediments. Liquefaction around the Rotunda pump tower created a large subsidence sinkhole. This new interpretation is based on McCall's (1812) literal meaning of *sinking the pump*, contrasts sharply with the common perception that this feature is a product of saltpeter mining. Sinkholes produced by the earthquake were common about the town of New Madrid located along the Mississippi River flood plane (Fuller, 1912, pp. 87-88). Sinkhole formation is due to redistribution of stratified sand deposits during liquefaction. The intensity of the earthquake in the cave for December was estimated as a Modified Mercalli Scale VIII, which is exactly at the medium strength necessary to produce liquefaction events in unconsolidated stream derived sediments. The Mammoth Cave sediments were saturated with leachate near the surface of the soil interface with the cave cavity. This is the right combination needed for subsidence of the pump tower into a sinkhole. Although earthquake-induced sinkholes tend to be concentrated near the epicenter, those developed in Mammoth Cave appear to be exceptions to this. The phenomenon was not limited to Mammoth Cave alone; a huge catastrophic liquefaction induced sinkhole opened up 60 miles northeast of Nashville near Carthage (Fort Bloant) in an Ordovician karst locality adjacent to Cumberland River (Figure 3-2). The sinkhole occupied "a track of land four miles square had sunk about four feet" (Anon., 1812, in Street and Green, 1984, p. A71). Horizontal distances between New Madrid and Mammoth Cave (~195 miles) and Fort Bloant near Carthage (~210 miles) are similar. There were also liquefaction induced earthquake cracks as far as Louisville, ~255 miles from New Madrid.

Figure 1-2 shows the location of three lift stations associated with the Mammoth Cave mining operation. According to McCall's letter, a pump station in the cave was "sunk three feet," but he did not specify which station. How may we determine which pump was "sunk" by the earthquake? Shortly before the earthquakes, the entrance station utilized buckets to lift the leachate out of the cave (Farnham, 1820) and there would not be pumps in the entrance until 1813 (Meriam, 1844). This leaves two pumps known to be actually located within the cave. The only pump station that exhibits a vertical discrepancy that would prevent gravity flow is the one in the Rotunda (Mullin, 1986, p. 17), which is described more fully in Chapter Four. After four major earthquakes and the obvious failure of the Rotunda pump, a level survey had to be conducted before hydraulic repairs could be attempted. A larger pump tower is conjectured to have been built around the existing structure and a second pump was installed on a higher platform drew water from the elevated water tank at the top of the old tower (Figure 4-13). With the tandem pump system, the hydraulic requirement needed to lift the leachate a minimum of 22.6 feet was satisfied to just barely reestablish gravity flow to the entrance (George and O'Dell, 1992; and George, 1990). This is based upon remnants of tower legs of longer lengths. Once fitted around the existing tower, these revealed they were of the right size needed to support a platform-mounted tank to maintain gravity flow of leachate. Field measurements and the survey are based upon an engineering transit survey conducted by the Historic American Engineering Record, National Park Service (Mullin, 1986).

The large depression about the pump tower and hoppers in the Rotunda is almost certainly a product of liquefaction subsidence and is only partly the result of land filling above and around the hoppers as spent earth was removed and discarded. Gatewood and Wilkins did not have to conduct a level survey to know the pump had been sunk 3 feet. The subsidence sinkhole would be immediately visible upon entrance into the Rotunda producing the same amount of awe tourists experience today seeing the saltpeter works. The effects on the pump tower are discussed in more detail in Chapter Four. The very large and relatively intact hoppers clustered around the pump tower represent new construction after the series of earthquakes on February 7th. None of these hoppers appear to have been damaged by the earthquake, although located in a known locality of soil liquefaction.

The effects of the earthquakes upon Mammoth Cave were not generally publicized, so that over time a popular mythology developed that the cave was earthquake proof. Early guidebooks and the patter of mid 20th Century tour guides represent the dry levels of Mammoth Cave as a safe haven from various disasters, e.g., violent storms and nuclear attack as well as earthquakes. Although upper level cave passages would certainly provide a refuge from storms, this does not hold true, obviously, for earthquakes or for detonations during nuclear warfare events.

The earliest account of Mammoth Cave as a safe haven is found in Binkerd (1869, p. 17), who notes: "since the cave has proved a safe retreat during a violent earthquake, it is hardly probable that it could be unsafe at other times." Binkerd's claim appears to derive from Wright (1860, p. 24), "thunder is never heard in the Mammoth Cave, and a gentleman who was in it at the time a shock of an earthquake was experienced on the surface of the earth, did not perceive it." Underground places have had a long tradition as being safe places to go in times of danger. Colleen Olson (2001, p. 116) recently explored the developmental fallacy of using Mammoth Cave as a fallout shelter during a nuclear holocaust. During the Cold War era in the 1960s, members of the National Speleological Society at the request of the Federal Government investigated the possibility of using caves across America for this purpose and concluded later that caves were not suitable for a number of reasons. Before the findings, hundreds of caves were outfitted with

POST-TRAUMATIC STRESS PRODUCED BY THE NEW MADRID EARTHQUAKES IN MAMMOTH CAVE

There were many reasons why those who were involved in the mining operation at Mammoth Cave during the earthquake series would prefer to avoid publicity about the effects. For those in the cave during the shocks, it was truly a traumatic experience. The National Center for Post-Traumatic Stress Disorder defines post-traumatic stress disorder as "a psychiatric disorder that can occur following the experience or witnessing of life threatening events" which may include natural disasters as well as combat situations. Persons suffering from the disorder "often relive the experience through nightmares and flashbacks, have difficulty sleeping, and feel detached or estranged, and these symptoms can be severe enough and last long enough to significantly impair the person's life."

Those who attempted to work in the cave during the earthquake period experienced not only the four major shocks spread through December, January and February, but also hundreds of lesser aftershocks that would still be strongly felt for several years after the main temblors. Under these circumstances, the apprehension of imminent death was so strong that the slaves staged worker strikes and even the supervisor refused to go back into the cave, not only at Mammoth, but in all the saltpeter mines across the region, where work halted for months.

This type of fear caused a major population shift out of western Kentucky after the New Madrid earthquakes. People left the locality by thousands, creating a depopulated wasteland and depressed economy. Abandoned prime real estate, businesses and farms could not be sold at any price. Western Kentucky became a place nobody wanted to live for fear of devastating earthquakes. Only after the Civil War did the area slowly repopulate with people having no firsthand memory from that early time.

Source: http: // www.ncptsd. org.

Civil Defense supplies as part of a feel good panacea needed to calm a troubled population during those anxious paranoid times.

The damage occurred from the quakes and interruption of processing at the Mammoth Cave works dealt a crippling financial blow to Wilkins, Gatewood and Gratz. Overnight, one of the greatest saltpeter producing caves in America teetered on the brink of financial ruin. Nor was Mammoth Cave alone in its difficulties. Cave mining operations throughout the region ceased production as result of the multiple quake episodes, including the largest operation, Great Saltpetre Cave. The industry was devastated (George, 2001a). Management disagreements promoted a hostile takeover by Gratz in late 1813, shutting Wilkins out of the business. This failed to save the operation, however, for within a few weeks production at Mammoth virtually ceased altogether (George, 1988). From all appearances, it seems Wilkins was the glue that gave Mammoth Cave its purpose as the nations preeminent saltpeter factory. Du Pont (1829) wrote, "the caves of Kentucky, which had furnished the principal supply until 1814 were then generally exhausted, the richest had been worked and could produce no more." Mammoth Cave was one of the "richest" and experienced some short-lived mining activity in 1814 (Meriam, 1844), no doubt from Dixon Cave and sparingly during the time of Ward's (1816) visit to Mammoth Cave in November 1815 and in 1816 (Anon.). There was still some western demand for saltpeter after the end of the war in 1815, which is consistent with post 1815 saltpeter mining in Wyandotte Cave, Indiana (George, 2001b).

Figure 4-1. Gothic Avenue in Mammoth Cave was the main passage leading down to Gratz Avenue into one of the principal mining areas of the cave. *The Great Republic Kentucky*, (1871).

CHAPTER FOUR

VIEW FROM THE WRECKAGE: REBUILDING THE SALTPETER WORKS

"Mammoth Cave, one of the greatest curiosities the country affords."

John H. Farnham, 1820

The earthquake damage left owners Charles Wilkins and Fleming Gatewood, Sr., with the task of orchestrating what amounted to a complete rebuilding of the saltpeter factory above and below ground. It was imperative to be back in operation as fast as possible. Not only were there contract obligations, the commodity price of saltpeter on the open market was ever increasing. From the interpreted collected historical record (George and O'Dell, 1992; George, 1989, 1990, 2001a) the following reconstruction scenario is offered.

Gathering their courage after the two initial shocks on December 16, mine workers cautiously re-entered the cave (Figure 4-1). While underground they had to contend with hundreds of aftershocks. Fear and trepidation diminished their productivity as repairs and mining progressed intermittently.

Workers made repairs and construction on the hoppers in Mammoth Cave only to have their handiwork dashed to the ground during the January 23 major shock and the "hard shock" of February 7, 1812. All of the newly constructed and repaired hoppers in Booth's Amphitheatre were damaged so as to render them inoperable. The great quakes damaged Hopper Nos. 1, 2, and 3 and subsided the Rotunda pump tower 4.7 feet. The February temblor was strong enough to rupture the pipelines in the cave. Although there is no direct physical or documentary evidence for this, pipeline breakage is often associated with quakes of that magnitude.

Surveying the damage, Gatewood was probably dismayed by the extent of repairs that would be needed and what it was all going to cost. The first thing that would have caught his eyes in the Rotunda was that the central pump tower room had subsided into a sinkhole. No matter how vigorous one might work the pump handle, leachate from the hoppers would no longer flow out to the entrance collection tank. The liquid just stalled in the pipeline and overflowed the pump's elevated collection tank. This hydraulic problem would need immediate correction for the mine to resume processing saltpeter. Labor problems compounded the dilemma of bringing the works back into operation. African-American slaves went on informal strikes after each of the great shocks and refused to enter the cave. The succession of aftershocks following the December 16th quake did not provide more than ten minutes respite between tremors (Brooks, in McMurtrie, 1819, p. 233) and kept workers in a state of agitation. The slave workers remained on the surface during the early winter months, even after the weather turned much colder. They may have taken refuge in sandstone rockhouses and rock shelters "where the hunters formerly took up their abode" at Mammoth Cave (Lee, 1835, p. 10). Even the cave manager and saltpeter maker, Archibald Miller, Sr., was so terrified he refused to enter the cave.

This unrelenting chaos, exacerbated by the hard shocks of January and February and nearly constant agitation of the earth, must have frustrated Gatewood to no end. The financial commitment needed from Gatewood to make extensive repairs was more than he was willing to bear. He solved his problems by selling his half interest in the cave to wealthy Hyman Gratz of Philadelphia on April 18, 1812, for $10,000 ($136,000 today). Newly capitalized, he purchased a cave south of Mammoth Cave along the Natchez Trace that became known as Gatewood Salt Petre Cave (present day Coach Cave on the Park Mammoth property).

Even as Gatewood began to disengage himself from the operation, new construction presumably began under the supervision of Archibald Miller, Sr. A new central processing station was built around the sunken pump tower in the Rotunda (Figure 1-2). Here, a new style of box hoppers with imbricate filters was constructed (Figure 4-7), based on one of the types used in Great Saltpetre Cave (Figure 2-1). This new filter system consisted of interlocking half round hollowed out logs. The lack of earthquake damage to this hopper style is convincing evidence for post February 7th "hard shock" construction. Gangs of V-vats continued to be used around the perimeter of the room. The tower in the Rotunda may have been taken apart and reassembled in a plumb position. A conjectured tandem pump tower fitted with two old English style manual wood pumps could have solved the problem of gravity flow of leachate to the entrance pumping station (Figure 4-13). Approaching the First Hoppers from the entrance gives the impression one is looking down into the bottom of a sinkhole full of wood structures. As the renovated operation came up to speed, discarded lixiviated earth from the V-vats and hoppers was spread out over the floor. The saltpeter apron gradually rose above the three hoppers. The apron also served a utilitarian purpose in bringing the oxcart service ramp above the hopper rims. This facilitated dumping of fresh saltpeter earth directly into the hoppers. The absence of discarded soils around the sides of Hopper No. 1 (Figure 2-7) suggests it was the last one built. It would have been imperative to stabilize hopper wall exteriors as fast as possible to prevent bursting outward from the weight of cave earth being processed. The walls of this hopper are noticeably bowed outward. This further implies that it was used only one time with the first charge still in the hopper.

The cave entrance pump tower associated with the external evaporation furnace complex originally used buckets lifted by hand (Farnham, 1820), but was upgraded by installation of tandem old English style hand "pumps" (Meriam, 1844; Mullin, 1986, p. 17). After the earthquakes, the two freestanding 20 feet tall furnace chimneys probably needed to be repaired, along with living quarters. Earthquake damage to structures in Louisville, farther from the epicenter, included fallen chimneys, collapse of gable ends in log buildings, and cracked brickwork in more substantial homes (Brooks, in McMurtrie, 1818).

By August 25, 1812, Hyman Gratz finalized his investment in the mine works, buying out Gatewood and acquiring the interests of all other prior owners of Mammoth Cave except for Charles Wilkins (Thomas, *et al.*, 1970, pp. 324-325). For a time, following the quake,

Wilkins and his new business partner continued to repair and upgrade the saltpeter operation. No documentation has been discovered to suggest what kind of improvements other than repairs were made in the cave. Reconstruction of the sequence of modifications to the operation relies primarily upon interpretation of physical evidence. The condition of the artifacts in the cave indicates that the saltpeter works was severely damaged by the New Madrid earthquakes of 1811-1812. The influx of cash from Gratz allowed significant repairs and retooling to be made in Mammoth Cave. The position of artifacts and spoil piles strongly suggests that box hoppers in Booth's Amphitheatre were abandoned and gangs of V-vats built north of the tourist trail. In all likelihood the pipeline in the cave needed repairing.

The late 1811, pre-quake workforce was increased from 20 or 30 to 70 slave laborers in 1813 (Farnham, 1820; Meriam, 1844). Even with additional manpower, the cave never regained its pre-quake production yield of 3000 pounds per week (McCall, 1812). Large numbers of inexperienced workers and the abandonment of the specialized tertiary method of saltpeter refinement implemented by Gatewood, contributed to quality control problems. More seriously, the saltpeter resource was being depleted, because nitrate-bearing soils had been mined out from all the passageways near the processing centers. Nearby Dixon Cave was purchased to make up the difference in production deficits (see Chapter Five). As a result of greatly reduced production output and quality problems, Wilkins and Gratz lost their contracts to supply saltpeter to the E. I. Du Pont Company, their largest customer.

HYDRAULIC SYSTEM IN THE CAVE

A historical interpretation of the hydraulic system in Mammoth Cave lends much to our understanding of early pioneer industrial technology. No documentation from the period of operation is known describing the mechanics as to how the system worked or stages of construction. We are left to reconstruct the operation from a very few published references, a handful of primary documents, and dispersed and fragmentary artifacts in the cave. The marvelous fieldwork conducted by Borresen (1942), Faust (1967), De Paepe (1986) and Mullin (1986) provides an excellent roadmap to these early times. Mullin's (1986, p. 16) watershed work encapsulated the dilemma confronting modern interpreters in that "many parts of the pumps, pumptowers, and pipeline are missing today and written evidence is limited. Only conjecture can be made about the details of the operation."

Horace C. Hovey (1882, p. 57) viewed the saltpeter works and offered his opinion as to how the manufacturing plant operated. Thor Borresen (1942) was the first to propose and draft engineering details of the leaching hoppers and the hydraulic system of pipelines and pumps in the cave. Field investigations by Faust (1967) and De Paepe (1986) relied heavily on Hovey and Borresen for their interpretation of the mine works. This research was synthesized in Mullin (1986) and combined with new engineering-architectural drawings, which added greatly to our knowledge of the pioneer mining operation. Although work by Borresen and Mullin was never published, it was used internally within the National Park Service to manage and interpret the artifacts and as a result became one of the cornerstones in the interpretation of Mammoth Cave history. George and O'Dell (1992) and George (1990) provided an account of the disruption caused by the New Madrid earthquakes, focusing upon damage to the hoppers and the hydraulic system associated with the Rotunda pump tower. Each interpretation has built upon the work of their predecessors. This chapter further develops the historical analysis of the hydraulic system, addressing the issue of the pumps used to move process water and leachate.

A complicated dual hydraulic system transported fresh water into the cave to the processing centers and moved leachate outward to the furnace complex for evaporation in the boiling kettles. Bringing water in could be accomplished with relative ease through simple gravity flow from a spring at the entrance, since the entrance area was at a higher elevation than the processing centers in the Rotunda and at Booth's Amphitheatre. Moving leachate outward from the hopper complex was a much more difficult undertaking for the same reason; every gallon of leachate had to be pumped uphill. This required the construction of three separate pumping stations to move the leachate outdoors in stages, in much the same manner as ships traversing the Panama Canal are elevated in sequential locks.

Leachate from the vats or hoppers in each processing center flowed through a connected series of wooden troughs that were inclined toward a large collection tank beneath a tall pumping tower. A

Figure 4-2A. Elevated saltpeter pipes in the Methodist Church. Diana Emerson George photograph.

simple, hand-operated wooden pump located atop the tower brought the leachate up into a holding tank, from which liquid was allowed to gravity drain to the next station. The maximum vertical distance that leachate could be raised at any station was restricted mainly by the ceiling height of the room and, to a lesser extent, by the inherent limitations imposed upon lift pumps by atmospheric pressure. Pumping stations were located at Booth's Amphitheatre, farthest into the cave and at the lowest elevation; at the Rotunda complex; and at the cave entrance, from where it was conveyed to the furnaces.

The plumbing system for both fresh process water and leachate consisted of log pipes placed end-to-end. Logs approximately 7-8 inches in diameter and 8-26 feet long were hollowed through using an auger, and the ends shaped into pointed male and recessed female fittings (Figure 4-2A). The male end of the pipe was inserted into the female, the tapered end indicating the direction of flow (Figure 4-2B). The connection was held together by friction and by an iron band tightened around the joint. The iron band also helped to prevent splitting of the ends. Generally, the pipeline was laid directly upon the floor of the cave, but in places was elevated using an A-frame structure of logs (Martin, 1851, p. 20) or heavy forked tree branches (Figures 1-12

Figure 4-2B. Detail of saltpeter pipeline connection. Diana Emerson George photograph.

and 4-2A).

Certain sections of the pipeline that are visible today are erroneous reconstructions made long after the mining era, when Mammoth had become a tourist attraction. Henry C. Ganter leased the cave and acted as manager from about 1888 to 1902, making a number of improvements to tour routes. One such improvement was the construction of the double elevated pipeline seen today in the cave near the Methodist Church, completed no later than 1889 (Ganter and Darnall, 1889a). In this reconstruction, the pipelines are supported on rock towers, a technique which was not used during the actual mining era. There is no record of the existence of this feature prior to this time. Ironically, Ganter's elevated pipeline has become one of the most photographed and described features in the cave (Figure 4-2A).

During the winter of 1812-1813 "the pipes in the cave burst" (McCall, 1813), forcing a halt to production until repairs could be made. This probably referred to the fresh water pipeline; depending upon where the blowout occurred there could have been as much as 50 feet of head pressure in the line. Pipeline ruptures were a common occurrence in early Cincinnati municipal water systems using wood pipelines (Pruse, 1973, p. 48).

Figure 4-3. Stone aquatint illustration of Booth's Amphitheatre pump tower with staircase into Gothic Avenue. Alexander Bullitt, *Rambles in the Mammoth Cave*, Morton & Griswold, Louisville, KY, (1845).

BOOTH'S AMPHITHEATRE

The pump tower in Booth's Amphitheatre was needed to lift the leachate 18 feet above the bottom of the collection tank into an upper reservoir (Figure 4-3, 4-4, 4-5, and 2-6). The elevated tank needed to be no larger than the receiving tank in the Rotunda (Mullin, 1986, p. 16). This way the Rotunda tank would not overflow providing the pump operator could keep up with receiving leachate discharge. During pumping, operators needed to have communication with each other; otherwise the leachate-receiving tank in the Rotunda would overflow. How was communication between the pump operators in Booth's Amphitheatre and the Rotunda resolved? The leachate pipeline between the two stations would have made a good acoustical telegraph. Sharp raps on the pipeline would signal the Booth's Amphitheatre to stop or start pumping. The leachate pipeline is buried in the ground just northeast of the Rotunda water tank and way beyond the pump operator's arm reach, requiring a signalman stationed where the pipe extends out of the ground. The easiest signaling device would have been a noise-making instrument such as a trumpet, whistle, or fireman's ratchet. With the amount of pumping going on in the cave, the

80

Figure 4-4. Wood engraving of pump tower next to Booth's Amphitheatre is similar to Alexander Bullitt's with the addition of more hardware scattered around the pump tower. "Mammoth Cave Kentucky," in *Ballou's Pictorial Drawing-Room Companion*, May 19, 1855.

area about the Rotunda pumping station must have been a wet sloppy mess from overflowing reservoir tanks and pump priming. This kind of housekeeping problem was a common occurrence in many industrial operations utilizing large amounts of liquid.

Tower legs measured twenty feet in height and supported a working platform at the top to hold a simple suction pump upright. Long after the saltpeter boom times, the tower collapsed and fell against the south wall just below the overlook of Booth's Amphitheatre and to the right of the Gothic Avenue steps. Early illustrations and photographs of the Booth's Amphitheatre pump tower show the gradual dismemberment of the structure, although sometimes considerable liberties were taken in depicting its position in the room. Alexander Bullitt's (1845) *Rambles in Mammoth Cave* shows the tower in standing position minus the pump. The lithographer-artist moved the tower far to the right to better balance the space and form of the illustration. An

Figure 4-5. Dynamic engraving of Booth's Amphitheatre showing the way the pump tower collapsed against the wall. First rendering presenting the tower in the correct position with respect to the water tank. Anonymous, *Mammoth Cave America's Great Natural Wonder*, (1883).

enhanced copy (Figure 4-4) providing more detail of the same artistic treatment shows the tower in 1855 with a large wooden body (possibly the pump) propped against the side of the structure (Anon., 1855). All of the illustrations in *Ballou's Pictorial Drawing Room Companion* (Anon. 1855) are redrawn copies from Bullitt (1845). By 1882 (Figure 4-5), the structure had collapsed against the south wall (Hovey, 1882, p. 88; Anon., 1883, p. 7; Ganter, 1892 in Hovey and Call, 1897, p. 26). Shortly thereafter, the legs were removed and presumably installed as hand railings for the walkways overlooking the hopper complex. To account for the removal of the tower legs, Borresen (1942, p.12) suggested, "perhaps the high platform ruined the appearance of the large room and was for this reason removed and made into a handrail." Mullin (1986, p. 16) observed the "hand rail along the visitors trail above the vats are assumed to be members of the Booth's Amphitheatre pump tower. Since these timbers average twenty feet long they support the concept of a pumptower of sufficient height to provide for gravity flow. A simple suction pump like the pump body which resides in the Rotunda could have accomplished this." At sometime after the removal of the tower legs, the collection tank between Hopper Nos. 4 and 5 was mostly destroyed by fire (Borresen, 1942, p. 12).

Details of the collection and transport systems at the top of the pumping towers have long been a subject of controversy. Most of the Mammoth Cave history has been orally handed down from generation to generation of guides. A few visitors recorded these stories and published them in newspapers, travelogues and guidebooks. Today novice guides observe seasoned guides deliver the story of Mammoth Cave and hone their craft by reading guide manuals. Mullin (1986, p. 16) favored a gravity drain system in which a free discharge was pumped into a large tank atop an elevated platform (Wood, 1841, p. 89). The leachate pipe probably extended out near the base of the tower tank to the next lift station collection tank. Mullin (1986, Plate 12-12) pictures an elevated leachate pipeline sloping toward the entrance cave passage. George (1990) and George and O'Dell (1992) adopted Mullin's model as the most practical. Equally so, the pipeline could have easily extended from the bottom of the tank, vertically down to floor level to take advantage of immediate hydraulic head pressure. Elevated storage tanks in modern public water systems are designed this way.

Borresen (1942), on the other hand, presented a different interpretation, in which the leachate-outgoing pipe was connected already to the pump (Figure 4-12C). Perhaps taking a cue from Hovey (1882, p. 57), he suggested that the leachate "was pumped into a second set of pipes, tilted so as to let the liquor flow out of the cave." Borresen concluded that the leachate pipe was connected directly to the spout end of the pump allowing gravity flow of the leachate to the next lift station collection tank. Faust (1967) and De Paepe (1986) favored the Borresen model. Their model was published before Mullin started her fieldwork.

Figure 4-6. Part of a wood pump column across from the Corkscrew in Mammoth Cave. Diana Emerson George photograph.

Why didn't Borresen adopt the reservoir tank scenario? He conducted his fieldwork in late 1940, during a time of management change at the cave and the setting of new priorities. There was a lack of interest by previous management in historic traditions, denying him critical information. The African-American guides had been recently discharged (Schmitzer, 1993, p. 256, 258) and replaced with a new cadre of Caucasian tour guides. As a result, much of the cohesive tradition of Mammoth Cave oral history was lost at this point in time. Furthermore, details of engineering construction were considered tedious and mundane compared to more entertaining stories that could be told about the cave. The exact mode of operation of the pump and pipeline were not considered of sufficient interest to include as part of the pioneer history, except the elevated pipeline at the Methodist Church. Only one obscure publication prior to Mullin's even mentioned the elevated tank (Wood, 1841). Classic descriptions of the Mammoth Cave saltpeter works are short on substance concerning engineering artifacts or the collective functioning of the system. Strong pacifist sentiments from the 1830s up to the Civil War and for at least several decades afterward tended to dampen guide recitations in regard to the saltpeter factory, a pattern also noted for Wyandotte Cave, Indiana, during this same time period (George 2001b).

At Mammoth Cave, stories and traditions as well as physical artifacts of the mining era were lost or deteriorated, as much from a lack of concern with historical significance as from the passage of time. The remaining artifacts and oral traditions have been preserved under the stewardship of the National Park Service, which acquired Mammoth Cave in 1941. It has taken decades to reconstruct the history of the cave, of which the elevated reservoir was one of these traditions.

CORKSCREW

Between Booth's Amphitheatre and the Rotunda is a short segment of an out of context pump (Figure 4-6), located across from the Corkscrew in Broadway. It is 6 ½ feet long and "is thought to represent the segment below the pump handle and head valve section" (George, 1990, p. 11). This pump lacks the refined wood craftsmanship of the Rotunda pump. Exactly where it was used in the hydraulic system is not known.

ROTUNDA

Wreckage of a shorter pump tower is still standing in the Rotunda (Figure 2-7, 4-7 and 4-8), consisting of three support legs 16 feet $1^{13/16}$ inches high along with some angle bracing. According to Mullin (1986, p. 17), the base of "the pumptower would have been 8 feet 9 inches by 8 feet 4 ½ inches (from center post to center post), which provide a platform for the pump operator to stand on as well as a space about 5 feet by 5 feet in front of the outlet hole which could have been for a holding tank."

An ornate hexagonal pump body lies prone on the ground in an out of context position near the Rotunda tower (Figure 4-12A). Between January 18-20, 1994, 32 tons of rocks dislodged by frost wedging fell from the ceiling and broke the pump in half. The pump column is 15 feet 6 ¼-inches long (Mullin, 1986, plate 9-12) and is missing certain key body parts, specifically the pump handle, waterspout, pump rod, internal foot valve, pump rod head valve and tailpipe. The missing tailpipe possibly measured 4.5 feet, which would have placed the pump handle at a comfortable working height at the top of the platform.

Figure 4-7. Early photographic large format cabinet postcard of the Rotunda saltpeter works shows a more complete pump tower. Photographic view by Carlos G. Darnall, March 11, 1889. Courtesy of the Gordon L. Smith collection.

"This would suggest that the pump handle was only about 20.5 feet from the floor of the collecting tank," (Mullin, 1986, p. 17).

Based on the extant remnants, the dimensions of the working pump assembly can be estimated. The tapered tailpipe was probably perforated or notched on its flat bottom to allow leachate into the pump column, with a stationary foot valve at the top. A similar period pump is seen in Eubanks'(1972, p. 47) illustration of an old English pump. Three feet above the tailpipe was a movable head valve connected to the pump rod. The head valve at the end of the pump rod rested in a valve seat 4.5 feet below the bottom of the open pump handle hole (Figure 4-12B). The spigot hole was "about 18 feet above the floor of the collection tank" (Mullin, 1986, p. 12). A curved pump handle rather than a straight one probably sported a counterweight to make it easier on the operator (Eubanks, 1971, p. 8). Manufactured Colonial and Pioneer era pumps often were constructed this way.

Mullin and the Historic American Engineering Record (HAER) team surveyed the saltpeter works with an engineer's transit to clarify differences in elevation. If this pump were used today, the pump would be required to lift the leachate 22.6 feet in order to gravity drain the

Figure 4-8. Photographic postcard view of the Rotunda pump tower. Card is postmarked October 23, 1907, Glasgow Junction, Ky. Courtesy of the Gordon L. Smith collection.

liquid past the gate at the cave entrance. Mullin discovered an interesting defect in the pump's hydraulic system. The spigot hole is "about four feet too low for gravity feed" to the entrance (Mullin, 1986, p. 17)! During the HAER team's fieldwork and final report writing, Mullin was unable to explain why the pump was too low or how the gravity drain problem was solved. From the available evidence, based on measurements of hardware and level surveys between key hydraulic points in the cave the suction pump system would not have worked. Without a working pump, leachate would have to be carried in buckets by hand or on the backs of oxen to the entrance. Mullin offered several possibilities as to why the pump is too short. Tops of the tower legs may have been shortened, or the tops of the tower posts may have been damaged in the fire. Possibly the leachate pipeline in Houchin's Narrows could have been buried 4 feet deeper. Perhaps Borresen's spigot-leachate pipe connection had some merit. A close examination of the spigot orifice however presents "a straight bore which would not allow a tight fit for a water pipe. (The pipe to pipe connections in the Mammoth Cave water system have tapered bores.) The cut also appears to be clean, suggesting that nothing has ever been jammed into it and sealed as a water pipe would need be" (Mullin, 1986, p. 17). At the time, Mullin was unaware of damage to the works caused by the New Madrid earthquakes.

Before the National Park Service acquired Mammoth Cave, many of the wooden artifacts were damaged or destroyed by fire, either accidental or deliberately set. In the early years, planks and timbers from the V-vats, crib hoppers, and other engineered structures served as sources for firewood used in bonfires to illuminate the Rotunda for tourists (George, 1989, p. 75). At the beginning of the 20th Century, the tower was greatly damaged in an accidental fire. John Nelson, one of the guides at the time (1882-1907), recalled "the pumping platform in the Rotunda was set on fire by one of the torches thrown by a guide. This happened about 1903" (in Borresen, 1942, p. 13). A photograph (Figure 4-7) taken prior to the fire shows a more complete structure although lacking the floorboards on the platform supports (Ganter and Darnall, 1889b). The tower posts are visually the same apparent height as today.

Two sets of pipelines are visible in Houchin's Narrows and one at the surface near the Entrance Gate. Excavations for the new gate did not encounter any pipelines deeper than the ones visible today (Crothers, 1996).

A leather hose coupling could have been connected directly from the pump spigot to the leachate pipe. This could have been a sewn leather hose or a later development utilizing rivets fastening the hose together that was invented in 1807 and immediately found use in fire departments (Marty, n.d.). Charles Wilkins was a civic-minded fire chief in Lexington, Kentucky, who was quick to embrace new technology, and could have had knowledge of this important firefighting invention as well as other hydraulic developments. The town had a fire engine with pumps (Staples, 1939, p. 67) in the Union Fire Company firehouse as early as 1804 (Leavy, 1942, p. 323).

The easiest way to solve this problem is to revise the conjectured length of the tailpipe from 4.5 feet to 8.5 feet long. This would fix the height problem, but presents three secondary problems. The pump handle would now be about 8-9 feet above the operator. Having the operator stand on a 4-foot tall box could easily solve this. A taller reservoir tank at the top of the platform would also be needed. The most significant problem concerns the pump lifting capabilities; the elevated position would require a pumping head of 22.6 feet and exceeded the design operational requirements against air pressure. The pump would be unable to provide the necessary lift needed to fill a reservoir of taller height because the technology of producing and maintaining a total vacuum inside these early industrial pumps was beyond the normal expertise of pump manufacturers. Well-made iron and steel suction pumps manufactured today have the same limitations of 20-25 feet (Driscoll, 1986, p. 580).

Borresen assumed a suction pump was used for elevation and gravity was the driving force to drain the pipeline from station to station. What Borresen didn't consider in his model was the inherent difficulty of trying to force leachate flow uphill over a long run of pipe with its own set of frictional and head pressure limitations. Even though the elevation difference between the pump spigot at the top of the Rotunda tower and the entrance was not great (about 5 feet). The maximum force provided by the tower pump would not have been enough to overcome the head pressure resulting from the great weight of water in the pipeline. It would have been impossible, given the relatively weak pump used and the non-watertight connections to push leachate up gradient over any significant distance. Vigorous hand pumping would simply force the water out of the pump handle hole as the head increased in the pipeline.

Mullin rejected these ideas, and so we are left with the reality that leachate would not gravity drain to the entrance using the existing pump and elevated reservoir tank. This is based on the assumption that the pump was a suction lift pump. If, however, the existing pump in the Rotunda was instead a force pump, the scenario becomes more likely. This possibility is discussed later in this chapter.

TABLE OF ELEVATIONS OF SALTPETER ENGINEERING CONSTRUCTIONS MAMMOTH CAVE (after Mullin, 1986)

Site Location	Distance from the Second Hoppers to Furnaces	Elevation msl	Elevation Difference Feet
Booth's Ampthitheatre			
Collection Tank	0	576.3	0
Rotunda Collection Tank	970	592.3	16
Top of Tower Platform		607.4	31.1
Top of Pump Body		612.4	36.1
Pump Discharge Orifice		610.2	33.9
Pipeline at Entrance Gate	1580	614.9	38.6
Furnace Foundations	1785	655	78.7

ENTRANCE

The furnace area outside the Historic Entrance, where leachate was concentrated in boiling kettles, was located forty feet higher than the pipeline at the entrance gate. Farnham (1820, p. 357), Anonymous (1853, p. 3), and Meriam (1844, p. 317) all refer to a third lift station located at the entrance of the cave. Anonymous (1853, p. 3) described the entrance lift as consisting of a windlass and bucket system. Traditional guide patter also referred to the use of buckets to move leachate from the pipeline to the furnaces. From Meriam (1844) we know that a system of pumps was installed in the entrance after the 1812 earthquakes as part of the repairs and improvements made to the works. Why, then, is the historic literature essentially devoid of references to pumps, when this was the primary post-1812 means employed to lift leachate out of the cave?

It may be that, during especially cold winter weather, the entrance pumps were frozen and workers had to use buckets on a temporary basis. Priming the pumps with hot water is one way to thaw out a frozen pump or leave open the upper check valve on the pump rod. This does not provide a satisfactory reason for the total omission of any mention of entrance area pumps in historical accounts. The explanation may reside in the traditions of early Mammoth Cave guides, who tended to select one version of events or circumstances that most struck their fancy and to recite this, as part of their tour patter, throughout their lifetimes. From a close reading of Mammoth Cave travelogues, one is often able to deduce the identity of the guide informant based solely upon on the type of information provided to the writer. Most of the guides concentrated on legends and folklore, but two famous African-American guides, Stephen Bishop and Mat Bransford, were celebrated for their technical expertise.

Stephen Bishop was the most knowledgeable of the African-American guides concerning cave science and local geology. His fellow guide, Mat Bransford, was even more technologically oriented and held in nearly as much esteem as Bishop. Bransford most likely supplied much of the engineering detail in accounts written decades after the mining era. Neither Stephen nor Mat had actually been present when the saltpeter works were active, being employed in 1838 to the new cave owners, Franklin Gorin and A. A. Harvey, to serve as tour guides. During the period just prior to their arrival, from 1828 to 1835, the one man who had the most direct and significant role at the mining operation, Fleming Gatewood, Sr., was employed at the cave as resident caretaker, manager, and guide. Gatewood had been at the cave prior to the earthquakes, when buckets were the dominant means of lifting leachate from the entrance. Post-quake, after Gatewood sold his share in the cave, Archibald Miller, Sr., became superintendent of the works and a pumping system was installed at the entrance.

For more than a decade, then, during Gatewood's tenure as manager of the cave as tourist attraction, the interpretation of the Mammoth Cave operation would have been strongly skewed towards the state of the works as it existed prior to the earthquakes. This view provided by Gatewood, as an acknowledged authority on the mining operation would have become embedded lore among the other guides and in turn passed along to Bishop and Bransford when they became guides. Even though Archibald Miller, Sr., became a guide at the cave after 1836, it is quite likely that such minor detail as the presence of a pump installed at the entrance after the earthquakes would not have been incorporated in an already well-established tradition of guide patter.

Figure 4-9. Classic steel engraving of the entrance to Mammoth Cave by Robert Montgomery Bird in 1837. Of all the renderings made of the entrance and interior views, this one illustration was reprinted numerous times. The large "boulders" in the lower right of the illustration are saltpeter kettles in another view of the entrance. Robert Montgomery Bird "The Mammoth Cave of Kentucky," *American Monthly Magazine*, (1837).

After Gratz purchased Gatewood's interest in the cave early in 1812, improvements were made to all areas of the factory system. Ebenezer Meriam (1844, p. 317) worked at the cave as a subcontractor and refers to "pumps" in the entrance in 1813. At least two pumps (Mullin, 1986, p. 17) were required to lift the leachate about 40 feet out of the cave, since this distance would have been beyond the operational capacity of a single suction pump. By the late 1830s, most of the lift structure was in an advanced stage of rot and was falling into the entrance. The engraving in Figure 4-9 shows two large wooden beams positioned across the entrance (Bird, 1837). The upper structure, built just above the mouth of the cave, has all the characteristics of an elevated pipeline connected into the furnace complex whose chimneys are visible to the upper right. The lower one is positioned down in the entrance opening. The same beam is pictured on Lee's (1835) *Map of the Mammoth Cave* from the vantage point of the vestibule looking out of the cave entrance (Figure 4-10). Other artifacts once located in the entrance area were a water trough below the spring and a dilapidated

Figure 4-10. Earliest known inside-out view of the Mammoth Cave entrance. Architectural engineer Edmund F. Lee pictures a number of dilapidated artifacts: fallen pump tower (lower left and upper left of center), V-vat (lower right of center), water pipe with leg supports or V-vat (far lower right), and catwalk-tower support beam across the center of the entrance. Edmund F. Lee, *Notes on the Mammoth Cave, to Accompany a Map* (1835). Courtesy of the Gordon L. Smith collection.

ladder covered in moss (Kite, 1847, p. 10). Martin's (1851) title page illustration of the cave entrance shows an over sized ladder-like structure with one leg attached to five cross bar members (Figure 4-11). As depicted, the size against two people for scale suggests the structure is part of a tower, although his description in the book is clearly of a ladder. Lee's illustration shows part of the pump tower collapsed on the ground in the lower left and upper left hand part of the cave entrance (Figure 4-10). Martin's rendering of later date is an exaggerated out of proportion ladder.

Most of the interpreters of Mammoth Cave history have concluded from available evidence that there was a wooden tower at the entrance, similar to the one in the Rotunda that supported two pumps.

Figure 4-11. Wood engraving of the entrance to Mammoth Cave showing a structure similar to part of a pump tower or ladder. Scale of two people in the entrance suggests it is part of the entrance pump tower. Yet, the text in Martin's book establishes it as a ladder greatly exaggerated in size. The actual pump tower had fallen down inside the entrance by 1835. Horace Martin, *Pictorial Guide to the Mammoth Cave, Kentucky*, Stringer & Townsend, New York, (1851).

The well-known spelean historian Burton Faust, for example, noted that the beams shown in Figure 4-9 "...were placed there to support a platform of some type for specific purpose.... for a second pumping station" (1967, pp. 53-54). Early published descriptions such as Bird (1837) and engravings such as those by Lee (1835) and Bird (1837) provide sufficient engineering details to offer a hypothesis as to how the entrance lift station may have been constructed.

Bird's (1837, p. 428) description of the entrance area notes "the presence of several mouldering beams of wood stretched across the mouth from ledge to ledge," referring to the lowermost of the timbers shown in the frontispiece of his Mammoth Cave article (Figure 4-9). These cross beams were the supporting members of a catwalk, possibly 5-6 feet wide, associated with the first or lowest of the two pumps. Vertical bracing beneath the structure kept it from sagging and collapsing.

Two collection tanks were located in the entrance area, one as a reservoir for fresh water and the other to receive leachate transported from the Rotunda by gravity flow. The fresh water tank was probably located near the center of the cave entrance, directly beneath the fall of water from the spring, and the leachate tank positioned to the left, in the direction of the south wall. Log pipelines connected to these tanks were built along the south wall and into the cave through Houchin's Narrows. A pumping tower was built directly above the leachate collection tank. To bring leachate up out of the sinkhole entrance to the furnace complex required a total vertical elevation of at least 40 feet.

From available evidence, the most logical configuration of the pumping system is to place two suction lift pumps on this single tower, one above the other. This is also consistent with Mullin's (1886, p. 17) interpretation. The lower pump would have been located about half way up the tower, and discharged leachate into a second tank at that level. Above this single stage would be a second pump and reservoir, from which leachate would flow naturally by gravity through a pipeline to the furnace complex. The tanks on the tower were probably not very large, due to considerations in supporting their weight, but obviously the tower would have to be of sturdy construction.

Fresh water was collected in "a large wooden reservoir, supported by stones piled up from the floor of the Cave" (Anon., 1847, p. 18).

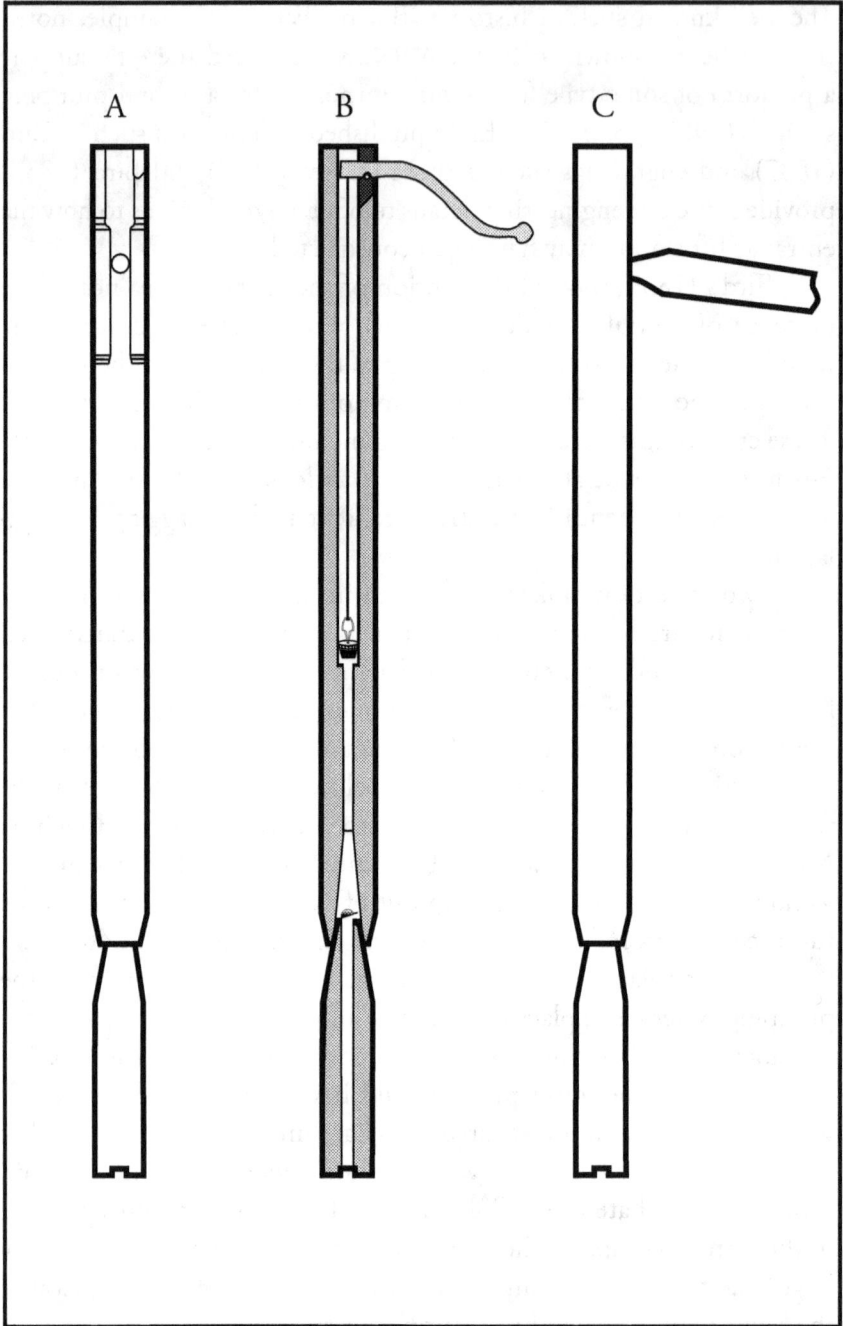

Figure 4-12. Three views of the pump in the Rotunda, (A) exterior view, (B) cut-away view, and (3) Borresen's pump configuration. After Mullin (1986).

The dry laid stone foundation gave elevation to the collection box, which provided the necessary hydraulic head needed for water flow to each processing station in the cave: Entrance, Rotunda and Booth's Amphitheatre. Each gang of V-vats and box hoppers had a dedicated log fountain positioned over the hoppers to irrigate the soils. In Houchin's Narrows today, one of the floor logs has a drilled out fireplug hole which suggests a hose with a spigot was inserted into it and used for watering the V-vats illustrated on Ridgely's eye draught map of Mammoth Cave (Figure 2-2).

The pipeline pictured in Bird (Figure 4-9) above the entrance and sloping away from the furnace complex is enigmatic. The pipeline might represent the hot water return needed to leach saltpeter more thoroughly and would also be needed to keep the operation running during the winter when the spring was frozen. But the pipeline seems to be in the wrong place to be associated with connections with the pipeline in Houchin's Narrows. Possibly this may have been a pipeline from or to Dixon Cave.

OPERATIONAL CHARACTERISTICS
OF THE ROTUNDA PUMP

The pump in the Rotunda was a positive displacement device designated as a single-acting piston pump and based on a design called an Old English Wood Pump (Eubanks, 1972, p. 47; Figure 4-12AB). This type of pump raises liquid by vacuum suction. Reference to the pump in the Rotunda as a suction pump is only discussed in 20th Century historical interpretations. Pumps of this nature are employed where there is a shallow draft water level less than 20 feet below the pump spigot. The collection tank below the pump has a maximum water depth of 2-feet and best fits this condition. A suction pump lifts water by moving a piston attached to a head valve up and down, creating on the upstroke a lower pressure inside the pump body than the outside air. Responding to the partial vacuum, air pressure pushing down on the water surface in the collection tank causes leachate to rise up into the suction pipe. Leachate enters the pump through the open foot valve during up stroke of the pump rod. As the upper pump body fills, water flows out the head valve and out through the pump spout on the down stroke as the foot valve closes. To make the pump work requires priming by pouring leachate or water into the top cavity of the pump.

Priming would be needed nearly every time the pump broke suction. Suction pumps were the most common type used in the 19th Century and capable of lifting water only 20 feet (Parker, 1976, p. 8; and Helweg, *et al.*, 1983, p. 12) or at most 22 feet (Somerscales, in Mullin, 1986, p. 28). Modern pumps of this type are able to lift water 20-25 feet (Driscoll, 1986, p. 580).

In theory, a perfectly constructed pump should be able to lift 33.9 feet of water at sea level. Modern pump manuals often round this figure to 34 feet (Driscoll, 1986, p. 595). Even the best pumps of this type built today are, however, not able to pump this high because of a number of design inefficiencies and circumstantial uncontrollable factors. Pump inefficiencies include leakage around joints, valves and fittings, and head loss due to friction within the system. Circumstantial factors include reduction in air pressure with increasing elevation above sea level, daily meteoric changes in atmospheric pressure, and changes in temperature, which affects the vapor pressure of water. Another consideration is net positive suction head (NPSH), which is the absolute pressure at the pump suction (in feet) minus the vapor pressure of water (in feet) at the pumping temperature.

The net result of the combined and variable influence of all these factors is that suction pumps operate at an efficiency considerably less than the theoretical maximum. The maximum lift for antique pumps of this type is little more than 20 feet. Lifting water to a height greater than this would require multiple stages, the use of buckets, or a different type of pump.

Fortunately, except for the entrance sink, there were no considerable changes in altitude through the main mine works area or the plumbing system would not have worked at all. The Booth's Amphitheatre pump was 18 feet long, raising water a sufficient height to allow gravity flow to the Rotunda station. The Rotunda pump elevated leachate received from both processing centers to a height of about 20 feet, from where it flowed to the collecting tank at the entrance. Like the Booth's Amphitheatre pump, the pump at the Rotunda drew leachate from a relatively shallow tank, which most likely further reduced pump efficiency due to cavitation. Cavitation occurs when the pump draws water mixed with large amounts of air into the pump column as the floor collection tank is sucked dry of leachate, much like trying to get the last drop of a beverage through a straw. The pump would have to be primed after each cavitation event. From the entrance station, the depth of the sinkhole presented special difficulties that would have required a two-stage pump system, if suction pumps were used.

FORCE PUMP OPERATIONAL CHARACTERISTICS

Although suction pumps were the most common type during the era, another type of pump could have been used in the cave. The force pump was often employed by farm, home, and industry when pumping depths exceeded 20 feet. Pumps of this nature lift liquid by means of pressure and are known as force pumps. These pumps have a long history of use that dates back to the third or fourth Century B.C., invented by the Greek, Ctesibius of Alexandria. Ctesibius first devised "the cylinder, the plunger, and the valve," the fundamental components of a hydraulic pump (Sarton, 1959, p. 344). Many refinements occurred over the centuries and suction pumps became one of the evolutionary types.

Travel writer, novelist, playwright and medical professor Robert Montgomery Bird, M.D. (1837, p. 438) uses the term "forcing pumps" in his description of the hardware at the Mammoth Cave saltpeter works. His information most likely supplied by Fleming Gatewood, Sr., guide-manager at the cave during his visit in 1833 and 1836. Mat Bransford, who was strongly influenced by Gatewood's recollection and interpretation of mine engineering, represented the pumps in the cave as "forcing pumps" (Anon., 1853, p. 3). Bransford arrived at the cave in 1838, a year after Bird published his travelogue. Bailey (1863, p. 23) mentions "a force pump" in the Rotunda. This information was obtained from his African-American guide, who, from the amount of technical information supplied was most likely Mat. Adam D. Binkerd (1869, p. 16) retained Mat's guide services through the cave and discussed the hydraulics of Rotunda pipes and pumps: "Through one line of these old pump logs, fresh water was conducted from without for the purpose of leaching the dirt, and through the other the lixivium was forced back by means of a hand pump, to the entrance." These four early 19th Century descriptions suggest a different type of pump, rather than a simple suction pump, was employed in this saltpeter factory. Three of these accounts are clearly based on Mat's tourist presentation. Only Mat was interested in engineering details; to the other guides, a pump was a pump needing no explanation other than its common name.

The possible use of force pumps rather than suction pumps must be considered in light of this evidence. To summarize: (1) some early post-mining accounts using the "forcing" pump terminology were in all probability derived from interviews with either Fleming Gatewood or Archibald Miller, former managers of the mining operation subsequently employed as guide-managers at the cave; (2) later antebellum accounts of mining fixtures and equipment were based upon interpretations supplied by knowledgeable guides such as Mat Bransford or Stephen Bishop, whose traditions were directly rooted in the training they had received from Gatewood and Miller; (3) forcing pumps gained national popularity after 1832 with the introduction of W. & B. Douglass Company's cast iron "Ctesibius style" pump (Eubanks, 1971, p. 47); and (4) substituting the use of force pumps instead of suction pumps would resolve many of the hydraulic problems associated with interpreting the operation of the pumping stations in the Rotunda and at the entrance.

The primary benefit of using a force pump is its ability to overcome the restriction of air pressure that limits suction pumps to a maximum lift of about 20 feet. Force pumps are able to lift water from depths up to about 150 feet! The weight of the water column at depths much beyond 150-200 feet tends to over power the operator's ability to lift it manually. Greater depths used animal power as the motive force to raise the water to the surface. For the shorter distances involved in the Mammoth Cave hydraulic system, a single force pump would have been more than adequate, eliminating the need for tandem pumps at the entrance.

Another difference between the force pump and the suction pump would have been in positioning of the two valves relative to the tower and pump body. The suction pump was designed to pull water upwards and would have its valves about the middle of the pump. A force pump, in contrast, pushes water upward and so would have its valves beneath the tower at the level of the reservoir. Merely moving the suction pump valve assembly closer to the floor does not make it a force pump.

Manufactured force pumps were made of brass or bronze and by the 1830s iron became the dominant medium in America. Several types of force pumps were in general circulation in 1810-1812. Both have long histories of use. The double cylinder Ctesibius model found use in firefighting. The other is a variation and consisted of a single cylinder pump invented by Samuel Moreland in 1675 (Usher, 1982, p. 341). Moreland's improved single cylinder Ctesibius force pump gained advantage by having the solid weighted plunger attached to the pump rod work "through a gland [airtight packing nut] and stuffing box." Construction of a force pump is based on the position of the valve cylinder along with dedicated ancillary hardware. The cylinder is a small unit attached to the bottom of the pump and contains two one-way valves. A solid piston connected to the pump rod that rides through a stuffing box insured an airtight system. The cylinder is the metal tube in which the piston works. Using heavy weights on the plunger, liquid could be raised to great heights. Small models were built for hand use. Pump strokes and operation of the valve assembly is exactly the same as in suction pumps, except the solid piston is inside the cylinder and the top head valve protrudes out the upper side of the cylinder. This is connected to the discharge line. Modern deep well high service vertical turbine pumps and submersible pumps use the same principle of force pump technology.

Modifications to the pump must be made to increase lift above the spigot. Once another valve is installed on the spigot, a hose or pipeline can be connected so that water can be pumped to greater height above the pump using the elevator force of water lifted from the cylinder in the bottom of the pump body. Fire wagons during Wilkins' time found ready use for force pumps because they were able to squirt a stream of water up to second and third story windows and rooftops at a safe distance away from the fire.

Could the existing pump artifact on the floor of the Rotunda be Bird's (1837) "forcing pump?" One of the necessary design characteristics is certainly seen in Borresen's interpretation (1942) as he pictures the end of the leachate pipeline inserted into the spigot (Figure 4-12C). There is a limit at which this system would work, given the pressure required to push many pounds of leachate up gradient through 610 feet of friction hold wooden pipeline. The pipeline would have burst along, not to mention exhausting the pump operator. The physical architecture of forcing pumps is completely different from the wood suction pump on the floor of the Rotunda.

There is no physical evidence the Rotunda pump was ever modified nor does the artifact exhibit force pump architecture or construction materials. The hydraulic system in the Rotunda was obviously designed for the use of a simple suction pump. This leads to the question as to why Wilkins and Gatewood, or Gratz, chose to install a suction pump rather than the more efficient force pump? There are a number of plausible explanations. The suction pump may simply have been the most easily obtainable, since it was the type in most common use elsewhere, or the pump maker may not have known how to construct the more complex force pump. Ordering a readymade pump from an east coast supplier was costly and time consuming. Importation from Europe was illegal from 1808 through the end of the War of 1812. There may have been no real benefit to be gained from the use of more costly force pumps prior to the New Madrid earthquake, since suction pumps would have had the capacity to elevate the leachate sufficiently to operate the system, just as in Booth's Amphitheatre.

Although both Gatewood and Bransford asserted the pump on the Rotunda floor was a force pump, the artifacts' internal evidence tends to contradict this. As this apparent suction pump is the only pump remaining in the cave, we must, in the absence of primary documentation, presume that all pumps associated with the system were suction pumps. We must qualify this observation, however, by noting that there is no specific evidence to indicate that this pump was part of the final engineering solution to correct hydraulic problems in the system. It may have been discarded in place after post-earthquake repairs or modifications were made. The force pump issue remains open until more evidence, archaeological or documentary, is discovered.

DISCUSSION

The imprecise and often conflicting descriptions of system elements by historic writers have led to some confusion in modern interpretations of the pumps used in the cave. Faust (1967, pp. 52-53) favored the term "lift pump" for the type used in the Rotunda. His operational description is clearly of a suction pump. Hill and De Paepe (1979, p. 255) contrasted the operation of this pump to "pitcher

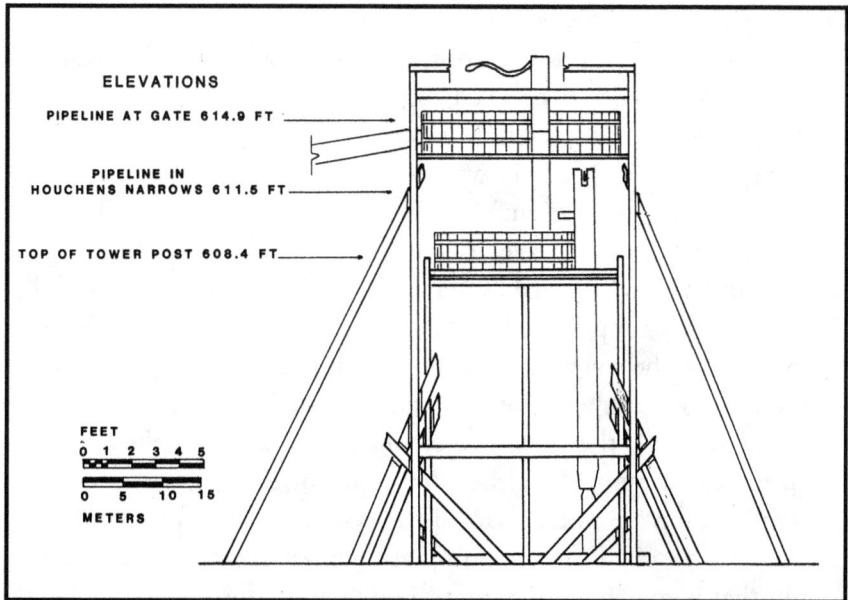

Figure 4-13. Conjectured Rotunda pump tower built after the major New Madrid earthquakes. The tandem pump tower helped to solve the hydraulic problem by reestablishing gravity drainage of leachate back to the entrance.

pumps" which operate in the same way as suction pumps. In their account, the hydraulic system is described as "a series of pumping stations [that] forced the liquor through the wooden conduit to the surface." Borresen's (1942) hypothesis of a pipeline directly connected to the pump spigot evidently influenced Hill and De Paepe to envision the word "force" as the driving mechanism to move water flow through the pipeline.

No one prior to Mullin (1986) was aware of the hydraulic obstacles associated with the Rotunda pump tower. The level survey under her direction established that the tower here was too short to allow gravity flow toward the entrance, the subsidence of the structure a direct consequence of the New Madrid earthquake. Without this elevation data, previous researchers, including myself, did not realize that flow from the Rotunda to the entrance would have been up gradient under these circumstances. If this was the case, the pump on the Rotunda tower would have required a direct connection to the pipeline to the entrance in order to maintain a positive pressure against the head pressure resulting from a higher elevation. This is unlikely because suf-

103

ficient force exerted at the pump to move water to the entrance would have been nearly impossible to achieve manually and, if possible, a pressured line would have leaked copiously from the log joints. Gravity flow is not pressurized and leakage would have been minimal.

Borresen (1942, p. 11) was well aware of this limitation, for he wrote, "there was no pressure feed water system in the cave. The fresh water brought into the cave, as well as the return of the peter water, could only be accomplished by gravity flow." Both Borresen and Mullin (1986) favored simple, straightforward interpretations of the hydraulic system. In their view, which the author shares, outflow of leachate was accomplished by gravity flow from elevated reservoir to floor-level reservoir through the cave, the elevated reservoirs supplied by platform-mounted pumps. Neither Borresen nor Mullin felt it necessary to require a force pump as part of the system. Both investigators were convinced that the Rotunda pump artifact represents a simple suction pump that is missing a number of body parts. This is the only largely complete (about 85%) historic pump present in Mammoth Cave today, and so it is upon the basis of this artifact that we must hypothesize the use of suction pumps in the system.

To solve the hydraulic problem of a too short pump tower, George (1990) proposed using out of context artifacts in the Rotunda to construct a conjectured tandem pump tower (Figure 4-13). The new tower was high enough to reestablish gravity drainage to the entrance collection tank. Two tower corner posts of longer length are found along the floor of the tourist trail in the Rotunda. Like the Rotunda pump or the tower post hand railing in Booth's Amphitheatre their position today is out of context. De Paepe (1986, p. 18) thought the posts along the tourist trail had been part of the entrance pumping station and had been transported into the cave at a later time. They are 23.5 feet long and mortised similar to the timbers of the existing Rotunda pump tower. These corner posts are of the right length needed to overcome minimum hydraulic problems that developed after the floor along with the tower subsided during the 1811-1812 New Madrid earthquakes. This led George (1990) to propose a tandem pumping station in the Rotunda (Figure 4-13).

The hydraulic system in Mammoth Cave was severely affected by the four hard shocks of the New Madrid earthquake and the hundreds of aftershocks. The subsidence of the Rotunda tower was the most serious problem, since this rendered the entire system inoperable, unable to convey leachate to the exterior of the cave. The pipeline itself was almost certainly affected as well, the vibrations of the earth springing apart the log-to-log connections and destroying the integrity of the pipeline. Earthquake damage to the works, to both the hydraulics and to the vats and hoppers in the processing center, post-quake repairs, and subsequent destruction, removal or repositioning of artifacts has greatly complicated the task of reconstructing the engineering of the Mammoth Cave saltpeter factory. Further adding to these difficulties has been a body of historic literature that is too often vague or misleading, sometimes including erroneous guide traditions such as Gatewood's, Bransford's, and Bird's mistaken identification of the Rotunda pump as a "forcing" type. In this chapter, as elsewhere, the author has attempted to weigh all the presently available evidence to provide the most reasonable interpretation.

Figure 5-1. Dixon Cave is a huge paleotrunk cave passage floored with limestone cobbles and blocks over massive breakdown. Saltpeter miners removed this material from the wall area and deposited them in the center of the passage. Diana Emerson George photograph.

CHAPTER FIVE

EXOTIC SALTPETER MINING TECHNIQUES IN THE MAMMOTH CAVE AREA

In Dixon Cave "we are rewarded by finding ourselves in the mightiest subterranean hall yet discovered."
Hovey and Call, 1897

S altpeter extraction as carried out by most cave mining opera-tions, large and small, generally consisted of excavating soils from various passageways within the cave, transporting the earth to vats or hoppers in some central processing area, and leaching out the water-soluble nitrate minerals. Nitrate deposits within caves are generally in the form of calcium nitrate, requiring underground operations to carry out a further step, filtering the original leachate through wood ashes or potash to promote a chemical conversion from calcium to potassium nitrate. Although some controversy remains as to the origin of cave nitrates, the most widely accepted theory holds that such nitrates are the result of near-surface microbial activity and are subsequently trans-ported to the subterranean environment by the movement of ground water (Hill, 1981, 1984; Hill and Forti, 1986). According to the seep-ing ground water hypothesis, ground water containing dissolved cal-cium and nitrate ions percolates through the bedrock in which caves are located and becomes concentrated by evaporation in soils or rock at the interface with the cave atmosphere. Where ground water seep-age occurs in sandstone, instead of limestone, fewer calcium ions are present and the depositional form tends to be potassium nitrate rather than calcium nitrate.

Customary mining procedure at sandstone shelters, described by Brown (1809) and substantiated by archaeological evidence (Coy *et al.*, 1984; Fig and Knudsen, 1984; Des Jean, 1997), was to pry apart or blast the nitrate-impregnated sandstone bedrock and pulverize it into gravel and sand. The sand, gravel and cobbles were placed into V-vats and the nitrate content leached with water in a manner similar to that employed at cave sites. Although shelter mines were generally much smaller operations than cave sites and, individually, possessed a lower total nitrate content, shelter sites were more economical for a number of reasons. Because sandstone is a highly porous material, impregnated sandstone bedrock provided a very high nitrate yield, more so than cave earth. Shelters were very numerous all along the sandstone cliftlines and could be worked by small teams of a few men, requiring no great labor force, except when the entire valley is considered. The mining environment was outdoors and needed no accommodation to constant darkness. Finally, because the leachate from sandstone rock was predominantly potassium nitrate, there was no need for the chemical conversion step.

Dr. Samuel Brown (1809, pp. 241-242) of Lexington, whose fieldwork took place during 1802-1805, observed that the miners of eastern Kentucky preferred to work shelters for saltpeter, rather than caves, because of the higher nitrate yield. Coy *et al.* (1984) documented a number of shelter sites in Kentucky's Daniel Boone National Forest and estimated there were probably hundreds of shelters similarly mined for saltpeter. Fig and Knudsen (1984), also investigating mining activity in the National Forest, described shelter sites in the Red River Gorge Geological Area. Within the Mammoth Cave region, sandstone rock mining took place at one rockshelter and three pseudokarst caves (caves formed in sandstone bedrock). Of these latter, Holley Cave in Edmonson County and Hatcher Saltpeter Cave, Hart County (Figure 1-3), provide clear examples of this form of mining activity (George, 1985cd). Hard-rock mining of sandstone for saltpeter was a common practice in eastern Kentucky, but rarely practiced in the western part of the state.

Hard-rock mining as carried on at shelter sites was seldom resorted to at caves, although the surface and near-surface exposures of cave bedrock were also impregnated with nitrates. Elevated nitrate concentrations in limestone at bedrock surfaces within the cave have been confirmed through empirical work by Hill (1981ab). There are a number of regional caves where hard-rock mining of limestone for its saltpeter content is definitely known to have taken place. Saltpeter Cave, for example, located in Crawford County, Indiana (Figure 1-3), near famous Wyandotte Cave, exhibits distinct evidence of the mining and processing of limestone rock (George, 2001, pp. 162-164).

In Tennessee, a considerable amount of rock mining took place during the pioneer era at Big Bone Cave (Troost, 1835, p. 239; Figure 1-3). Long after the operation ceased production, geologist Gerard Troost visited the site in the company of one of the early miners. He observed various indications of mining activity and, according to his guide, "the earth from the floor is not preferred by the workman; they often take the lower part of the sides of the cave, even peeling off about an inch deep from the rock, which they say is more productive." Support for this statement was supplied when D. T. Maddox (1813, p. 175) observed the saltpetermen and heard "nothing but the indistinct echoes of hammers and pick-axes." Lexington (Kentucky) antiquarian, world traveler, merchant, and saltpeter broker John D. Clifford purchased most of the saltpeter made at this cave after its discovery in 1806. Mammoth Cave owner Wilkins knew him well, for they had mutual interests in saltpeter, Indian artifacts, and Indian mummies found in caves. Both had mummies, unearthed by saltpeter miners, on public display in Clifford's Cabinet (natural history museum) in Lexington.

Tantalizing items of correspondence suggest saltpeter rock mining was considered for some western Kentucky caves. Abel Morgan of Russellville, Logan County, wrote Thomas Jefferson on December 5, 1812, about a cave, "which is supposed to be valuable. it consists of stone very strongly impregnated with petre, likewise a quantity of dirt. the quantity of Rock is indescribable. there appears enough for 100,000 lbs weight of petre." He requested a treatise on methods of saltpeter extraction from the rock and Jefferson's "own ideas on the subject." Jefferson's reply on January 11, 1813, recommended Morgan secure a copy of Samuel Brown's paper on saltpeter or contact Dr. Brown in New Orleans or his "friends on the spot." Warren County Land Survey Book records an entry dated December 26, 1811, referring to Abel

Morgan's 50-acre land survey containing Joel Hampton Saltpeter Cave (possibly Savage Cave, Logan County; Figure 1-3).

William N. Blane (1824, p. 271), a wealthy Englishman who visited the United States during 1822-1823, explored Mammoth Cave. Upon reaching the Second Hoppers, the method of saltpeter extraction was explained by his guide: "The earth, that is mixed with the fragments of broken rock, contains the saltpetre, and used to be carried in a small cart, drawn by oxen, to both Hoppers, where it was washed." Examination of the north lixiviated wall of Hopper No. 2 today reveals a large fraction of angular gravels mixed with the soil matrix (Figure 2-6).

The only other reference to saltpeter rock mining comes from the *1820 Federal Census of Manufacturers* (p. 104) for Hart County. The James M. Cannon Saltpeter Cave utilized "Rock Dirt Ore" from the cave. They processed "Ten ton of Rock and Dirt," generating an annual market value of $2400.00 ($43,900.00 today) in saltpeter sales. This was one of the last active commercial saltpeter mines in the state. The only known saltpeter rock mine in Hart County is Hatcher Valley Saltpeter Cave (Figure 1-3), a pseudokarst cave developed in sandstone, which may be the Cannon Cave.

When all the evidence is weighed, there are only six caves in Kentucky that can definitely be identified as sites where mining and processing of limestone rock was carried on to extract nitrates. George's (1985a) discussion of the occurrence and distribution of saltpeter mine sites in Kentucky notes minor evidence of rock mining in Breeding Saltpeter Cave in Adair County, including what locals call a "lime kiln" near the entrance, and strong evidence of industrial mining displayed at Dutch Creek Cave (Cumberland County) and Short Cave, Jim Cave, Dixon Cave and Mammoth Cave (all in Edmonson County). The available physical and documentary evidence for Dixon Cave provides a good case study for this unusual form of saltpeter mining (Figure 5-1 and 5-2). Short Cave is discussed in Chapter Six with comparisons made to Dixon Cave.

DIXON CAVE

By the end of 1813, all significant saltpeter-mining activity had ceased at Mammoth Cave, as was true for many other sites throughout the western frontier and as far as Missouri. Yet, Wilkins and Gratz

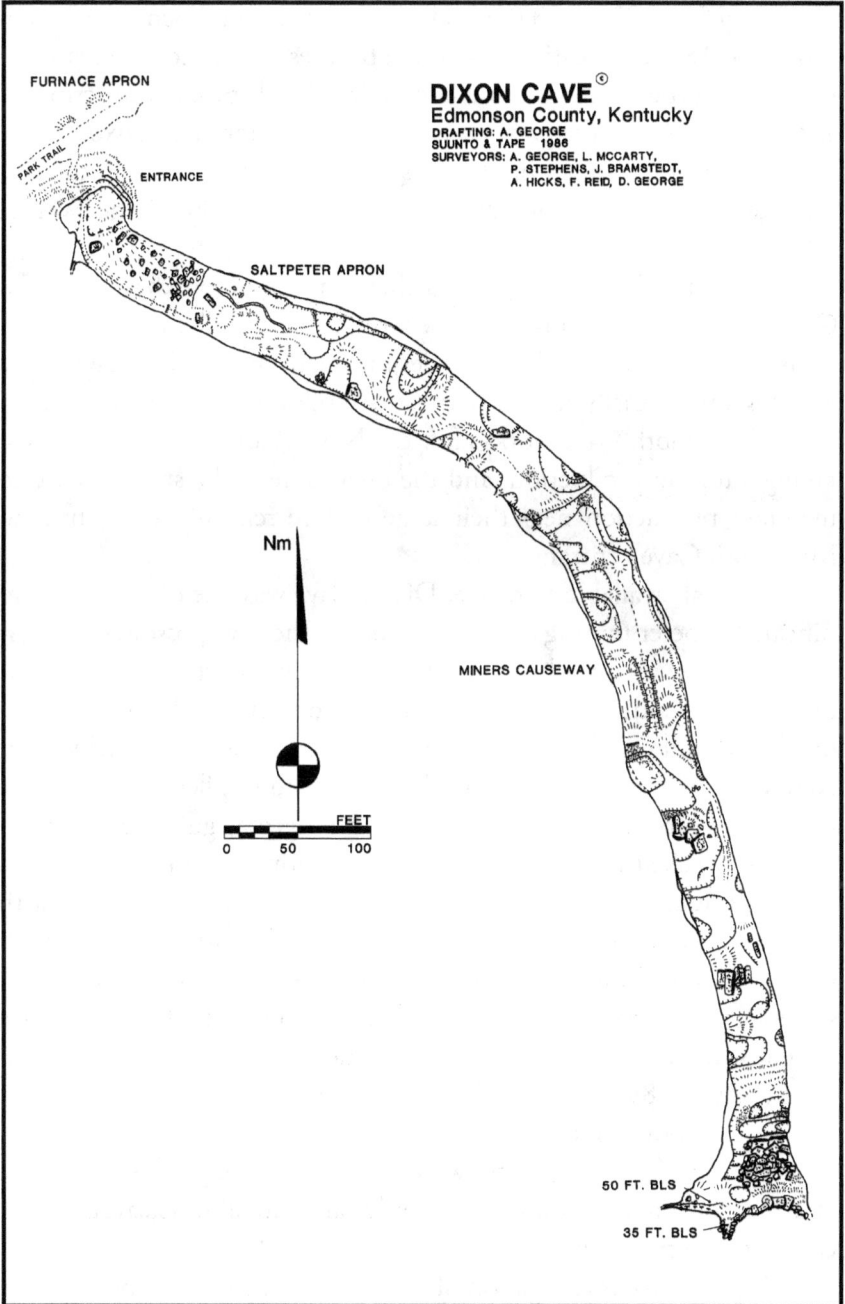

Figure 5-2. Cartography of Dixon Cave, from the author's survey made with a Suunto compass and tape. Broken rock veneer floor has been omitted from the map.

purchased $20,000 ($238,000 today) of potash from Ebenezer Meriam (1844) in 1814, indicating that these business associates were still involved in saltpeter mining and processing. With production crippled at Mammoth Cave, the partners moved their operation to Dixon Cave, less than a quarter-mile from the Historic Entrance of Mammoth. This little cave was mined for saltpeter during the height of the War of 1812.

Gratz and Wilkins expanded their empire by purchasing Dixon Cave in April 1813. This purchase would help fulfill contract obligations; because Mammoth Cave, despite many miles of passages, was running out of easily mined saltpeter supplies; repairs and rebuilding of the Mammoth Cave works after the New Madrid earthquakes were taking a toll on production; and the owners needed a stopgap cave to maintain production near their large surface refining center next to Mammoth Cave's entrance.

From all available evidence, Dixon Cave was one of the most significant saltpeter mining sites in Kentucky. The cave possesses processing artifacts, widespread physical traces of mining activity, and a well-documented tradition of saltpeter mining. Beyond the V-vat remnants on the breakdown slope in the entrance vestibule lies a rocky floor composed of fragments and blocks of limestone piled in tall heaps. Over the years, since the end of the mining era, guidebooks and a number of scientific articles have described how workmen moved this immense quantity of rock to gain access to the nitrate-bearing earth beneath. Nineteenth-century speleologist and indefatigable Mammoth Cave promoter Horace C. Hovey, known as the father of American speleology, observed that every rock from the base of the entrance breakdown slope to the end of the passage has been moved at least once (Hovey, 1897, p. 291). This would have been an astounding feat of physical labor, amounting to displacement of more than 30,000 tons of rock in an area 50 to 60 feet wide and 650 feet long. This Herculean effort, according to tradition, was undertaken to allow excavation and conventional processing of underlying cave soils.

An extensive investigation of Dixon Cave, carried out by the present author over a period of several years, suggests that traditional interpretations of the Dixon Cave saltpeter operation are mistaken as to the intent and nature of the work carried out there. Only limited quantities of cave soil were mined and processed for saltpeter here; Dixon Cave was primarily an operation dedicated to the hard-rock mining of limestone for its nitrate content. The many accounts that depict the overturning and restacking of the entire massive quantity of rock needed to intercept the soil/breakdown interface in the cave are legendary rather than factual. This did not take place. Published accounts dealing with the actual methodology of Dixon Cave mining came into print long after the mining era. Dixon Cave is floored with natural breakdown overlain with a thick veneer of limestone rubble placed there by hand. This rubble, consisting largely of small breakdown, was excavated from near the walls of the cave to expose specific limestone bedrock intervals. No cave sediments are exposed anywhere in the lower half of the main trunk, except in several small anastomoses, crawlways, and the upper terminal end of the cave. The colossal spoil apron in the entrance vestibule is composed almost entirely of hand-milled limestone gravel and smaller fractions.

Dixon Cave (Figure 5-1 and 5-2) is a large abandoned paleotrunk passage separated from Mammoth Cave by an area of extensive and impenetrable breakdown collapse. The cave is 650 feet long, 50-60 feet wide and up to 70 feet high. According to tradition, the formerly open connection between the two caves collapsed during the early days of saltpeter mining. The stratigraphic position of similar rock formations and passage size suggest that Dixon Cave was a down stream extension from the Methodist Church segment in the area of the Historic Entrance.

Ebenezer Meriam's (1844) account of a visit in 1813 describes activities in Dixon Cave, where workers "digging for saltpetre earth at its extremity, have been heard within ten feet of the Mammoth Cave." Hovey (1882, p. 70) wrote, "persons in [Dixon] cave can make themselves heard in the other, as was proved by the miners in 1812, whose picks could be heard as stated." Contemporary spelean historian Duane De Paepe (1979) demonstrated the authenticity of these old accounts through experiments in sound conduction. The late Frank Reid and the author used induction radios at the terminal end of the cave. The vertical electronic signal indicates the cave is only 35 feet below ground and located 179 feet from the historic marker (now removed) near the steps into Mammoth Cave. The radiolocation position in the cave is below the edge of a small sinkhole.

Historically, Dixon Cave was known as Saltpetre Cave as early as 1798. For over 17 years it was a source of saltpeter for various entrepreneurs including Valentine Simons, John Flatt, the three brothers George, Leonard and John McLean, Charles S. Morton, and, finally, the venture consortium of Charles Wilkins and Hyman Gratz. From the number of mine operators connected with the cave, it must have been a valuable source of saltpeter.

Morton subcontracted mining in his cave to John and Henry Dixon (Hill and De Paepe, 1979, p. 248) from whom the cave's name is derived. Wilkins and Gratz expanded their saltpeter empire by purchasing Dixon Cave on April 20, 1813 from Morton for $400.00 ($5100.00 today). For Morton, this represented a loss since he originally paid $600.00 ($8930.00) to the McLeans in 1808 (Thomas, *et al.*, 1970, pp. 324-325). Morton may have thought he had exhausted the economic resource, having excavated the limited soil exposures in the cave. Wilkins, a successful Lexington merchant, was a shrewd salesman and probably reinforced Morton's belief by offering a fraction of the cave's potential value. Low sale prices usually implied the saltpeter cave had been nearly worked out. On the other hand, the value of Mammoth Cave had increased by about 33% at the time Gatewood sold his share in 1812.

Morton's sale is consistent with the total state of affairs governed by the depletion of saltpeter resources throughout the Midwest. In December 1812, a Green County saltpeter cave was advertised in the *American Statesman* for half its value of just a year before. By purchasing, for a low price, a cave believed to be nearly mined out, it is clear Wilkins and Gratz planned to exploit the cave in a different manner than Morton had practiced. There were direct payback advantages associated with the purchase. The cave could be harvested quite a few times a year. The saltpeter rock mine resource in terms of nitrate strength was comparable to soils in Mammoth Cave! Saltpeter mining in Mammoth Cave was spread out over several miles of passage while Dixon Cave spanned a modest 650 feet of saltpeter rich passage. It was probably Wilkins and Gratz who conceived mining rock rather than limited soil resources in the cave. Hard-rock mining had already been done in several areas of Mammoth, Jim Cave and Short Cave (named for Wilkins' brother-in-law Peyton Short). As early as September 30, 1810, Wilkins' brother-in-law Frederick Ridgely's cousin Levi Brashear from Nelson County, Kentucky, mined Wyandotte Cave and saltpeter impregnated limestone rock from nearby Saltpeter Cave, Crawford County, Indiana (George, 2001).

Evidence of saltpeter mining activity seen today in Dixon Cave consists of rock stacking, trail building, soil excavations in a few side passages and, predominantly, by signs of lateral highwall mining and balcony alcove mining in bedrock. Artifacts consist of V-vat remnants, burnt wood torch material, small gluts (pointed sticks used to break rock with a maul), log poles, digging sticks, tally marks, lamp seats and faggot slashes. Some of these artifacts could be prehistoric, especially the log poles, digging sticks and faggot slashes. Regional caves, and particularly Mammoth, contain many traces of prehistoric people. De Paepe (1981, p. 103) recorded the existence of a beveled-edge wood pry bar in Dixon. A saltpeter paddle has also been found in the cave (Hill and De Paepe, 1979, p. 261).

The original leaching center and furnaces were located outside in front of the entrance (Hovey and Call, 1897, p. 7). Remains of two furnace aprons are located north of the entrance and nature trail. One of these could have been a calcining furnace mentioned by Meriam (1844, p. 328). It would be needed to break down the limestone into smaller fractions. Assessing the magnitude of the work that went into making the cave into a saltpeter mine, Hovey (1897) describes:

> Every foot of the floor was searched and overturned long ago by the industrious miners, who carried the nitre-bearing earth outside to the vats and boiling-tubs whose ruins are yet visible. The miners left the rocky fragments within the cavern piled in what might be described as transverse billows, of which we counted eighteen; each were being forty feet through at the base, and rising thirty or forty feet above the true floor. At the extreme end the mass of earth and rock do not seem to have been disturbed.

Hovey's use of the phrase, "nitre bearing earth," clearly shows his belief that the operation was more or less conventional, focused upon excavating and processing cave soils only. This indication is reinforced by his observation (1899, p. 50) that *every block and fragment of those massive ridges was laid there by the old saltpeter miners. By this means they got at the peter dirt to be carried outside for further treatment"* [emphasis added]. In this statement, and in a further description (Hovey and Call, 1897, p. 7), the writers are under the impression that leaching operations were all conducted outside the cave entrance. And for good reason, since there were several visible mound structures located out beyond the entrance. They were halfway correct, but missed the V-vat signatures on the spoil apron inside the cave. Identification of highly deteriorated V-vat remains is often difficult, ridge dumps appearing to the untrained eye as merely soil hummocks separated by narrow depressions.

WATER SOURCE AND DESCRIPTION
OF LEACHING HOPPERS

A small spring and seepage drips provided a seasonal water source at the entrance of Dixon Cave. Observations by the author indicate the spring and drip water sources are not functional from July thru September; only during the fall, winter, and early spring months is this water source active enough to supply a saltpeter-processing factory. Charles S. Morton apparently had this seasonality in mind when he purchased the cave on January 22, 1808. His contract agreement with the McLean brothers ran only to April 22 that same year (Thomas, *et al.*, 1970, pp. 324-325). The spring would have been most active during this three month wet season. Morton continued to work the cave, probably seasonally, to April 20, 1813, when he sold his interest to Gratz and Wilkins. The April 20 date approximately marks the usual end of the annual Dixon Cave mining season when the spring began to dry up. During Morton's tenure, saltpeter mined from Dixon Cave was manufactured into gunpowder at his farm, just south of Pilot (Morton's or Bowden's) Knob in Russellville, Logan County (Hoss, 1916, p. 41). The lack of a perennial water source in the cave was a serious problem; water would have to be piped from the entrance spring at Mammoth Cave or, far less likely, pumped up from Green River. Presumably, Wilkins and Gratz could only mine the cave seasonally as did their predecessors until they solved the need for a continuous supply of process water. This was well within their capabilities, financial resources, and proximity to other spring water sources.

Although a few vats had been initially erected outside the entrance to assess the potential saltpeter yield of the cave, the actual leaching operation was established for a time inside the cave. The remains of ten rectangular shaped V-vats are located about 105 feet inside the cave, positioned on the lower entrance breakdown slope atop a large salt-peter apron. Dampness in the entrance area has promoted decay and deterioration of the wooden V-vats, reducing them to a series of low rectangular hummocks and indistinct mounds of earth. Surface inwash has eroded through several of the vats and down through the complete length of the saltpeter aprons (Figure 5-2).

The ten vat remnants are associated with a series of what appears to be at least five cascading tiers of saltpeter aprons. The dimensions of the two highest aprons are smaller than V-vat size and may not be connected with hopper construction. The upper buttress is very small with a 3-foot high dry stacked rock wall. The lower buttress is about 6 feet square. These may, instead, represent landings for wood steps installed during the short-lived commercialization of the cave for tourism. Alternatively, the six-foot square base is large enough to have supported a pump tower.

To make the leaching station operational, a pipeline would have to be constructed from the spring to the V-vats. Buckets could have been used to remove collected leachate from the cave. There is no physical or documentary evidence that Wilkins and Gratz installed pumps to make the task easier. At least three suction pumps or one force pump would have been required. One thing is certain about Wilkins and his saltpeter business partners: they always went first class and spent whatever it took to make the operation modern and efficient.

The vertical sequence of the hoppers on tiers of saltpeter aprons suggests leachate water may have been allowed to flow from the highest V-vat into the lower vat on each tier. This way the leachate became increasingly concentrated.

V-vats in Dixon Cave measured 8 feet long, 3 feet high and had an external log support structural frame that grouped 3 or 4 hoppers together in a gang. Channel logs are embedded near the top of two saltpeter mounds, suggesting the vats were empty at the time miners abandoned the site. Another partial section of channel log is found 175 feet from the entrance dripline near the right wall on the west side, 6 feet long, 15 inches wide and 10 inches high. Two parallel V-notch groves extend along most of its length. The mouth of the channel log has either rotted away or has been broken off. This missing piece would have had a shallow concave V-notch similar to those in Longs Cave. Cross-sectional log diameter is similar at both cave sites.

Miners made an obvious attempt to recycle processed lixiviated saltpeter soil and rock by shoveling it into 5 feet high heaps along the left (east) wall in the entrance vestibule. Some spreading along wall ledges and stacking of the spoil is also evident along the west wall. This is one of the few examples of deliberate recycling of saltpeter earth in the Mammoth Cave region. Dixon Cave recycling would be consistent with the French practice in Paris Basin saltpeter mines during this time period. Modern chemical analysis shows regeneration of Dixon Cave nitrate concentration in these soils is exceptionally high after almost two hundred fallow years (Hill, 1981). In contrast, the growth of salt-peter spoil aprons around vats from discarded processed soils cannot be considered a form of recycling.

CONSTRUCTION OF WORKING BAYS

A *working bay* is a new term devised to describe a specific kind of cavity produced in caves or rockshelters during the mining of soil or rock (Figure 5-3). Quarrying of cave sediments or bedrock produces a niche that is bounded on three sides by an excavated highwall face. Away from the highwall working face of the cave wall, tailings and/or breakdown built up to form artificial ridges perpendicular to the working face are called lateral tailing ridges. The approach from the center of the passage trail usually has a gentle to steep slope away from the transverse trail toward the working face. These features are not restricted to the floor of Dixon Cave. There are balcony alcove working bays that are found on high narrow ledges above the rocky floor in Dixon Cave. They take the form of excavated niches (usually) without lateral tailing ridges.

Dixon Cave pit bay mining is the natural extension in the development of the working bay. Pit bays are the result of excavations made to reach deeper nitrate impregnated horizons in rock or soil (in other caves), and have vertical or steeply sloping walls. Excellent examples of pit mining are in the Historic Section of Mammoth Cave and, at one time, Short Cave.

In Dixon Cave, the miners probably exploited deposits of nitrate-

Figure 5-3. Working bay excavation along the main passage wall in Dixon Cave. Diana Emerson George photograph.

rich soil in anastomosis areas, side passages, and in the upper terminal end of the cave before attempting to tackle cave sediments below the breakdown mass in the trunk passage. It is not reasonable to presume it took 17 years of labor before the idea dawned on the managers of the saltpeter works that the bedrock-soil interface lay too far below the breakdown. Most certainly the prior owners of Dixon Cave tried to reach the nitrate rich clay soil and gave up the effort.

Experience in Mammoth Cave would have discouraged any major commitment of resources to what would have been, in any case, an essentially futile exercise. In Mammoth, as the easily accessible saltpeter soils were mined out, the next step would have been to start moving breakdown to expose soils in distant passages beyond the Giant's Coffin (Figure 1-11). Wilkins would have been well aware of the immense labor needed to accomplish this, since his work force had previously shifted considerable weight of rock in the Rotunda and Audubon Avenue areas.

Miners in Short Cave removed "from four to six feet" of breakdown "before you enter the clay impregnated with nitre" (Wilkins,

1820, pp. 362, 366). An excellent example of pit mining is found along the south wall of the Methodist Church in Mammoth Cave (Figure 1-2). The amount of labor effort is truly mind-boggling, especially since much of the breakdown is the size of modern day subcompact cars! The majority of eastern Kentucky saltpeter entrepreneurs facing obstacles of this kind tended to abandon the site for easier prospects (Brown, 1809, p. 243).

The certain difficulty and expense of such an undertaking was among the factors that motivated the Gratz/Wilkins partnership to, instead, move part of the mining operation out of Mammoth Cave, through the purchase of Dixon. If they were going to move massive quantities of breakdown, it was better to do it in a small cave close to their main surface processing plant. At Dixon Cave, the most likely interpretation of site evidence indicates that shifting of pre-existing breakdown was mainly for the purpose of facilitating bedrock mining at the walls of the cave, including the construction of 24 working bays and 7 balcony alcove sites.

Evidence of hard-rock mining is based upon a close examination of the working bays. No cave sediment is present at the base of the excavations. An intentional effort was made to build dry stone laid walls trending away from the highwall excavation face. This helped to stabilize a growing spoil pile of excavated breakdown rock placed between the rock walls. To make access easy, most of the working bays have a shallow sloping approach ramp directed toward the highwall working face. The working highwall face displays pickax and maul marks. Some highwall mining areas and all the alcove balcony sites show evidence of undermining of the wall, forming niches. Many of the bays have wood fragments, burnt wood torches, gluts, soot on the working face, tally marks, faggot slashes on walls, log poles and other wood objects. In a number of working bays there was considerable effort to reduce wall rock to hand size-cobbles, which were subsequently further broken down into gravel size. Wall staining from lamp soot in the working bays indicates the original level of breakdown prior to excavation (Figures 5-3). Breakdown was moved away from the wall working face and not selectively worked. This was needed to exposed specific stratigraphic intervals that were individually mined along the free face of the highwall. The width, depth and slope angle of working bay approaches probably represent penetration events at the end of Dixon Cave's mining era.

Workers moved breakdown boulders and blocks away from the wall to the center of the cave passage. In this way a transverse trail was built up along the crest of natural breakdown in the center of the passage (Figure 5-1 and 5-2). Some of the bays are 20 to 30 feet below lateral tailing ridges and from 3 to 17 feet below saddles of the traverse trail. The bays range from 10 to 40 feet across at the highwall working face. Toward the rear of the cave the width and depth of working faces decrease. Once the working bays were constructed to a desired depth, a layered dry stack rock wall was built on one side of the excavation, perpendicular to and out from the cave wall. It was common practice for miners to work the complete length of a cave passage in progressive stages. First breakdown was removed from the area to be mined out and stacked in some location out of the way. Miners would then excavate rock for processing and possibly refill the excavation with breakdown rock being excavated from an adjoining site.

The workers may have applied some of these techniques in Dixon Cave. Bedrock wall surfaces show extensive evidence of having been worked with pickaxes, mauls or blunt instruments (gluts). Construction of deeper satellite bays within some working bays suggests attempts were made to lower the breakdown base from the center of the passage, then extending the new working depth toward the wall.

MINERS CAUSEWAY

The Miners Causeway (Figure 5-2) was a truly monumental building feat (De Paepe, 1979). Construction of the leading edge of the Causeway represents efforts to remove excess breakdown from the working bays. The difference between elevation of the upper and lower traverse trail ridge is 20 to 25 feet. Breakdown was removed from the working bays and stacked along the leading edge of the Miners Causeway from the back of the cave toward the entrance. The terminal breakdown slope at the end of the cave was excavated to form a highwall that extended the mine exposure area along the wall surface.

There is a critical point at which placing breakdown on a 10-foot wide lateral ridge presents a stability problem with greater height resulting in collapse. The miners' solution was to build up the grade and

Figure 5-4. Narrow ledge snakes off from the Miner's Causeway and leads over to a balcony alcove excavation site. Diana Emerson George photograph.

narrow the transverse trail. Leading up to the Causeway, the trail had to be wider in the main part of the cave to accommodate greater foot traffic. As the spoil mound grew from the working bay excavations, a central cleft with steps was built in the center of the leading edge of the Causeway and fortified with a dry stone laid wall. Probably this was the transit route for miners returning from the V-vat complex to the back working bays. A shallow graded trail was built next to the east wall on top of the leading edge of the Causeway (Figure 5-2). This was probably the avenue for miner and oxen traffic from the back working bays transporting sacks laden with rocks to the final processing area near the entrance. The Miners Causeway solved two engineering problems, what to do with spoils from the working bays, and how to control the miner traffic flow pattern.

BALCONY ALCOVE SITES

Balcony alcove mining sites are present mostly in the front half of Dixon Cave (Figure 5-2). On the east wall, a ledge approach from the saltpeter apron traverses about 50 feet to two balcony sites. This is directly above the deepest working bay in the cave. Two alcove sites are found immediately across the passage at a similar elevation. Below the alcove sites, breakdown rock is stacked higher along separation ridges next to the wall in the cave. Position of the ridges suggests the base supported a ladder to gain direct access to the balcony-working bay. The west wall along the saltpeter apron has been subjected to highwall mining.

From the west side of the north slope of the Miners Causeway one approaches a narrow 2-foot wide ledge (Figure 5-4). Soot and wood torch fragments litter the trail along with faggot slashes on the wall. By inching out on the ledge for 120 feet, another alcove mining site can be found. This somewhat precarious site could have been accessed from along this ledge or by ladder. The easiest way to work it would be to excavate rock and let it fall to the floor of the cave where it could be collected. The wall below the ledge trail has also been worked. Across the open cave passage on the east side of the north slope of the Miners Causeway is another balcony alcove mining site. On the west wall, halfway between the Causeway and the terminal end of the cave, is one additional balcony alcove-mining site.

STRATIGRAPHIC ZONATION OF MINING SITES

Previous interpretations of the stratigraphic sequence at Mammoth Cave National Park have been invaluable to identifying the rock units exposed during highwall mining in floor working bays and balcony alcove mining sites in Dixon Cave. Palmer's (1975; 1981) field guide and illustrations of stratigraphy and Hill's (1981a, p. 113) description of rock intervals from the rim of the Dixon Cave sinkhole entrance to the top of the lower apron of leached soil were of particular significance in this regard. Based on these reports, it is apparent that five stratigraphic intervals in the Ste. Genevieve Limestone were selectively worked along the length of the Dixon Cave trunk passage (Figures 5-2 and 5-5).

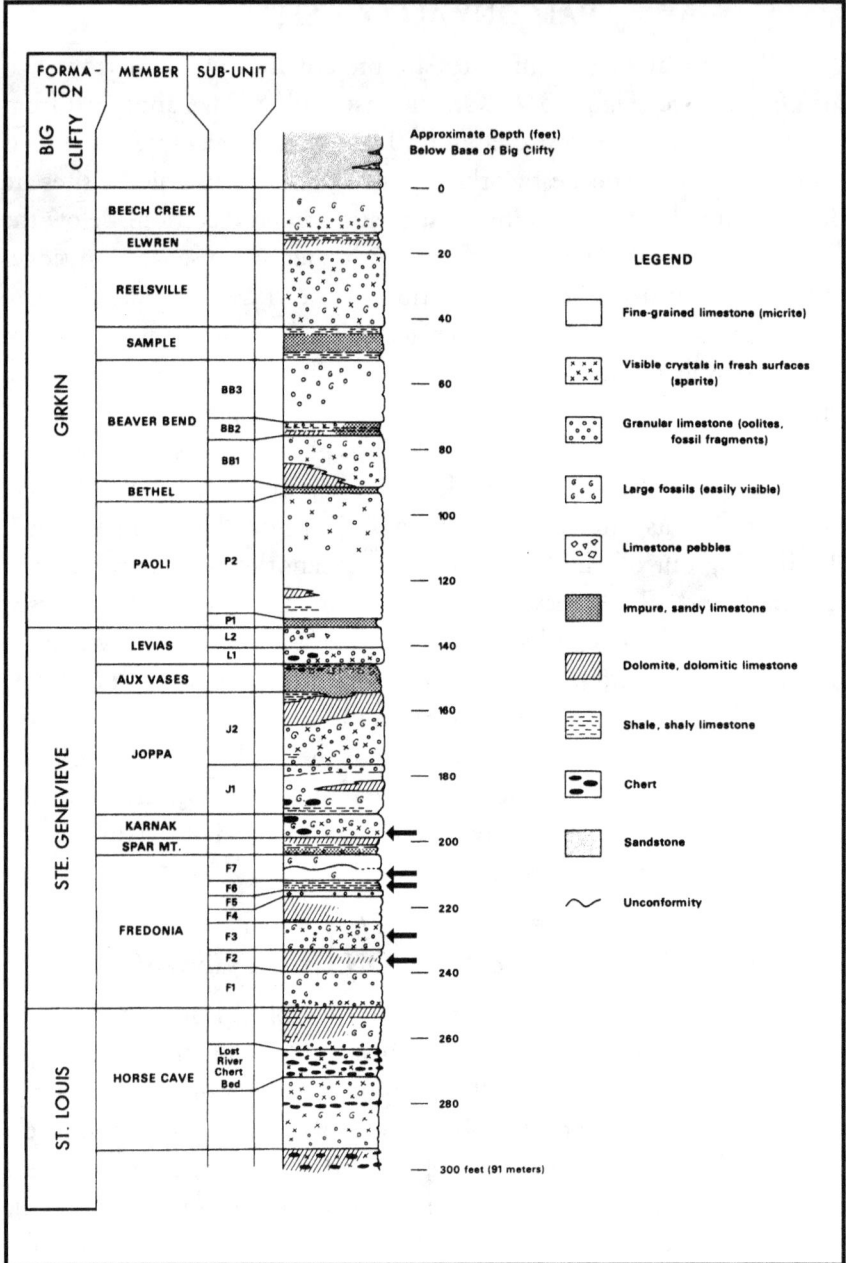

Figure 5-5. Stratigraphic section in the Mammoth Cave National Park (modified from Palmer, 1981). Arrows indicate selected rock units mined by Dixon Cave saltpeter workers.

The Karnak Limestone Member was excavated in three terminal working bays at the south end of the cave. The lower unit of the F-7 zone of the Fredonia Limestone was selectively worked adjacent to the entrance vestibule saltpeter apron, in 6 balcony alcove sites along the first half of the cave, and in 1 balcony alcove and 8 working bays in the last half of the cave. The shaley F-6 zone was also excavated in the front half of the cave. The upper F-3 zone was mined in the first working bay, just north and west of the leading edge of the Miners Causeway. The F-2 zone of the lower Fredonia was selectively worked in the front half of the cave at floor level.

The F-7 zone is a highly fractured unit with large pressure (stress) release limestone wedges or flakes with closely spaced vertical fractures. Wedge dimensions range from 0.5 to 1 feet by 0.1 to 0.3 feet thick. Some of these limestone wedges are friable and easily broken. Gypsum wedging in the fractures promotes exfoliation. Pressure (stress) release jointing combined with exfoliation made this rock interval easy to mine. One to two hundred pounds of rock from this zone could easily be removed by hand even without tools. Deeper working bays expose the F-2 zone in the Fredonia. Sulfate fracture fillings also occur in this unit. There are a number of examples where the laborers undermined into the lower Karnak, F-7, F-3 and F-2 units. Such activity, marked by the use of pickaxes and mauls gives credence to the idea that saltpeter miners were excavating bedrock rather than soil or the widespread breakdown on the floor of the cave. At present, no evidence has been found to suggest the miners scraped the fine veneer of dirt from breakdown on the floor of the cave or penetrated nitrate rich cave soils below the breakdown mass. Instead, breakdown was moved to expose selected cave wall rock units targeted for rock mining. The evidence of tool marks visible on upper and lower Fredonia limestone verifies Hovey's (1882, p. 70) account of pickax noises from Dixon Cave heard in the Historic Entrance area of Mammoth Cave.

MAMMOTH CAVE

In Mammoth Cave, evidence of wall rock mining is found along the west wall in the Rotunda. The Levias Member, Aux Vases Member and Ste. Genevieve Limestone outcrop along the wall behind the V-vat ridge dumps (Figure 2-8). Apparently the miners first attacked the shaley upper interval in the Aux Vases. They continued their work following the wall into Audubon Avenue along the north wall concentrating below the Levias and possibly in the upper Aux Vases. The only well-defined example in the Historic Section of pit mining through breakdown is found along the south wall across from the Methodist Church. At this location is the interface between the cave soil and breakdown that was exposed by the miners. The excavation extends down along the bedrock of the cave wall and displays signs of being selectively mined along a twelve-foot stretch. This would place the base of the excavation in the shale interval at the top of the J-2 zone in the upper the Joppa Member.

Calcareous shales can be rich in potassium (Pettijohn, 1957, pp. 343-346) and the potassium radical could easily attach to the nitrate chemical radical. These rock intervals would therefore have been a very desirable unit to mine. Ground water capillary flow through and or along the shale also helps to transport potassium nitrate rich solutions into rock intervals directly below.

Shale and rock was excavated and carried over to a processing station situated on top of a massive breakdown area across from the Corkscrew. The area consists of a veneer of sorted cobbles and gravels spread around islands of block breakdown. Intriguingly, some of the *worked* gravels are under some of the massive blocks of breakdown. This suggests the massive blocks of breakdown were placed on top of the gravels after the gravels were manufactured. If so, could these be among the pieces of breakdown reported to have fallen during the 1811-1812 earthquakes (Ward, 1816)? Or, possibly, was this a working site for prehistoric selenite miners?

CONTENTS OF SALTPETER HOPPERS

Excavated areas in the anastomoses and side passages of Dixon Cave have soil deposits of a medium red-orange color. Saltpeter hoppers examined at Mammoth Cave and other local saltpeter caves contain a red-orange, silt, clay-rich earth similar to sediments found in cave passages. In contrast, Dixon Cave V-vats and aprons contain about 65-85% limestone gravel mixed with a dark gray to gray, fine to coarse-grained limestone fraction. Size of the limestone gravel ranges from 1/8-1 inch in diameter. Friable limestone and shale (probably from the F-6 zone) make up part of the total vat mixture. The hopper contents are uniformly gray, matching the general color of limestone in the cave. The vat matrix color and high percentage of limestone gravel in the hoppers is further support for an interpretation of mining activity at Dixon Cave that indicates bedrock mining, rather than the excavation of soils common to the great majority of saltpeter caves across the state.

Additional evidence to indicate bedrock mining in the cave comes from the frequent occurrence of gravel piles through the cave, usually in association with a working face at the cave wall. Alternatively, such piles might indicate sites where rock dust and fine fractions impregnated with saltpeter were sifted out, or possibly, on-site manufacture of gravel used to improve the later-era tourist trail along the transverse ridge in the cave. Dixon Cave was infrequently shown to the general public in the 19th and 20th Centuries. The extent of tourist trail improvement is not known. The most likely interpretation seems to be that there were at least 9 sites where workers, during an early phase of the operation, made a concerted effort to reduce wedges and slabs of rock mined from the cave walls into smaller fragments, gravel of 1-2 inches in diameter. Meriam (1844, p. 328) noted the presence of a calcining furnace outside the entrance of Mammoth Cave. There are also the apparent remains of one or more furnaces outside the entrance of Dixon Cave. One of these could be a calcining furnace. Meriam's mention of a calcining furnace at Mammoth suggests that a more advanced technology was later applied to lessen the labor intensity of gravel production.

When limestone (calcium carbonate) is heated in a furnace to temperatures between 900°-1100°F (500°-600°C), the material is decomposed to calcium oxide (CaO) and carbon dioxide (CO_2). This is also the first step in the manufacture of cement, a process that predates recorded history.[1] Calcium oxide is softer than limestone rock, and more easily reduced to smaller fractions. At a saltpeter rock-mining site, such as at Dixon or Mammoth caves, rock would have been transported to the calcining furnaces, partially broken down, and then milled on-site into dust and small gravels no larger than 1/8-1 inch in diameter. The process was only partial, rather than a complete transformation to calcium oxide. The sole function of the calcining furnace was to heat limestone rock only up to a temperature needed to fracture the mass sufficiently to make it more friable. The process stopped short of converting the entire mass into calcium oxide, a white powder called quicklime. The inert white powder signature is not present in the V-vats or spoils aprons in the cave. This suggests the calcining process was not carried to a quicklime completion. A milling machine could have been used to crush the friable limestone and was probably similar to one described by Arnow (1984, p. 288). The reduced fractions were then ready to be leached for their nitrate content. Preparation of nitrate-impregnated sandstone from rockshelters used an analogous method consisting of boiling the rocks in a kettle to breakdown the cementing material holding the sand grains together (Fig and Knudsen, 1984).

It seems rather unlikely that workers would transport the friable limestone back into Dixon Cave from the furnaces. Possibly, a series of vats or hoppers were built outside the cave entrance that deteriorated or were later dismantled so that no visible artifacts remain today. In times past more physical evidence was present outside the cave entrance. Hovey and Call (1912, p. 7) report "the industrious miners ... carried the niter-bearing earth outside to the vats and boiling-tubs whose ruins are yet visible." It appears, however, that at Dixon Cave, as at other large-scale saltpeter *factory* mining sites including both Mammoth Cave and Great Saltpetre Cave, there have been sequences of techno-logical and organizational changes overlain upon prior forms. At Dixon Cave, the present interpretation, subject to revision as new information comes to light, is that during the initial phase, miners reduced rock to gravel by strenuous hand labor at working faces within the cave and placed these fractions into V-vats whose remains are still extant within the cave. During a later phase of the operation, rock fragments, rather than gravel, were transported outside to calcining furnaces for an easier method of reduction, and, possibly, leached in an area adjacent to the furnaces. This would nullify the use of a multi-staged pump tower in the cave. A leachate pipeline could have been built between Dixon and the central evaporation furnaces at Mammoth.

CHEMICAL STRENGTH OF NITRATES IN DIXON CAVE

Figure 5-6 is a bar chart showing nitrate concentrations (ppm) in Dixon and Mammoth caves (Hill, 1981a, pp. 113, 117-118). Sampling sites are located in the vicinity of historic saltpeter mining areas. Nitrate concentrations in Dixon Cave wall rock are comparable in strength to

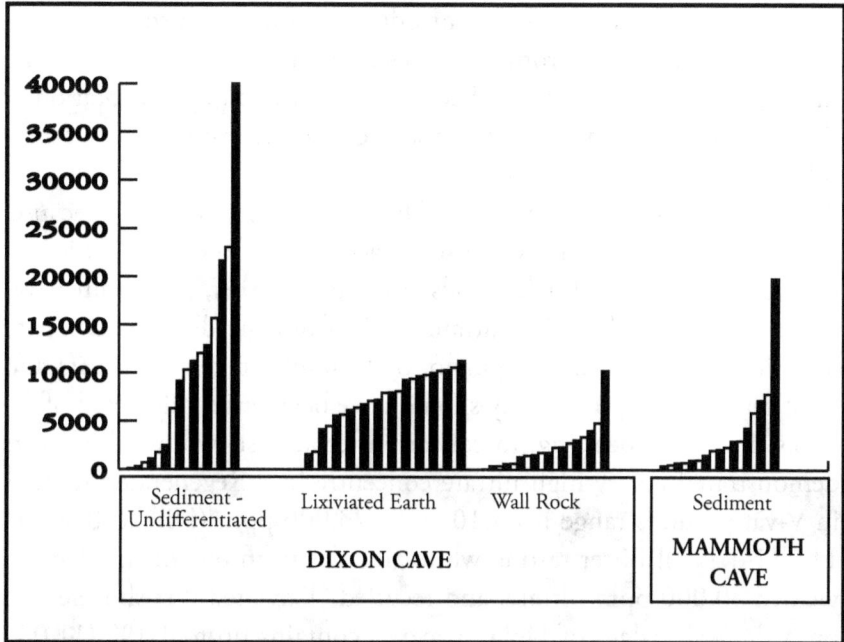

Figure 5-6. Chart comparing nitrate concentration (ppm) of soils and bedrock in Dixon and Mammoth caves (from Hill, 1981a).

nitrates in Mammoth Cave soils. A great departure in nitrate concentrations in Dixon Cave occurs when undifferentiated sediments consisting of soils, lixiviated earth, white nodules and white pockets along with recycled lixiviated material are graphed against nitrate levels in Dixon Cave wall rock. These processed earths have significantly higher nitrate values than wall rock, which suggests, there are vertical intervals of wall rock containing nitrate values higher than Hill's (1981a) chemical sampling demonstrates. Wilkins had to have known about elevated nitrate yields prior to purchasing Dixon Cave. He had ample opportunity to clandestinely establish this during off-season when mining was suspended for want of process water.

Hill's (1981a, pp. 113-114, 117) core drilling experiments for nitrate concentration in the wall rock of Dixon Cave verifies high nitrate level in native bedrock. The first few centimeters (¾ to1 inch) into rock have the highest concentration of nitrates, decreasing with depth. After 30 centimeters (1 ¼ inch), nitrate concentration is still into the thousands of parts per million (ppm)! Hill proposed vadose seepage of

129

ground water as the vector for introducing nitrate rich solutions into the cave environment from the surface forest litter zone. Percolating through the bedrock, nitrates become concentrated by evaporation at the interface between the rock (or soil) of the cave and the cave atmosphere.

Hill's watershed research in Dixon Cave is significant because, on the one hand, it supports historic accounts of the regeneration of nitrates in previously leached soils, and on the other, undermines traditional theories of in-situ nitrate origin from the decomposition of organic matter such as bat guano. Soil samples taken from vats and spoil piles, which presumably should have been largely depleted of nitrates through processing, in contrast after almost two hundred years demonstrated a very high nitrate concentration. Regenerated nitrates in V-vat mounds range from 10,298 - 23,000 ppm (Hill, 1981a, pp. 113-114, 117)! Bitter tasting white globules from one of the hoppers yielded 40,000 ppm nitrate; and recycled "lixiviated dirt shoveled up onto the wall ledges of Dixon Cave ... contains up to 1.1% (11,000 ppm) nitrate" (Hill, 1981b, p. 253).

Many of the traditional theories of the origin of cave nitrates suppose that these minerals originate within the cave environment, either derived from the atmosphere or as a byproduct of bacterial decomposition of accumulated organic material. Most common among these theories is nitrate derivation from the droppings of bats, or guano. Several authors including Hill, have observed that nitrates are found in caves that are not known to be past or present bat habitats. Of all the samples taken from Dixon Cave during Hill's investigation, those from directly beneath a pile of bat guano at the end of the cave had the lowest nitrate concentration. Low nitrate values were also found outside the cave around the entrance sinkhole in an area subjected to rainfall and natural leaching of any nitrates. Inside the cave, nitrate concentration increases dramatically as the rocky floor is approached (Hill, 1981a, p. 113). "In almost all of the drill samples and hand specimens collected, the outer layer had the highest nitrate content," because the highly fractured nature of the F-7 zone in the upper Fredonia Limestone offers maximum surface area for saltpeter-impregnation into all sides of each rock wedge. Interestingly, Hill also noted that, within the cave, nitrate concentrations tended to decrease with distance away from the entrance. Earlier researchers had also observed this phenomenon. Graham (1827, p. 176) reviewed Longchamp's theories of nitrate origin, based upon Antoine Lavoisier's experiments in French saltpeter caves and quarries.

> [A]t Roche Guyon, that in the caverns or pits which were very deep and had but one issue, nitric acid did not appear in the deep parts, but only at the entrance. The same observation was made by that celebrated philosopher in the tufa quarries of Touraine. The nitric acid is formed only in places which contain porous rocks or light soils, possessing carbonate of lime, moisture, and a constant circulation of air.

Although the chemist of Lavoisier's era did not possess a methodology that would allow them to determine actual concentrations of calcium nitrate, they were able to test for nitric acid as an indicator for saltpeter formation in rocks and soil. The nitric acid was believed derived from the atmosphere (discussed in Chapter Six).

Potassium nitrate has been identified as the primary nitrate mineral in sandstone rockshelters mined for saltpeter in eastern Kentucky (Coy, *et al.*, 1984, pp. 54-57). Samuel Brown (1809, pp. 239, 243) called this "rock saltpeter" and reported it "is greatly preferred by our merchants and powder makers, and commands a higher price." In caves, nitrate deposits are almost exclusively in the form of calcium nitrate rather than potassium nitrate. In specific geologic circumstances, however, potassium nitrate deposits may also occur in limestone caves. Kenneth Tankersley (personal communication, August 18, 1986) identified high levels of potassium nitrate in sulfate fracture fillings and crust at Mammoth Cave, Lee Cave and Salts Cave. Dixon Cave is a truncated segment of Mammoth Cave and in the same rock units. Hill's (1981, pp. 118-119) investigation verified the occurrence of nitrate in sulfate speleothems in Dixon Cave.

Hill's (1981a) identification of greatly elevated nitrate levels in wall rock and recycled lixiviated V-vat contents supports observations made by Craig (1862, p. 312). His descriptions of Paris Basin underground quarries and Ceylon (Sri Lanka) cave sites match mining activity and occurrence of saltpeter in limestones from Dixon Cave. Craig, surprised by the circumstances of saltpeter occurrence, noted that these sites "belong to a class by themselves, or at least to have strong points of dissimilarity from any other known instances. In both localities wrote

Craig (1862, p. 312), "the face of the rock, when chipped off, is found to be impregnated with nitrates, which renew themselves on the exposed surface twice a year or oftener." He continues:

> In these caves [Ceylon], as well as in the French quarries, it is only to the depth of a fraction of an inch below the surface of the rock that the nitrates are found, and after this thin coat has been removed it requires from one to six months for the fresh surface to become impregnated. In both these instances the conditions under which nitrification goes on are very similar, taking place on the surface of a porous rock which is continually moist, and exposed to a warm temperature, for in France the nitrates form only on a southern exposure, and mainly during summer. The action is a more rapid one than that of the ordinary nitrification of the earth in caverns, and is to be distinguished from it. The formation of nitrates on the surface of a rock is said to take place to a less extent in other localities, among them in some caves in this country, but the nitrification in our western caves appears to be, mainly at least, that of the earth on their floors. (p. 312).

The time span proposed for regeneration of nitrates in American caves ranged from uncertainty (Brown, 1809), 3 years (Meriam, 1844), to 3-5 years (Mitchell, 1805).

Mining and processing sandstone bedrock for nitrates was a common practice in shelter sites throughout eastern Kentucky and was described in some detail by Samuel Brown's 1809 monograph. Brown, whose Great Saltpetre Cave was for a time Charles Wilkins' main competition in the saltpeter mining business, is silent on the subject of mining limestone for nitrates. Wilkins was almost certainly aware that mining of carbonate rocks for saltpeter was carried on at European sites. Two French encyclopedias of the era (Diderot, 1790, p. 169; Buffon, 1789, pp. 182-183) provide descriptions of mining sites and methods employed on the Continent to extract saltpeter from underground limestone and chalk quarries in the Paris Basin. Buffon's encyclopedia was, in fact, among the early purchases made by Brown as a contribution to Transylvania University in Lexington.

Bedrock mining for nitrates in caves, in contrast, was rare in Kentucky. A number of the caves in the state where rock mining was conducted belonged to Charles Wilkins, his relatives, or business associates. As an educated man and one of the financial and social pillars of the Lexington community, Wilkins may have read of the European practices. Regardless, in 1803, Wilkins was visited in Lexington by a relative who was very likely well aware of French mining methods, having resided in France, periodically, for 17 years in the very place carbonate rock mining for saltpeter was carried on. This was William Short, who, for Wilkins, was his "French connection."

Figure 6-1. This European rendition of Gothic Avenue inspired awe and wonder of cave exploration. Engraving is titled, *Die Mammuths-Höhle (Mammoth Cave) in Kentucky.*

CHAPTER SIX

THE FRENCH CONNECTION

Louis-Alexandre Duc de La Rochefoucauld is "one of our most illustrious and most knowledgeable academics" in France.

Georges LeClerc Buffon,1798

The brothers William (b. 1759) and Peyton (b. 1761) Short, native Virginians and graduates of the College of William and Mary, seemed destined for great things. For the level headed and thrifty William, success came naturally. At an early age, the gifted elder son came to the attention of Thomas Jefferson and became part of the statesman's family, mentioned by him as an unofficial adopted son and later serving as Jefferson's private secretary. From this promising beginning, William indeed moved on to great accomplishments as an American diplomat and international financier. His life was long, comfortable, and distinguished, secure in power, wealth, and the recognition of his countrymen.

Peyton Short was, in every respect, the exact opposite of his older brother. Free-spirited and cocksure, he viewed life as an endless adventure. Kentucky frontiersman, explorer, land developer, and irresponsible investor, he was constantly embroiled in scandal of one sort or another, usually revolving around some get-rich-quick scheme. Time after time, Peyton's reckless ways took him to the edge of financial disaster, and each time he was rescued by his steadfast brother. William cared deeply about his younger brother and made sure Peyton came to no harm, although his brother's behavior exasperated him greatly. As William's biographer noted, Peyton "rarely had bothered to answer William's letters from Europe and had showed little respect for his success" (Shackleford, 1993, p. 139). Peyton would always be an impractical dreamer, and always in trouble.

The biography of William Short, *Jefferson's Adoptive Son*, by George Green Shackleford (1993) is a richly detailed treatment of his life as an international statesman. Fortune smiled upon the perennial bachelor, who invested wisely, lived frugally in his later life and died a millionaire in 1848 at the age of 91. He left the bulk of his enormous estate to his favorite nephew, Peyton's son Charles Wilkins Short, M.D., the botanist. The Shorts were a solid and respectable Virginia family, connected by marriage to Thomas Jefferson, future President of the United States (1801-1809). Jefferson took note of his wife's nephew William at an early age, viewing him as someone possessing exceptional qualities, and took it upon himself to guide the career of the young man he often fondly referred to as "his adopted son." In 1783 Jefferson penned a referral to James Madison, noting that William, while inexperienced, possessed "a peculiar talent for prying into facts" (Ford, 1892-1899, p. 318). This character trait was no doubt one of the reasons that Jefferson had earlier enlisted William to aid in the final editing of his *Notes on the State of Virginia*, published in 1782.

William, who graduated from William and Mary College in 1779, soon found himself thrust into the center stage of international politics under Jefferson's patronage. In 1784, Thomas Jefferson was sent by the Continental Congress to Paris as a commissioner empowered to negotiate commercial treaties, and succeeded Benjamin Franklin in 1785, as Minister Plenipotentiary to France. Jefferson brought his protégé William to Paris to serve as his private secretary. The young man traveled widely through Europe and gained valuable experience in international affairs. He rubbed elbows with the rich and famous, scientists and writers, in elegant surroundings in the Court of Louis XVI. Shortly before Jefferson's return to the United States in 1789, William was promoted to the post of Chargé d'Affaires and represented America during the turbulent years of the French Revolution.

Jefferson arrived in France on July 31, 1784, and was soon followed by William who departed America on October 7, 1784. Although he was initially determined to stay only a short time as Secretary of the Legation, Short was to remain in France for 17 years. During his early years in France he was fond of sharing stories of his brothers bold western adventures. Parisians were spellbound by these accounts of Peyton's exploits in the Kentucky wilderness as a frontiersman, Ma-

Figure 6-2. Exterior of the remodeled 13th Century chateau in La Roche Guyon and Norman era castle on the hill overlooking the Seine River.

jor in the militia, land speculator, and personal friend of Daniel Boone (Shackleford, 1993, p. 28). Boone and Benjamin Franklin were the two Americans most admired in France.

In the summer of 1785, Jefferson and Short were invited to a gala reception in a refurbished 13th Century chateau west of Paris in La Roche Guyon (Shackleford, 1993, p. 21; Figure 6-2). The English writer Arthur Young visited the location in 1788 and thought it was "one of the most singular places I have been at. The chalk rock has been cut perpendicularly, to make room for the chateau" (Betham-Edwards, 1900, p. 145). The most striking attribute of the chateau is that part of the building was constructed inside an underground chalk quarry and was connected with a secret underground tunnel from the chateau up to a Norman era castle high on the palisade overlooking the Seine.

The American delegation were guests of the munificent Louis-Alexandre Duc de La Rochefoucauld, 53 years old and close in age to Jefferson, and his second wife, the beautiful duchess "Rosalie" Alexandrine Charlotte Sophie de Rohan-Chabot, who at 23 was nearly the same age as William. The Duc was an enlightened nobleman, elected to honorary membership to the French Academy of Science, with wide-ranging interests that included experimental agriculture, estate garden design, mineralogy, and all geological phenomena. So impressed was Jefferson, he considered the Duc a "son of science" (Rice, 1991, p. 73). A frequent guest was the naturalist and encyclopedist Georges LeClerc Buffon (1798, p. 182), who characterized the Duc as "one of our most illustrious and most knowledgeable academics" in France. Rochefoucauld's fascination with science derived from early youth, from tutors and the influence of his mother, the Duchess d'Enville. Visiting the estate in May, 1785, Abigail Adams described the elderly Duchess in a letter to her sister: "She is the most learned woman in France; her house is the resort of all men of literature, with whom she converses upon the most abstruse subjects" (Rice, 1991, p. 74). The Duchess collected intellectuals and Americans with the same passion others devoted to collecting furniture or fine art.

Nor was the sophisticated Duchess d'Enville the only intellectual female in the household, for Rosalie shared her husband's interest in natural history (Shackelford, 1993, p. 21). Even though the marriage was ostensibly one of convenience, a common bond of interest in science enlivened their union. Their home was a lively resort for a cross-section of French intelligentsia, including the noted chemist and commissioner of the Royal Gunpowder and Saltpeter Administration (Régie des Poudres et Saltpêtres), Antoine Lavoisier. He was "the protagonist of the chemical revolution and the most influential person in the scientific world at large" (Gillispie, 1980, p. 51). Another significant contact for William Short was Pierre Samuel du Pont de Nemours, the General Commissioner of Commerce, who had played an important role in negotiating the treaty that ended the American Revolution and became a close friend of Jefferson. Du Pont's son, Eleuthère Irénée du Pont, would found the du Pont gunpowder mills in Delaware following emigration of the family to America, and was the most significant purchaser of saltpeter from Mammoth Cave.

William was a handsome young man who somewhat resembled the young 1970s movie star, Beau Bridges. With a silver tongue and a knack for reciting verse, he easily charmed the French ladies and especially Rosalie. William developed an attachment to Rosalie that matured into a romantic relationship lasting their lifetime. He was a frequent guest at the chateau and Hôtel de La Rochefoucauld in Paris.

Figure 6-3. Underground chalk quarries have been converted to troglodyte garages in La Roche Guyon. Quite a few families still occupy these troglodyte houses.

The Duc de La Rochefoucauld was an experienced mineralogist. In June 1787, the English agriculturist, Arthur Young, visited the Duc while vacationing in the south of France in the Department of Languedoc. While taking hikes in the Pyrenees, they were able to examine "the minerals (an article for which the duke de la Rochefoucauld likes to accompany us, as he possesses a considerable knowledge in that branch of natural history).... serves well to keep our time employed sufficiently to our taste" (Betham-Edwards, 1900, p. 37).

La Roche Guyon is a distinctive location on the north side of the Seine River. Along the edge of the main street of the town and for several miles west are numerous multi-level underground quarries (Figure 6-3). These were excavated for chalk building stone used to construct the old fortifications on the hill and some of the residences during the Middle Ages (Figure 6-2). Many of the tunnels had been converted into troglodyte homes by the time of Young's visit in 1788 (Betham-Edwards, 1900, p. 146). Others had old saltpeter artifacts within from prior operations (Gallispie, 1980, p. 69), presumably from the time of the Hundred Years' War (1337-1453) between France and England. The practice of mining saltpeter at that time also often entailed manufacturing gunpowder on the spot. French forces took the fortification away from the Normans in 1449. In another time and another war, German Field Marshal Erwin Rommel used the chateau as his headquarters to direct his troops during the Allied Normandy invasion of 1944.

The Duc's scientific interest was far ranging and included detailed experimental investigations into the origin and occurrence of saltpeter in France. The French Academy of Science offered a cash prize in 1776 for the best paper on saltpeter. By 1786, the Duc had submitted two for publication. One was coauthored with Jean-François Clouet (Professor of Chemistry and Metallurgy) as *Mémoire sur des terres naturellement salpêtrées existant en France*. The other, *Mémoire sur la génération du salpêtre dans la craie*, dealt with the area around La Roche Guyon. Experiments conducted in his underground chalk quarries revealed saltpeter from lixiviated rocks would rapidly regenerate (in 2 to 6 months). This was something saltpetermen had known for centuries, but had received scant attention from the scientific community. Carrying the observations further, he concluded, "in high places, where the air is purer, nitrification is almost null." The free circulation of "putrid air contained in the lower parts of the atmosphere" (Diderot, 1790, p. 177) penetrated through porous rock near the surface and accounted for nitric acid formation, yielding saltpeter. "Putrid air" was believed to be the receptor needed to supply the nitric acid to the underground environment. This was a shocking idea to Antoine Lavoisier after 1776 (who observed the Duc's initial experiments), since scientific opinion had long favored an animal/organic source for saltpeter in rocks and soil. He reversed his opinion once the Duc's arguments and results were published. Lavoisier conducted further investigations along the same lines in these and other quarries in the area.

Experimental work into the origin and regeneration of saltpeter initiated by the Duc de La Rochefoucauld and carried on by Lavoisier enabled a more concentrated rock mining operation around Tours and Chinon. These saltpeter factories continued well into the time of Napoleon, supplying perhaps 10% of the national demand (Gallispie, 1980, p. 69). Evreux (in the 1820s) is the closest active site to La Roche

Guyon, 22 miles west, where saltpeter from rock was harvested "seven or eight times every year" (Phillips, 1823, p. 189, in Gale, 1912, p. 10). The saltpeter workers mined the walls and ceiling by scraping efflorescences and excavating layers of rock and leaching the product in barrels. Most of the abandoned quarries today are garages and storage sheds and, for a few in La Roche Guyon, troglodyte dwellings, quaintly reminiscent of Hobbit houses.

FORMATION OF SALTPETER IN CAVES

For most of the Renaissance and well into the late 1800s, the origin of saltpeter in underground places was a mystery and remains somewhat controversial today. Lewis (1989, pp.68-69) summarized a number of competing modern theories for the origin of saltpeter. At the time the Duc de La Rochefoucauld began his research, two concepts vied for acceptance, the nitric acid theory and the organic substance theory. The first proposed the atmosphere as the source of nitric acid that formed saltpeter in the ground, while the organic theory was as popular if not more so (Johann Rudolph Glauber, in Graham, 1827, p. 172), relying upon dead, decaying, animal or vegetable material as a source. This could be investigated experimentally by growing saltpeter in compost heaps. The organic theory concept had staying power, for we still read in popular references that bat guano is the source of saltpeter in caves. Late Renaissance chemist John Mayow hypothesized saltpeter was a "substance" that resided in the atmosphere. Covering much of the same territory, Nicholas Lémery refined the saltpeter theory about 1675, by adding, "saltpeter ... derived its acidity directly from acid particles in the atmosphere" (Lewis, 1989, p. 68). The discovery of nitrogen in the air would help change the way people looked at the origin of saltpeter.

A Swedish druggist, Carl Scheele, and a Scotch botanist, Daniel Rutherford, discovered nitrogen independently in 1772. Lavoisier was the first to recognize nitrogen as an element and in 1790 J. A. C. Chaptal introduced the name "nitrogen" to indicate that the element is a constituent of nitre – potassium nitrate (Hersh, 1968, p. 454).

The Duc de La Rochefoucauld won over Antoine Lavoisier's support to the nitric acid theory in which nitrates are generated by putrid air interaction in rocks and soils. Longchamp (1823) departed from the traditional interpretation, favoring nitrogen in "the air and not from organic substances" (Lewis, 1989, p. 69). Graham (1827, p. 172) summarizes Longchamp's theory with "There is reason to doubt the original proposition of Glauber, and which as far as regards the nitric acid has been the prevailing theory to the present day, that formed by the decomposition of animal and vegetable substances" and "for nitrates [to] form and are found in materials and in places which contain no vegetable or animal matter, and which have never been exposed to the emanations of animals." An English expatriate, Joseph Priestley, in 1809 championed a "weak nitrous acid produced in the atmosphere causes deposition of saltpeter" (Lewis, 1989, p. 69), and a concept originally identified years earlier by Rochefoucauld and Lavoisier. David Dale Owen (1856, p. 169) best characterized thinking in the mid 19th Century on the formation of Mammoth Cave saltpeter, in that "many of these limestones are of such a composition as to be acted on freely by the elements of the atmosphere, which, in the form of nitric acid, combine with the earthy and alkaline bases of calcareous rock, and give rise to the formation of nitrates, with the liberation of carbonic acid." Not until 1877 did Schloesing and Müntz determine a living biological agent caused nitrification. S. Winogradsky in 1890 isolated the actual bacteria responsible for nitrification in soils (Gale, 1912, pp. 33-34). The origin of saltpeter in caves, however, remained elusive.

Hess (1900) and Nichols (1901) debated opposite points of view over the origin of saltpeter in caves. Hess (1900) rejected the bat guano organic theory and offered a different interpretation. The ultimate origin of cave saltpeter, he proposed, is from surface dwelling nitrifying bacteria in soils. Rainfall and ground water carry soluble nitrates from the surface into the cave environment where they are deposited. Ground water flow line theory is a staple concept in modern hydrogeology to understand the movement of water through soils, rocks, and caves. Nichols (1901) countered the argument and rejected the ground water flow line theory in favor of bat guano. The argument languished until the late 20th Century as more researchers investigated caves as a science. Burton Faust (1967, p. 27) favored the ability of bacteria in dry caves to "convert atmospheric nitrogen into calcium nitrate" in the soil profile. White (1976, p. 316) briefly mentions, "there is some evidence that nitrogen-fixing bacteria (*Nitrobacter*) are responsible.... By and large, the question remains open."

Carol A. Hill (1981) reexamined, experimented, and refined Hess's (1900) theory of cave saltpeter. The ground water seepage theory maintains nitrates are produced by bacteria in the forest litter profile found outside and above a cave passage. Ground water flow lines carry the nitrates downward where cave passages act as a hydraulic sink, causing convergence of flow lines and fostering the evaporation of ground water and depositing nitrates near the cave-air interface.

The Nitrogen Cycle is one of the cornerstones of biological processes, although rarely mentioned in the speleological literature covering the formation of saltpeter in caves. Only recently has the Nitrogen Cycle been elevated to its rightful place in the cave environment by Northup and Lavoie (2004, p. 507). They found, "the processes of ammonification, nitrification, denitrification, and nitrogen fixation have all been documented in caves." This helps to settle the argument that the formation of saltpeter is associated with luxuriant populations of microbacteria living in caves. Some are responsible for ammonification and two bacteria (*Nitrosomonas* and *Nitrobacter*) are involved in nitrification. Until recently only a handful of bacteria were known from Kentucky caves. In Jack Bradley Cave, Pulaski County, Kentucky, Hazel Barton identified 111 *new species* of bacteria inhabiting the grotto (Burke, 2005, p. 66), a phenomenal feat in bacterial identification from caves thought to have limited microbiological life. One would not expect Jack Bradley Cave to be the exception rather the norm for all caves of the region.

The origin of saltpeter in caves centers on the microbiological interaction of a number of bacterial genera. Nitrates produced by bacterial activity chemically combine with calcium radicals in soil or rock forming calcium nitrate (niter). The porosity of saltpeter impregnated sediments or rock type determines the ease of growth and quantity of saltpeter available for harvesting.

Range of Values of Porosity (%)

(after Freeze and Cherry, 1979; and Ford and Williams, 1989)

Clay 40
Silt 35-50
Sand 25-50
Gravel 25-40
Sand & Gravel 25-35
Karst Limestone 5-50
Limestone 0-20
Chalk .... >40

In Mammoth Cave during the saltpeter era, "clay...produces 6 lb of Salt Petre to every bushel, the sand produces one to the bushel" (Ridgely, 1811). Higher porosity of clays and silts favors greater populations of bacteria growing along environmental surfaces, because there is a greater surface area in the pores to grow. Chalk rocks in northwestern Europe have porosity values > 40% (Ford and Williams, 1989, p. 21). Favorable renitrification conditions in high porosity rocks are why the French chalk quarries could be harvested 6-8 times a year. Rapid bacterial growth is reflected by the regeneration of saltpeter in well-aerated lixiviated saltpeter soils, an environment that is hostile to denitrifying bacteria.

Two different models thus account for nitrates in caves, rockshelters, quarries and even in the basements of domestic dwellings: ground water flow line seepage theory and in-situ bacterial growth using the Nitrogen Cycle. The interaction between these two models makes nitrate formation possible in different environments. Positively charged ammonium ions attach themselves to negatively charged clay colloids. Rainfall on the surface or pore solution flow through rock and soils will not flush out the ammonium, because it is locked up in its place of origin. In contrast, nitrate ions are negatively charged and hence are not held in the clay or rock. These ions can be easily leached from soils and rock. Cave soils and cave passage walls nearest the floor act as a hydraulic sink for converging ground water flow lines, which transport nitrate rich solutions into the cave, resulting in deposition of nitrates. The Nitrogen Cycle, utilizing a host of in-situ bacteria, also accounts for saltpeter production within cave soils and bedrock.

DENITRIFYING BACTERIA AND SALTPETER RECYCLING

Saltpetermen found that, by digging deeper into the cave soil pro-file, nitrate yields tended to decrease with depth. They stopped digging when the concentration of nitrates was no longer profitable. They had no adequate explanation for the observed phenomenon. By experience, they would excavate only the surface of soil banks, leaving most of the deposit in place. There are examples of this in Gratz Avenue of Mammoth Cave. Pit mine excavations rarely went any deeper than ten feet, as in Short Cave.

The main reason for diminished nitrate yields in the cave soil pro-file is due to the Nitrogen Cycle of which denitrifying bacteria plays a central role. These are anaerobic bacteria and must live in a low to no oxygen environment and are found deeper in the soil profile. Bacteria responsible for nitrification in soils require an environment high in oxygen. These are called aerobic bacteria and live at the top of the soil profile.

During the saltpeter era only a few cave owners made an effort to recycle lixiviated soils. Two prime examples are Dixon Cave and Great Saltpetre Cave. In Great Saltpetre Cave the lixiviated soils were removed from the hoppers and transported outside the cave. The soils were allowed to dry in the sun and then the dry mud was crushed to pea and gravel size. This deposit was taken back into the cave and sown like seeds in side passages, sometimes filling up the passage entirely. There it would lie fallow for renitrification to occur. Raking with a tool or simply crawling through the gravel soil helped to aerate the gravel and speed up the nitrification process. Recycling in Dixon Cave amounted only to dumping and shoveling wet lixiviated soils on and against the cave walls.

WILLIAM SHORT AND THE FRENCH REVOLUTION

During the Duc's time, atmospheric air, especially "putrid" air, was believed to serve as a chemical origin for many elemental com-pounds and as the cause of medical maladies unexplainable by any other means. The Duc's research led him to propose two requirements for the growth of saltpeter: air circulation and open porosity of the rock or soil. Another hundred years would elapse before bacteria were discovered as the cause for nitrification.

Frequent trips to the chateau would have given William many opportunities to become familiar with the saltpeter experiments being conducted by the Duc and Lavoisier in the underground quarries. At that time, Europeans performed physical experiments to discover unknowns. American scientists did not have this expertise, choosing instead to let the Europeans with a long record of advancement do the work. France at the end of the 18th Century dominated the world of scientific advancement. The Duc was probably delighted by the chance to explain his work to the intelligent and inquisitive young man. William already had a passing acquaintance with saltpeter mining from his work on Jefferson's *Notes on the State of Virginia*, which contained several references to saltpeter caves. Excavating the soil of caves in America for saltpeter was fairly straight forward, but here along south facing cliffs, saltpetermen mined and leached bedrock for nitrates.

William was present during the start of the French Revolution, the Reign of Terror, the establishment of the Directory, Napoleon Bonaparte's rise to power, the Consulate and the first few months of the Empire. Early in the uprising, word reached him the Duc had been arrested, and while being transported to Paris was overtaken by the mob at Gisors on September 4, 1792. De la Rochefoucauld made a public-spirited plea in favor of the revolution and human rights but to no avail, as he was stoned to death in front of his wife and mother. The Terror also swept up Antoine Lavoisier and sent him to the guillotine on May 8, 1794; the French courts stated bluntly, "The Republic has no use for savants." Rosalie was imprisoned for ten months (Ward, 1937, p. 137). These tragic events depressed William greatly, who expressed his troubled feelings in letters sent back home to Jefferson (Shackleford, 1993).

Political wrangling freed Rosalie from prison. She sought shelter in La Roche Guyon and in the protecting arms of William. By now, he had become a household fixture at the chateau. As the revolution churned and aristocratic heads rolled, Rosalie commissioned William to hide the family fortune out of the country, and he invested considerable sums in United States Government bonds. Both became wealthy as a result of these transactions.

William always had an active interest in scientific experimentation and progress. At La Roche Guyon he witnessed experiments in more efficient saltpeter mining, which could have applications back home in America. There are no specifics in his correspondences to enlighten us as to exactly what he saw in the quarries. He did possess a scientific and analytical mind and a wide general knowledge of natural science. One of Short's biographers, Samuel Ward (1937, p. 140), described his "delightful library.... [containing] much of the best in literature, history and science of the time. Numbering some 3000 volumes, preponderantly French works which Short had brought back from Paris, the library in its day ranked among the 5 or 6 most important in this country." When he returned to America in 1802, he was soon elected a member of the American Philosophical Society in July 1804 (Shackleford, 1993, p. 142). This membership was a high honor, for to be elected required a substantial reputation in the scientific community. He attended meetings, took an active interest in new discoveries and conversed with the scientific luminaries for the rest of his life (Shackleford, 1993, p. 169).

PEYTON SHORT'S RUINOUS CAREER

Peyton lived in the shadow of his older brother, never measuring up to expectations and a constant financial drain on his family and associates. Peyton was a poor money manager, a braggart and a raconteur of the fabulous. William considered him a disappointment and wished he would do better with wiser investments. He tried to escape creditors by going on exploring ventures in Florida, checking out land opportunities in the Indiana Territory near Vincennes or visiting relatives in up state New York. He was always one step ahead of urgent posts demanding payment. On the rare occasions that he wrote to a family member, such as his brother William or brother-in-law Charles Wilkins, the letter was filled with thin excuses as to why he could not, just then, meet his obligations. Creditors, especially Charles Wilkins and Frederick Ridgely, ultimately stripped Peyton's fortune from him. He lost everything: thousand of acres of land, including his Green River lands with the fabulous Short Cave, and his showcase Greenfield plantation near Versailles, Kentucky; numerous slaves; and even his children, who were distributed to relatives for up bringing. Despite his failings, he was well liked by acquaintances. Peyton was a "man of wit" wrote William Leavy (1942, p. 257). His son, Charles Wilkins Short (and Richardson, 1879, p. 122) recalled his fathers' best attributes.

> Those who knew him, say that he had a wonderful talent for conversation, which with his fine education and mental culture made him a most agreeable companion; that in his happy days his wit and humor were unbounded and "could have passed muster with Swift and Poe, and the 'brilliants' of their day."

In his early years in Kentucky, Peyton was held in high esteem as a Lexington merchant (1791) and land developer around the town. He owned and subdivided the northwestern part of pioneer Lexington for homes. West Short Street signifies his importance to the community. He was a sterling real-estate salesman with a gift for gab, but also an easy mark for *El Dorado* schemes, including purchase of property in Christian County, Kentucky.

William "was condescending about Peyton Short, whose removal to and reckless land speculation in Kentucky he attributed to his 'poor & good' brother's 'too lively imagination'" (Shackelford, 1993, p. 177). Peyton may be visualized as a slick tongued *Elmer Gantry* type with evangelistic zeal when it came to buying and selling land. He believed his own pitch and saw only gold on the horizon. His enthusiasm fostered a Pied Piper following to fabulous lands and business opportunities.

One of his milk and honey sales presentations enticed his brother-in-law, Charles Wilkins, to move his lucrative Pittsburgh, Pennsylvania, mercantile business to a frontier village called Lexington, Kentucky. Silver-tongued Peyton convinced Charles that this was his opportunity to be in on the ground floor to riches. Peyton, himself, was on the way to this Promised Land. Peyton's family moved to Lexington in the fall of 1791 (Short and Richardson, 1879, p. 4), and conceivably, Wilkins relocated at about the same time. This was a move Wilkins would soon regret as the reality of his new circumstances placed him in the middle of hostile Indian country. Indian attacks were, however, on the wane and by the end of the decade there was peace on the frontier. Nevertheless he came to believe this relocation was the worst thing he had ever done and never forgave Peyton, blaming him for many of his future misfortunes. Despite Wilkins' initial trepidation, after a few rough years things worked out rather well. He became one of the town's primary citizens, as banker, entrepreneur and patron of the arts and highly educated. Through the efforts of men like Wilkins, Lexington became *the* manufacturing center and first crossroads of culture in western America.

Financial security eluded Peyton. As soon as success came within Peyton's grasp, it vaporized as a mirage. His supposed wealth in land holdings was rotten at the core, acquired through a self-generating Ponzi scheme based on hocking existing land holdings and borrowing money from family and business associates to purchase new properties and to pay interest on old debts. By 1809 the mounting pyramid of land debts was enormous, and his empire began to crumble. From his brother William, "sums of money were constantly advanced to help him out of difficulties, and the same generous help was extended to his brothers children after his death" (Short and Richardson, 1879, p. 88).

Returning to America in June 1802, William tried to put his own financial and real estate holdings back in order, especially those mismanaged by Peyton's handling of their father's estate. He unexpectedly went to Lexington, Kentucky, in August 1803 to assess Peyton's management of their assets (Shackelford, 1993, p. 179). He stayed with his sister Jane, wife of the "friendly and worthy" Charles Wilkins (Shackelford, 1993, p. 140). It was here William discovered the true nature of Peyton's mismanagement of their properties and investments. His brave frontier brother and successful investor was nothing more than a charlatan, who had been disguising the truth of their ruinous financial situation. William was livid with anger, and his ire was due to far more than the loss of their father's estate. According to William's biographer Shackelford (1993):

> William was convinced that all of the Shorts had lost money in Peyton's hasty sale of the land and slaves of their father's estate and his speculation in large tracts of land in Kentucky and Ohio. William was questioning, rather than denunciatory, of Peyton's actions until after he visited Kentucky. Once having learned the facts, however, he was furiously indignant at

him and remained so for the rest of his life.... In his last years William wrote to a nephew [John Cleves Short] how much he had disapproved of his brother's "making the desperate move to Kentucky under the delusion of acquiring at a single leap a magnificent fortune. Such sudden starts never had any charm for me. But my poor brother completely deceived himself, and by his correspondence me, too, for from his letters I was under the full impression that he was most prosperous until I came back to this country and went to visit my family in Kentucky. I then had the mortification to see the real state of things" (pp. 139-140).

William could maintain a cool and even temper during the most intense negotiations with powerful heads of state, unruffled by the most severe diplomatic adversity. Only brother Peyton was able to disturb his composure. Peyton's land holdings began to unravel after his second wife, Jane Churchill, died in May 1808. His children were divided among relatives as he struggled with her loss and his impending financial ruin. He elected brothers-in-law Wilkins and Frederick Ridgely to hold his power of attorney, promising them great financial rewards to help him get out of debt. The sale of large tracts of real estate, his Versailles plantation (Greenfield) and slave holdings was authorized on October 21, 1809 (Kentucky Court of Appeals Books O-U, p. 142). Peyton owed $10,000 ($140,000 today) *in cash* to Ridgely alone at this point in time as well as an unspecified amount to Wilkins.

Peyton evaded his responsibilities the following month and was well on his way in November 1809, on a journey of exploration down the Mississippi into the area around Mobile, Alabama, and Pensacola, Florida. This trip, which lasted two years, was a scouting mission to assess new land purchase possibilities needed to rebuild his fortune (Hamlin, 1910, p. 3) in the land of alligators, snakes and swamps. He never cured himself of this land acquisition addiction. It haunted him the rest of his life.

A large proportion of his slaves had been sold to Thomas Hart, Sr., to satisfy part of the money owed to Hart (*Kentucky Court of Appeals Book N*, p. 258). Possibly, Short's remaining slaves went to work at Mammoth Cave. By 1813, his land empire was reduced to the Greenfield estate (Shackelford, 1993, p. 140), and finally, even the house was sold (Short and Richardson, 1879, pp. 120, 130).

Despite Peyton's manic desire to acquire land and his desperate financial hardships, his free spirited ways should not be interpreted as lazy. Extroverted and steadfastly independent, he was humbled to the point of apathy when told by family members to put his financial life in order. He stayed alert for opportunities to solve his financial troubles. He tried to do this by being a hard worker and marching to a different drummer. As businessman, he was a risk taker in an all out gamble. His mental character was that of a dreamer. T. E. Lawrence's *The Seven Pillars of Wisdom* aptly described men of Peyton's disposition.

> All men dream, but not equally. Those who dream by night in the dusty recesses of their mind wake in the day to find that it was vanity; but the dreamers of the day are dangerous men, for they may act their dream with open eyes, to make it possible.

Peyton's dreams excited others, but in the end, his was all talk. On the other hand, brother-in-law Charles Wilkins actualized his dreams into success.

Broken in spirit and finances, for a time Peyton operated a mill near Frankfort (Short and Richardson, 1879, p. 121). When his son, Charles Wilkins Short, M.D. moved to Hopkinsville, Christian County, Kentucky, in 1817 to set up a medical practice, Peyton followed later and settled twelve miles south of the town. Financially strapped, he spent his declining years still using credit and spending money he did not have, isolated, periodically penniless and later in poor health. He died at the age of 64, on September 1, 1825, leaving his son Charles the burden of paying off the remaining notes.

SHORT CAVE

During William Short's 1803 visit, Lexington was a fountainhead of scientific endeavors, and often referred to as the "Athens of the west." The community was home to inventor, silversmith and gunsmith Edward West Jr., viticulturist and inventor John James DuFour, and scientific polymath Samuel Brown, M.D., as well as many other intellectuals and Transylvania University, the first institution of higher

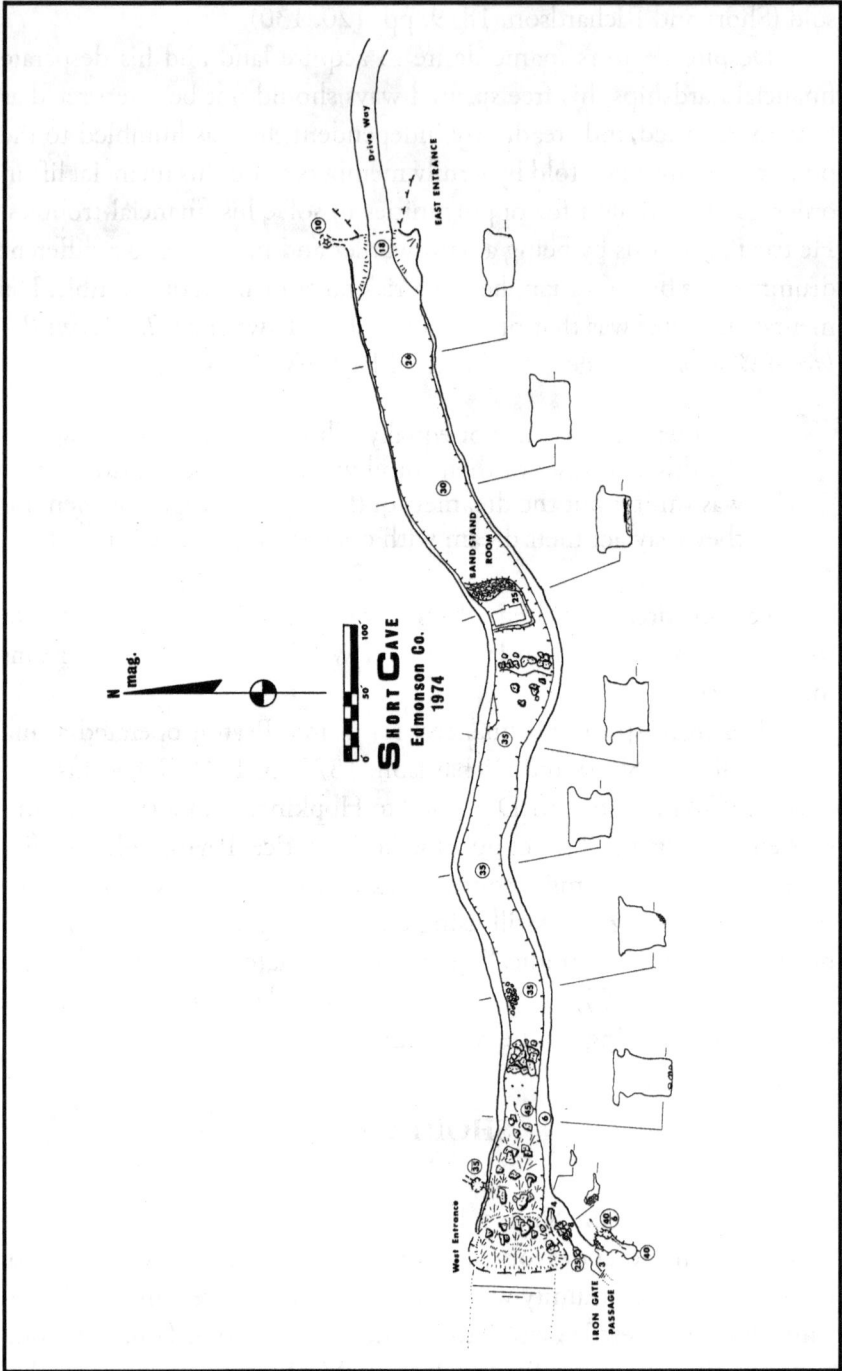

Figure 6-4. Brunton compass and tape map of Short Cave.

learning west of the mountains. Often compared to Philadelphia in development, Lexington was close knit with a strong sense of community development. Taverns served as community meeting houses, forums for scientific discoveries and intellectual discourse. Medical instruction connected with the university was given in the homes of Frederick Ridgely, M.D., and Samuel Brown, M.D. Just a year before (1802) French naturalist Andre Michaux had briefly visited while on a botanical expedition through the West. Chemist, mineralogist, pre-Lewis and Clark explorer of the Missouri River, and Philadelphia saltpeter processor George Hunter, M.D., made Lexington home for a short time. Hunter stayed to settle an estate and launch a field excursion to Great Saltpetre Cave with Brown to assess its investment potential and saltpeter output. By 1805, Brown and Lexington merchant Thomas Hart, Jr., purchased the cave, modernizing it with a new style of leaching equipment invented by John James DuFour. The cave produced 50% more saltpeter than did Mammoth Cave years later (George, 2001, p.72-74). During Peyton Short's period of prosperity, he built a luxurious plantation called Greenfield in the vicinity of Versailles, Kentucky, as befit a man of property and enterprise.

Peyton took shortcuts to riches and if the endeavor generated cash, so much the better. Occasionally, investments rewarded the perennial dreamer. In pioneer times, three businesses dealt in cash transactions: salt brine, saltpeter, and gunpowder manufacturing. By 1803, there were two powder factories in Lexington and by 1810 the number had grown to five (O'Dell, 1995). Peyton witnessed the kind of commerce being transacted by saltpetermen and the amount of money changing hands. Profits were staggering and it was in cash money, something most people did not have, favoring barter instead. He owned considerable lands in the Green River locality and on one of these properties was a saltpeter cave called Short Cave.

Short Cave is a huge paleotrunk passage, 800 feet long, 50 feet wide and 18-45 feet high and a close analog to Dixon Cave in physical morphology (Figure 6-4). The length of the cave in pioneer times apparently was greater than today's map indicates. Charles Wilkins (1820, p. 363; and Rice, no date) noted the cave was not large, perhaps three quarters of a mile in length, although Meriam (1844, p. 317) stated the length was a quarter of a mile. Terminal breakdown at the end of the trunk has truncated the cave completely, thereby reducing the total length that can be traversed today.

Location is everything in any business enterprise. The Barrens represented a vast grassland prairie crisscrossed by trails and sparse settlements connected by the main thoroughfare called the Natchez Trace. In the Mammoth Cave area, present day Interstate 65 and Federal Route 31W follow this early transportation route. Short Cave is located just north of the Natchez Trace, and found today north of Park City near Diamond Caverns, nestled within the Dripping Springs Escarpment (Figure 1-3). It has been called The Mummy Cave, Briggs' Cave (after J. B. Briggs) and Jan's Cave, named for Diamond Caverns prior owner's daughter, Janet Rowsey. Active saltpeter mining possibly dates prior to 1805 to late 1814. The cave was used as a mushroom farm and a cold storage produce warehouse between the years 1898-1922 or later by J. B. Briggs. By the late 1950s, the Diamond Caverns management periodically exhibited Short Cave to tourists, a practice which continued well into the early 1970s. Today the cave is used as a concert hall and as a place for banquets and dances.

Short Cave is arguably the third most historically significant Kentucky cave after Mammoth Cave and Great Saltpetre Cave. Pioneer events taking place in Short Cave helped propel Mammoth Cave into the most famous cave in the world. Out of context and in context Indian artifacts from the Early Archaic, 9500 B.C., to Late Middle Woodland, 200-600 A.D., have been identified from the cave (Sneed, 1986, pp. 33-34). Even rarer Indian artifacts were accidentally discovered during the mining era. As saltpeter miners moved breakdown boulders to exposes nitrate-impregnated soils, stone box crypts full of grave goods with Indian mummies were sometimes accidentally discovered. The public was astounded when they read reports of these discoveries in books, newspapers, and journals of the day.

Early in its mining history, estimated to be in 1805, a number of mummified bodies were dug up in the cave (George, 1994). Peyton's original description of the discovery has not been located. But an embellishment (worthy of Edgar Allan Poe) was collected and recorded in the travel adventures of Thomas Ashe (1808). Peyton apparently used his best story telling ability to dramatize the discovery to family members who then retold the event with the addition of significant embellishments. Ashe probably acquired the story from William Goforth, M.D., or Peyton's father-in-law Judge John Cleves Symmes near Cincinnati, Ohio. Both men are prominently mentioned in Ashe's book. Rather than one or two mummies, hundreds sounded more dramatic and well within Ashe's sphere of fantastic reporting of manufactured history and geography. Ashe dropped the name and changed the locale of the cave to Lexington, Kentucky, and romanced the story as the Lexington Catacomb. Ashe never visited Lexington, the Barrens of Kentucky, or Short Cave, but he extracted enough information from gazetteers, histories, and contacts in Cincinnati, to weave the tale of a catacomb with hundreds of mummies lodged in niches and buried near pioneer Lexington. European catacombs were originally excavated for limestone and chalk rock used in construction of buildings. Some of the underground quarries became catacombs for the burial of the dead in Paris and in Rome. Ashe's description of the mummies is exactly like real Indian mummies discovered in Short Cave. Even the arrangement of passages attributed to the Lexington Catacomb favors Short Cave. The legend of the Lexington Catacomb is still covered by the local news media, especially around Halloween.

Indian mummies found by saltpeter miners were very different from the preserved bodies found in Egyptian tombs. Indian mummies from this Kentucky cave were wrapped in layers of deerskins and a feathered cape, while Egyptian mummies were wrapped in linen bandages. These Indian mummies were complete bodies and appeared to the saltpetermen as recently deceased. All of the mummies were injured in someway before death or postmortem death. Opening the stone box crypts, the superstitious saltpetermen were frightened, thinking the mummies were demons or other infernal beings. To make certain the mummies were dead and would not come back to haunt them, they clubbed, or shot some of them, and at least one mummy was cremated in a saltpeter furnace (George, 1994).

Five known mummies were recovered in Short Cave from the time period 1811-1814. A child was found in August 1811 by the saltpeter miners. Word reached Charles Wilkins at Mammoth Cave, and he rode over to his brother-in-laws cave to retrieve the artifact for his collection. He discovered to his mortification that the body, along with most of the grave goods, had been destroyed in a saltpeter furnace.

Figure 6-5. Interior view of Short Cave from the entrance. Asphalt pavement improved the cave for Diamond Caverns tours in the 1950s and 1970s. Today the cave is used for banquets, parties, dances and concerts.

The skull was retrieved. He offered a reward for a complete mummy, and in late September 1811, Fawn Hoof (an adult) was discovered and sent to Mammoth Cave for storage (Figure 2-5). Tourists witnessed the mummy and later the Mummy's Seat in Gothic Avenue. The travel book, *Health Trip to the Tropics* by Parker Willis, named the mummy Fawn Hoof in 1853. Three additional mummies were discovered in the late summer of 1814, and Wilkins sent them to east coast museums.

An antiquarian by the name of Nahum Ward viewed Fawn Hoof in 1815, and wrote glowing accounts of her and the extensive passages in Mammoth Cave. The 1816 *Wonders of Nature* newspaper article was published all over America and Europe. His descriptions of the cave and mummy acted as the springboard needed to thrust Mammoth Cave into the public spotlight. Fawn Hoof resided briefly in Clifford's Cabinet in Lexington, Kentucky, along with another mummy excavated from Big Bone Cave, Tennessee. This one belonged to John D. Clifford. Nahum Ward acquired temporary custody of Fawn Hoof and exhibited her to east coast cities as a traveling exhibit before releasing her to the American Antiquarian Society in Worcester, Massachusetts. Fawn Hoof's public exhibition and newspaper accounts made the mummy and Mammoth Cave famous on both sides of the Atlantic. Not only did the common man want to see the mummy, they wanted to see where she was unearthed, which, erroneously according to Ward (1816) was in the far reaches of the Mammoth Cave.

Mining era artifacts from Short Cave have not survived. Everything has been removed and there is no obvious evidence outside the cave. During the late 19th and 20th Century, the front half of the cave was backfilled and level graded for the construction of a cold storage warehouse and mushroom farm. During the mid 20th Century the front half of the cave was blacktopped with asphalt to accommodate vehicles carrying tourists from Diamond Caverns (Figure 6-5). The end of the trunk passage was opened to the outside during a failed attempt to install a railroad for tourists from the Diamond Caverns Hotel through the cave. Backhoe and bulldozer activity has extensively remodeled the character of the floor between the two entrances.

Assessing the size of the Short Cave mining operation is difficult. What we do know is that there was a saltpeter furnace and ash piles outside the cave. Water sources are found in the two side passages in the present cave. The miners were industrious and moved four to six feet of breakdown to expose saltpeter-impregnated soils (Wilkins, 1820, p. 363) to facilitate excavation through at least ten feet of soil (Wilkins, 1820, p. 362). None of these features are presently visible in the cave except the excavation of limestone wall rock for saltpeter. On first impression, the interior morphology of the trunk passage exhibits all the characteristics of a modern underground rock quarry as Wainscott (1974, p. 45) observed years earlier.

High-level trunk cave passages in the Mammoth Cave area have solution features called scallops on the walls. These cup shaped features are formed by the dissolving action of slow moving ground water through the conduit. Scallops are absent from most of the walls in Short Cave and Dixon Cave in areas excavated for rock. Highly fractured limestone in two areas in the Short Cave trunk passage was worked for nitrates. The lower walls have been excavated in a manner similar to Dixon Cave (see Chapter Five), although the working bays are more subdued. The other locality, found below the ceiling level, is what looks like a wide prototube. A natural prototube incised by a trunk canyon passage has a concave bedrock floor directed toward the center of the passage. This one consists of a flat floor or ledge, artificially incised at least 4 feet into bedrock and extends the length of the cave along both sides of the passage. The height varies from 4-5 feet, making it possible for a person to walk and stoop-walk the complete length of the passage along these two opposing ledges. This is similar to the balcony alcove sites and walkway ledges in Dixon Cave. The Short Cave lower wall working bays look like shallow niches in the walls. These two features are analogous to the mummies' niches and shelving described by Thomas Ashe (1808).

William Short is considered to be the "French connection" for the introduction of an exotic method of saltpeter mining seen in a few caves of the pioneer West. William's visit to family relations in Lexington in 1803 would have been the opportune time for such an industrial technology exchange. He saw a growing industry of powder factories supplied by locally mined saltpeter. This industry was a lively conversation topic with visitors to Lexington during this time period. Andre Michaux and George Hunter waxed eloquently on the subject. William Short followed a year later and without doubt experienced the same euphoria from people associated with this developing industry.

The technique of mining and processing limestone rock for nitrates has its roots in underground French chalk quarries. William lived in this locality during the time the industry was in full swing. His friends, the Duc de La Rochefoucauld and Antoine Lavoisier, studied and published works on the origin of saltpeter, methods of mining chalk for nitrates, and conducted experiments in saltpeter regeneration in underground quarries. These sites are found next to the chateau where William lived off and on for seventeen years in La Roche Guyon. He had an inquisitive scientific mind and would have been eager to understand the process as he did with other kinds of scientific investigations.

The French method of scraping rocks for efflorescences and breaking up wall rock to leach nitrates is unique. We see the same techniques used in a few caves, especially those owned by William Short's family relatives. Peyton probably exploited the technique early on in Short

Cave. Charles Wilkins carried on the concept in Mammoth Cave, Dixon Cave, Jim Cave, and Short Cave. Another family member, Levi Brashear, employed the methodology in Saltpeter Cave next to Wyandotte Cave, Indiana. Mining limestone rock for nitrates was extensively employed in Big Bone Cave, Tennessee. Wilkins' close friend, John D. Clifford purchased most of the saltpeter from the cave and may have applied the French technique in Big Bone Cave.

Figure 7-1. Stone lithograph illustration of Wilkins' Arm Chair in Gothic Avenue. Later in the commercial life of the cave, its name was changed to the Devil's Arm Chair, emblematic of new place names associated with the infernal regions. William Stump Forwood, *A Historical and Descriptive Narrative of the Mammoth Cave of Kentucky*, J. B. Lippicott & Co., (1870).

CHAPTER SEVEN

CHARLES WILKINS AND THE WAR OF 1812

*"We doubt if victory could have been won in the war
of the Revolution, or in the War of 1812, without the aid
of the saltpeter caves of Virginia and Kentucky."*
Horace C. Hovey, 1899

Charles Wilkins became involved with Mammoth Cave during the prime of his life. He was about 47 years old in 1810, an astute and experienced businessman with a hard-driving personality well suited to carving out a niche in frontier society. He never extended credit or made loans without some kind of surety. If a person owed him money it was advisable to settle the debt promptly. Wilkins' correspondence reveals an individual without an ounce of apparent warmth, all business from the time he got up in the morning to late at night. With a busy schedule and a hyperactive Type A personality, he found little time to explore his "twenty-five mile" long Mammoth Cave (Wilkins, 1820, p. 363).

Wilkins' hand was visible everywhere in the social and economic life of Lexington, his new Kentucky home. He purchased stock in new companies and businesses, sponsored inventors, provided venture capital for novel agricultural experiments, and gave generously to the community and to Transylvania University. He invested tens of thousands and made millions in today's dollars during a time when people were rich in land but poor in cash and the economy was largely based on barter. By 1803 he was one of the directors of the Kentucky Insurance Company Bank (first in Kentucky) with William Morton as president (Leavy, 1942, p. 56). Any potential relationship between William and Charles S. Morton, owner of Dixon Cave is not known. Above all, one thing Charles Wilkins knew well was how to make money.

Wilkins was born in Pennsylvania about 1763 and brought up learning the trade in his father's general store. He became a successful importer-exporter at an early age, and became well connected with prominent east coast companies. At Peyton's urging, Charles relocated to Lexington about 1791. Probably less than a year later, on June 10, 1792, he married Jane Short, Peyton's sister (Short and Richardson, 1879, p. 4). Although Charles and Jane never had any children of their own, the couple always provided a warm and caring home for their nieces and nephews whenever brother Peyton was out of town. Wilkins died at Greensburg, Kentucky, aged 64, on September 15, 1827 (Short and Richardson, 1879, p. 4), while visiting one of his ironworks investments. Wilkins' heirs sold his Mammoth Cave interest back to Hyman Gratz for $200.00 ($4110.00 today) to settle his estate on June 28, 1828.

Lexington was centrally located to the saltpeter-producing regions of the state, the caves in the surrounding arc of Mississippian Period limestones and Pennsylvanian Period sandstone shelters of eastern Kentucky. Because of this fortuitous circumstance, and the community's position at the hub of the existing road network, Lexington was destined to become the market center of the state during the early nineteenth century and, in particular, the focal point of the saltpeter trade. The first commercial powder mill in Kentucky was established here in 1793, and by the outbreak of the War of 1812 a cluster of gunpowder factories in the central Bluegrass took advantage of close proximity to the saltpeter market. By the middle of the first decade of the century, an increasing volume of saltpeter arrived at Lexington from producing sites in the hinterland, to be consumed by local mills or transshipped to large eastern manufacturers such as the Du Pont Company (O'Dell, 1989; 1990; and 1995).

One of Lexington's most prominent merchants, Wilkins was well connected within the saltpeter infrastructure as commodity buyer and reseller, owner of producing saltpeter caves, and as an industrial salt manufacturer. He knew many people connected with the business and had a sound grasp of the various processes of saltpeter extraction. He was well-read, had assembled an impressive library, and possessed a keen interest in natural history and Indian artifacts (*Last Will and Tes-*

tament, 1827). In his industrial ventures, whether the manufacture of pig iron, salt brine or saltpeter, he hired others with the day-to-day specialized knowledge to run and manage his operations.

By the time of William Short's visit in 1803, Wilkins was a very wealthy man. His fortunes continued to grow, and by 1809 he had already branched out from his mercantile store and invested heavily in the salt brine industry and owned producing wells and springs in eastern Kentucky and in the Illinois Territory. These investments generated enormous amounts of cash. Increasing international tension created lucrative investment opportunities during the first decade of the new century. Wilkins was quick to take advantage by developing a large trade in saltpeter to supply gunpowder factories. Hundreds of saltpeter mines were opened in Kentucky as the market price for the commodity increased after 1802. Robert Montgomery Bird, M.D. (1837, p. 434), writing many years later, described those hectic times:

> the price of that article was so high, and the profits of the manufacturer so great, as to set half the Western world gadding after nitre caves – the gold mines of their day. Cave hunting, in fact, became a kind of mania, beginning with speculators, and ending with hair [sic.]-brained young men, who dared from the love of adventure the risks that others ran for profits.

Bird could well have been writing about Peyton Short's ruinous investment ventures. O'Dell (1995, pp. 83-84) observed, "during the saltpeter boom from 1808-1814, many Kentuckians combed the mountains and valleys of the cave regions. It was probably the greatest era of cave exploration prior to modern caving clubs, and was motivated mainly by profit." Wilkins' family members and business associates started early in their quest for saltpeter riches. Wilkins' cousin, William Henry Harrison, Territorial Governor of Indiana (1800-1812) and future President of the United States (March 1841-April 1841), visited the fabulous Wyandotte Cave in 1806, located not far from the future State capital on personal land he would lay out in Corydon. During that same year Wilkins' intellectual friend, John D. Clifford, a future resident of Lexington, purchased most of the saltpeter from Big Bone Cave, Tennessee, and continued to do so for many years.

Peyton was probably mining Short Cave before 1805 and digging up Indian mummies in the process (George, 1994, pp. 62-63). As a result of Peyton's disastrous financial escapades, Wilkins gained full administrative control over his cave by October 21, 1809 (*Kentucky Court of Appeals, Books O-U*, p. 142). Overseeing Short Cave's management placed Wilkins in a position to observe saltpeter mining first hand in caves next door. Short Cave adjoined another piece of real estate containing two caves, later called Mammoth Cave and Dixon Cave. He would have seen the investment potential and the bountiful resource available.

Wilkins' business plan was simple. Eliminate middlemen and become a direct supplier by owning producing caves with known saltpeter resources. Hire others to manage and work the factory. Strive to produce more saltpeter cheaper and of better quality than his competition was capable of producing. Embrace and install the most modern technology available. Sell the finished product slightly below the going market rate to increase sales.

These ventures by Wilkins and other Kentucky entrepreneurs were part of a larger, national movement in manufacturing. International tensions and conflicts disrupted trade during the early nineteenth century and promoted the development of American manufacturing self-sufficiency. During the Colonial Period, America supplied raw materials to Britain and received finished goods in return. This system was satisfactory to all until just prior to the Revolution, when the mother country embarked upon an exploitative course in its trade relations with America. This situation prompted efforts to build a manufacturing base and reduce dependency upon Britain. Following the Revolution, however, America returned to the status quo, continuing to import most finished goods from Britain despite the establishment of a number of manufacturing firms.

The availability of high-quality British gunpowder, imported at low cost, tended to discourage domestic manufacture of both saltpeter and gunpowder with two significant exceptions. In the east, Eleuthère Irénée du Pont established a gunpowder factory in 1802 on the Brandywine River in Delaware that would soon become the largest, state-of-the-art, powder mill in America and critical to the country's needs in the war years ahead. To the west, on the frontier, difficulties in transporting manufactured goods across the mountains, combined with ready access to abundant saltpeter resources, encouraged the local development of saltpeter mining and its dependent industry, gunpowder, simply as a matter of convenience.

As long as the flow of international trade continued uninterrupted, there was little real incentive to develop large-scale saltpeter operations in the United States. During the first decade of the nineteenth century, however, trade between America and Europe was anything but smooth. In a sense, the war between Britain and America had never truly ended in the west, despite the Treaty of Paris in 1783. The British endlessly delayed abandonment of their northwestern forts, such as Detroit, while continuing to encourage their Indian allies in conflicts with the settlers. In Britain, merchants and manufacturers were alarmed by the incipient industrial revolution incubating in America and the development of potential competition for British goods.

Commercial and political tensions among the United States, Britain, and Napoleonic France led to an exchange of inflammatory economic edicts. As tensions escalated, war between Britain and America became a real possibility. War fervor was strongest in the west, where Lexington residents eagerly followed the growing hostilities in the *Kentucky Gazette*. Henry Clay and other "War Hawks" who believed war was necessary to preserve overseas markets and American sovereignty fanned the flames of public sentiment, and land-hungry speculators contemplated the vast tracts of land in Canada. Under these circumstances, war materials such as saltpeter suddenly became critical to national survival. With increased demand, the price for Kentucky saltpeter began to rapidly escalate.

TRADE WARS: PRELUDE TO THE WAR OF 1812

The increasingly hostile relations between the United States and Britain during the first decade of the new century were, in a very real sense, an extension of the larger struggle then embroiling Europe (Horsman, 1962). The War of 1812 was essentially a sideshow compared to Britain's full thrust in countering the French threat. Had Britain been able to direct its full attention and military might to North America, the outcome might have been very different. The long war between France and Britain (1793-1815) engaged many nations. In February 1793, swept by revolutionary fever, France declared war on Great Britain, believing their arch-rival to be itself on the brink of revolution against the monarchy. The initial sympathy many British felt for the French Revolution evaporated following the execution of Louis XVI in January 1793, and the European war entered a new phase upon the assumption of power by Napoleon, who was crowned Emperor of France in 1804. Though adept at maneuvering large armies across the continent, Napoleon was defeated by the British on the battlefield at Waterloo on June 18, 1815.

The long duration of the European war can be attributed to the very different strengths of the two major players. France, fielding a conscript army, was nearly invincible on land, whereas Britain controlled the seas with the globe's most powerful navy. This was a recipe for an enduring stalemate. At sea, Britain strove to destroy French commerce, both directly and indirectly through intimidation. Britain used the threat of its overwhelming naval power to interfere with overseas shipping, and attempted to shut down all neutral trade with France. The European war was a golden opportunity for the United States to be neutral, with export trade rising from $20 million in 1790 to nearly $140 million by 1807.

Beginning with the outbreak of war in 1793, the British government issued a series of increasingly restrictive Orders in Council intended to halt neutral trade with France and its colonies. These orders allowed for the confiscation of cargoes and ships deemed to be in violation. In 1796 France declared its intent to respond in kind and treated neutral vessels carrying goods for Britain in the same manner. In other words, government sanctioned high seas piracy. In 1806, both France and Britain declared blockades that prohibited coastal trade. The American merchant fleet was thus threatened with confiscation by both sides in the war. Anti-British sentiment in America was further inflamed by British impressment of American sailors, most notably the 1807 *Chesapeake* incident.

The initial American response to the British and French actions was the 1806 Non-Importation Act. This act forbade importation of specific British goods and was intended to force Britain to relax trade restrictions on neutrals. The Non-Importation Act was soon superceded by the stronger Embargo Act passed by Congress on December 22, 1807, which forbade all international trade to and from American ports. The United States extended the scope of the Act to inland waters and land commerce in January 1808, to eliminate the growing trade with Canada.

The effects of the Embargo Act on U.S. commerce were disastrous. American ships of the merchant marine rotted in harbor, and the southern cotton economy was wrecked. Resistance approached the point of rebellion and forced replacement of the Embargo Act by the Non-Intercourse Act of 1809, which lifted all commercial prohibitions except against Britain and France. This act proved unenforceable and was in turn suspended by the Macon's Bill No. 2 in 1810, which allowed resumption of trade with Britain and France.

This series of American trade legislation, intended to apply economic pressure upon Britain and France, had virtually no effect upon the policies of those nations, but instead further disrupted the American economy. British and French warships continued to hunt American merchantmen and impress American sailors, violations of American sovereignty that ultimately led to the War of 1812. Without foreign trade, America was forced back on the pathway toward manufacturing self-sufficiency. As war with Britain came to appear inevitable, the foremost need of the nation was ordnance, including those materials needed to manufacture gunpowder. Prior to the trade restrictions imposed on both sides of the Atlantic, saltpeter for America's limited gunpowder manufacturing capacity was readily available, imported cheaply from the British Crown Colony of India. Elimination of this source, first by trade restrictions and later by coastal blockade, stimulated the saltpeter-mining boom in America and led to inflation of the commodity price.

WILKINS' SALTPETER EMPIRE

The earliest documentation of Wilkins' purchasing large quantities of saltpeter (10,000 pounds) is a letter from Archibald McCall (saltpeter purchaser for the Du Pont Powder Works) to du Pont on November 14, 1808. By 1809 Wilkins was running advertisements in local newspapers for saltpeter and paying "*cash*." He was probably making large saltpeter purchases in the Lexington market before this time period. Tantalizing McCall (1806) correspondence from 1806 describes an individual with expertise and capability in supplying large quantities of saltpeter to east coast manufacturers. This unidentified person had 20,000 pounds of Kentucky saltpeter for sale, and may have been Charles Wilkins. John D. Clifford, major saltpeter broker and merchant residing in Philadelphia, took up residence in Lexington about 1808 (Peter, 1882, p. 279). He had established connections with Lexington years before when he married Molly Morton (daughter of banker William Morton of Lexington, who was Wilkins' banking business partner) on June 17, 1804 (Staples, 1939, pp. 206-207). The move was probably made to be closer to Molly's relatives in Lexington and his Big Bone Cave in Tennessee, from which he obtained most of his saltpeter supply. Thomas Hart, Jr. and Samuel Brown offered stiff competition to everyone from 1805 onward with the saltpeter mined in Great Saltpetre Cave and satellite caves along Crooked Creek. Their "Big Cave" works provided the engineering blueprint from which Mammoth Cave benefited and prospered for a time as the most modern saltpeter factory in America. Hart and Brown would have been the most prominent saltpeter merchants in Lexington during McCall's 1806 correspondence. By 1812, Samuel Trotter, James Maccoun and John Wesley Hunt would join ranks with Wilkins and Clifford as saltpeter brokers.

From day to day business at his mercantile store, Wilkins acquired detailed knowledge of mine locations and people involved in the business. He traveled to these sites around the state to purchase saltpeter and arranged to have it shipped back to his store where it was repackaged in barrels for shipment. Rough saltpeter of inferior grade was subcontracted to others for purification (Wilkins, 1809). Wilkins was not a speculator in saltpeter, but a broker supplying saltpeter on contract to many powder factories, both local and east coast plants.

Economic stimuli in addition to trade restrictions affected the market price of saltpeter. Something of a knee jerk reaction occurred every time the War Department purchased a large parcel of saltpeter. Manufacturers took notice and raised their selling prices. Wilkins had to meet their demands and pass on the increase to clients. His major customer, du Pont, often balked at the price jumps, but had no recourse other than to capitulate and accept higher material costs.

Operation of Short Cave as a saltpeter mine acted as the proving grounds needed for Wilkins to gauge the full scope of being a direct source of a strategic commodity. To eliminate dependency on saltpeter producers and middlemen and increase his profits, Wilkins and

Louisville resident Fleming Gatewood, Sr., purchased Mammoth Cave on January 1, 1810, for $3000.00 ($42,300.00 today). Wilkins' Arm Chair (Figure 7-1) in Gothic Avenue commemorates Charles Wilkins involvement at the cave. This purchase assured a steady supply to fulfill contract obligations to Du Pont and other powder mills. Even with these new investments, Wilkins continued to purchase saltpeter from others through the end of the war.

Advertisements in the *American Statesman* on January 14, 1812, announced that "Charles Wilkins CONTINUES TO GIVE the HIGHEST PRICE, IN CASH for SALT PETRE." and on December 12, 1812, noted that Wilkins, "continues to pay CASH for Salt-Petre." "Cash" payments were a considerable enticement at a time when specie was in short supply and barter was the most common medium of exchange. This was doubly profitable since saltpetermen would load their empty wagons with provisions from Wilkins' store before driving back to the mines. His Lexington competitors ran similar notices. Most advertisements soliciting saltpeter were placed during the winter months when supplies were slow coming in from the mines. Most saltpeter was mined and delivered in the summer and fall when road conditions were ideal, prior to the winter season of mud and mire.

War was declared against Great Britain on June 18, 1812. The declaration fostered an immediate need for addition powder to fill Government magazines. The War Department had prepared for the advent of war with a strategic reserve, and prudence dictated continued stockpiling of saltpeter and gunpowder. America's saltpeter mines were already operating in high gear as the market price climbed yet again. With Mammoth Cave and satellite caves as resources, Wilkins was able to sell to du Pont a better quality and lower priced saltpeter than his competitors. Du Pont never paid more than 32 cents ($3.82 today) per pound in 1814 for Kentucky saltpeter (George, 1988, p. 20) even when the market price soared to a dollar a pound in selected places ($11.80 today)! After the declaration of war, the market price of saltpeter increased. Buying and selling saltpeter became a phenomenal business endeavor. "The saltpeter buyers in Lexington must have felt slightly dazed as hundreds of thousands of pounds of saltpeter passed through their hands amid demands of 'more, more!'" (O'Dell, 1995, p. 93), and the price skyrocketed.

Speculators and war profiteers purchased saltpeter and held the commodity until the price increased substantially, selling it at an artificially inflated profit (just like crude oil today). This activity promoted an investment bubble of the same order as the Holland tulip mania in the 1630s, Florida real estate in the 1920s, silver in 1979-1980, and the more recent Internet bubble. Like most raw materials, such as iron ore or hemp fiber, there was a limited market for saltpeter, consisting of the relatively few manufacturers of gunpowder. Gunpowder, however, was in demand both on a retail basis for civilian applications such as shooting powder for small arms and blasting powder, and on a wholesale basis by the Government for military use. Saltpeter hoarding forced the price of both saltpeter and gunpowder upwards throughout the nation. Hardest hit were the larger powder mills, mainly located on the east coast, who were locked into government contracts based upon pre-bubble material costs. Powder makers were outraged as saltpeter kept edging higher, sometimes seeing increases from week to week. This was the economic weight that threatened to break the backs of east coast powder factories. Owners of many powder factories banded together and formed a cartel to institute price controls, and for a time the market price did decline (O'Dell, 1995, p. 93). By 1814, some saltpetermen had rebelled and stopped mining. There was little product on the local market, giving the appearance "the Kentucky saltpeter industry had vanished virtually overnight" (O'Dell, 1995, p. 95). Other reasons for the scarcity included hoarding of the commodity by speculators and the depletion of this natural resource.

Mammoth Cave saltpeter was shipped to Pittsburgh where John Wilkins, Jr., Quartermaster General for the Western States during the War of 1812, served as middleman for his brother Charles. John stockpiled saltpeter in his warehouse and sent shipments eastward to du Pont and other customers. He may have had a more direct financial hand in the Mammoth Cave operation than is presently known. The demand was so great Wilkins had difficulty maintaining a constant supply. As hostilities with Great Britain intensified, neither Mammoth Cave nor the rest of the Kentucky mines combined were able to meet powder mill demands. Interruption of production by the New Madrid earthquakes, quality control problems, and exhaustion of easily accessible sites diminished the amount of product coming to market across the Midwest and south (George, 1988). Ultimately, Gratz and Wilkins were not able to satisfy du Pont's saltpeter supply quotas even with supplementing their production with saltpeter from other caves. They lost their du Pont contracts, because of a number of factors: (1) saltpeter from their other caves was considered inferior; (2) quality of the Mammoth Cave product declined; (3) availability of refined saltpeter from Mammoth was interrupted by the 1811-1812 earthquakes; and (4) they could not meet production shipping dates to du Pont's factory in Delaware. Wilkins just shifted gears and sold what he could to du Pont competitors who were not as conscientious about quality control.

Du Pont had preferred Mammoth Cave saltpeter because it was less expensive and of such high purity that it did not need further refining, thus eliminating a processing step he would have had to conduct in his factory with higher labor costs. In 1810, the Du Pont factory was the largest in the nation with 200 competitors spread out over sixteen states (Dutton, 1942, p. 46). At the onset of the War of 1812, the War Department "awarded only a small part" of its total national need to Du Pont (Dutton, 1942, p. 46). Government contracts amounted to only a fraction of his total output. Primary revenues for the company were from sales of commercial shooting and blasting powders. Although little if any of Du Pont's powder was used during the Battle of New Orleans, there were military engagements where Du Pont powder was employed decisively (Dutton, 1942, pp. 49-50):

> The mills' importance to the American forces was greater than is indicated by the total of 750,000 pounds of powder that can be definitely identified as military orders. This powder was exclusively for the Army. The Navy bought through its own agents, usually from local dealers in the principal ports. Through such dealers, Du Pont sold powder to ships of war and to privateers, contributing to such victories at sea as that of the *Constitution* over the *Guerrière*, the capture of the *Alert* by the *Essex*, of the *Frolic* by the *Wasp*, and the sinking of the *Peacock* by the *U.S.S. Hornet*. The American privateers captured more than 300 enemy ships during the first year and a half of the war.

The Mammoth Cave operation began to recover from the effects of the earthquake as workers' fear of being underground waned and work resumed. Mining had returned close to normal by 1813. Improvements, in addition to simple repairs, included installation of tandem pumps in the entrance, and building a taller pump tower in the Rotunda, along with three new box hoppers augmented by V-vats. Although production was still less than before the earthquake, Wilkins sought to remedy this with the purchase of Dixon Cave from Charles S. Morton on April 20, 1813. Most of the mining thrust was thereafter directed toward Dixon Cave, which had abundant supplies within easy reach of its entrance.

The acquisition of Dixon Cave was not Wilkins' first attempt to extend his revenue base. Great Saltpetre Cave represented a valuable jewel if only he could get his hands on it. The first opportunity was presented in 1810. Samuel Brown's business partner, Thomas Hart, Jr., who handled all the administrative and management of the saltpeter works out of Lexington, died on November 26, 1809 (George, 2001a, pp. 90-92). This threw the operation into disorder as Brown tried to handle some of the management at long range from his plantation near Fort Adams, 34 miles south of Natchez. It was Brown's responsibility to pay off debts incurred by his and Hart's investment at the cave. Hart's executors weren't moving fast enough, so the Lexington court appointed new executors on July 9, 1810, to speed things along. One of the new appointees was Charles Wilkins. Brown and Wilkins were not good friends because of political differences revolving around the Aaron Burr conspiracy years earlier.

AARON BURR CONSPIRACY

Many of the details of the peculiar enterprise that became known as the Burr Conspiracy and America's first civil war, remain unknown today. Aaron Burr, Vice-President of the United States during Jefferson's first term, had doomed his political career when he killed his political enemy, Alexander Hamilton, in a duel on July 11, 1804. Burr fled the scene of the crime, and later became America's first most wanted man. Distancing himself even further in an attempt to rebuild his fortunes, Burr apparently set about to build a personal empire in the West, planning a military expedition with two goals: to foment rebellion in the newly acquired Louisiana Territory and establish a separate republic, and possibly to seize Spanish possessions in North America. Burr was relying upon discontent in the west for support, where many believed that regional interests were ignored by eastern politicians and merchants.

Traveling through the west in 1805, Burr recruited a number of followers and began to assemble arms, ammunition and powder, leaving, however, a host of rumors in his wake. The secret conspiracy, unknown to Burr, soon became widespread public knowledge. Gunboats were built in Marietta and Louisville, locations that were stocked with men, weapons and a military command structure. On December 9, the Ohio militia captured some of his boats and supplies at a Marietta shipyard, and raided his "fortress" at Blennerhassett Island. Despite these blows, he determined to carry on. To Burr's dismay, however, at a late December rendezvous on the Ohio River, less than 100 men of his anticipated "army" appeared. From Louisville, a fleet of gunboats was launched and headed south. His fleet was interdicted and captured down river. Burr traveled another route and surrendered to authorities at Bayou Pierre, just above New Orleans, after failing to recruit more than a handful of volunteers on a trip down the Mississippi. Burr was conveyed to Richmond, Virginia, to be tried in February 1807, for treason before a federal court with a raft of co-conspirators in the trial of the century. Although the case was so badly mishandled by the prosecution that Burr was acquitted, he fled the country in fear for his life and remained abroad until mid-1812.

Charles Wilkins saw the treason trial as a perfect opportunity to inflict harm upon his future competitor Samuel Brown, and supplied information to the court intended to implicate the Brown family in the conspiracy. At this time Wilkins motives are not clearly known. The extent of Samuel Brown's entanglement in the conspiracy, if any, is unclear, but on at least one occasion he acted as a courier to deliver a letter to one of the principals, and may have supplied gunpowder for the expedition. No members of the Brown family were charged or brought to trial, but Wilkins made certain that they were tried and convicted in the court of public opinion. By April 1806, Samuel was so dismayed by the stain upon his reputation that he departed Lexington and moved to Fort Adams, Louisiana Territory, and finally north of Huntsville, Alabama.

DEMISE OF THE SALTPETER INDUSTRY

Facing financial pressure through the courts, Brown was required either to settle the accounts or have the cave sold against his will. Because of the Embargo and Non-Intercourse acts, Brown's cash reserves had evaporated. Cotton grown on his plantation found few buyers and his plight was symptomatic of the depressed southern economy everywhere. Using delaying tactics and borrowing from his family, he was able to show good faith in trying to pay down the debts. Brown continued his efforts to pay back the loans, only to falter in late 1813, and the cave was sold to Robert M. Lewis. Ultimately, the loss of Great Saltpetre Cave was of no great economic significance, for the saltpeter bubble was about to burst and render all such operations unprofitable.

In the interim, Wilkins and Gatewood purchased Mammoth Cave on January 1, 1810. Here was a cave far larger than any other known in America, with many more miles of passage than Great Saltpetre and hence a far greater saltpeter resource. Mammoth Cave should have been a gold mine, so to speak, but management problems, the earthquake, and the end of the war prevented realization of its potential. Management disagreements prompted Gratz to shut Wilkins out of decision-making and profits in late 1813 (George and O'Dell, 1992, pp. 21-22). Gratz must have had a controlling financial interest in the cave and Wilkins probably knew something like a hostile take over was about to occur. Wilkins made arrangements with his old Mammoth Cave partner Gatewood who had sold his interest to Gratz in 1812, and finalized purchase of Gatewood's Salt Petre Cave (present day Coach Cave) on January 29, 1814. The cave is about 8 miles south of Mammoth and only a mile south of Short Cave. Here Gatewood had continued to use his tertiary method of purification that had made Mammoth Cave saltpeter famous for its quality (George, 2001a, p. 21). Wilkins, who had a penchant for hiring experts, may have kept Gatewood on as supervisor of the operation. Wilkins also continued to mine Short Cave. In the late summer of 1814, three new Indian mummies were unearthed (George, 1994, p. 78).

At the height of the mining boom, a sour note intruded. Across the state, as the most easily accessible passages were mined out, saltpetermen were faced with decreasing yields, and fewer new caves and rockshelters were being pressed into service. Depleted caves with falsely inflated yields were being offered for sale in December 1812 (Sidebottom's Cave, Green County), at half the price received for such sites during the previous year (Anonymous, 1812). Other desperate cave owners *salted* worn out saltpeter soils, as at Pruett's Saltpeter Cave (Warren County) in September 1812, to fraudulently sell at a higher price to gullible investors (*Rice & Sterrett vs Perkins & Perkins*, 1814). Charles S. Morton sold Dixon Cave to Wilkins and Gratz on April 20, 1813, for less than he originally paid.

The end of 1813 represents an important turning point in Kentucky saltpeter mining history. It was almost as if the industry lost all motivation as operators tried to cope with diminished reserves in the caves. Many other caves certainly were located, tested and considered viable, but the amount of money required to establish a major mine works was astronomical. A few men with strong backs could not establish and operate a significant cave factory, although this is the mythological image conveyed by reading contemporary accounts of saltpeter mining. It took a company with enough capital, organization and manpower to build a saltpeter factory. Another important limiting factor was location; transportation costs dictated that only those caves located near a road were economically viable for development. The largest saltpeter factories were all located near major transportation routes of the era even though they might appear today as isolated in the hills. Alexander Scott, one of the prior owners of Great Saltpetre Cave, lobbied and won a spur road connection in 1804 with the State Road in eastern Kentucky (George, 2001a, pp. 36-37).

At the beginning of 1814, the war shifted into high gear just at the time saltpeter mines in the West were being exhausted of their saltpeter resources (George, 1988, p. 15). This strategic intelligence, if the British had known it, might have prompted a continuation of the conflict and, possibly, resolution of the war in their favor. Few people were aware of an actual supply problem, instead attributing scarcity to hoarding by speculators. With less saltpeter available to the market, the commodity price kept going up in accord with the law of supply and demand. Speculation also had a role in creating scarcity and inflated prices, particularly in the early years of the boom. Pricing in an investment bubble is often a measure of a person willing to pay any cost in the expectation of immense future profits. This is often referred to as the *bigger fool theory* of investment. The *Fool* must sell his share to a *Bigger Fool* to realize a profit before the price drops or the bubble bursts. The *Bigger Fool* is left holding an investment bag full of air. During the saltpeter boom, as soon as large lots of saltpeter came on the market, speculators snatched them up. Late in the investment bubble, powder mills instituted price fixing that helped to put a cap on what they were willing to spend on saltpeter purchases. Price controls produced only checkered results. To stay in business and meet contract obligations, these powder factories were forced to pay inflated prices unless they were fortunate enough to have a direct source, as in the case of du Pont contracting virtually the entire production of Mammoth Cave. After du Point voided its Mammoth Cave contracts due to availability, quality, and shipping problems, the company was required to obtain new and more expensive saltpeter supplies from other Kentucky caves. Gatewood, the master saltpeter maker, had already offered du Pont high quality weapons grade saltpeter as pure as he had produced at Mammoth Cave. Wilkins moved quickly to regain Gatewood's existing contract obligations.

In 1814, the British commenced an invasion of North America. Landing on the Potomac below Washington, they marched into the city and burned public buildings including the White House. The British pushed on to Baltimore but were repulsed by strong defenses. Late in the year a large land battle was crystallizing in New Orleans, even as diplomats almost half a world away hammered out a treaty in the Netherlands. The Treaty of Ghent was arranged to everyone's satisfaction on Christmas Eve, 1814. Now it became a race to get back to America, and have the document ratified by Congress before further bloodshed. It was not to be. While the ship was at sea, the Battle of New Orleans erupted on January 8, 1815, culminating in a major American victory. The document reached American shores on February 11th, the very day Fort Bowyer, Alabama, surrendered to an advancing superior British force. British expeditionary forces re-grouped to attack Mobile as the Senate quickly ratified the document on February 16th, and declared a formal end of the war on the following day. As the British prepared to take Mobile, news arrived of the peace.

News of the Treaty spread across the nation and sparked general celebrations in towns and villages. Fireworks, parades and rifle salutes acclaimed victory in America's *second war of independence* (Horsman, 1962). Despite all the hullabaloo, nobody really "won" the war. The conflict ended in a truce with warring parties pulling back to old geographic boundaries. In reality, the ending of the war had far more to do with political pressures exerted by London merchants' concerned over the loss of American trade, than with any military actions. Ironically, after the war Britain became our staunchest ally.

As celebrations quieted it didn't take long for most of the saltpeter mines to close. With a glut of the commodity on the market, there was no need either for the U.S. Government or large eastern mills such as Du Pont to continue purchasing in quantity. The collapse of the saltpeter investment bubble reverberated through the West. Prime producing saltpeter caves lost nearly all value almost over night. Many investors, mine owners, and speculators (the Bigger Fools) were ruined financially. Mammoth Cave's part owner Hyman Gratz was forced into bankruptcy despite everything he could do to stave off creditors. Wilkins, on the other hand, had been shut out of the management and profits at the cave since late 1813, but this also freed him from associated liabilities, a blessing in disguise. Wilkins was a survivor; diversification with interests in fire insurance, rope manufacturing, banking, salt production, and manufacturing of pig iron used in fabricating domestic and industrial ironware, provided a substantial cushion against calamity in any one industry.

THE DAYS AFTER THE WAR

The War of 1812 worked many changes in America, not least of which was a new nationalistic spirit in which the sense of unity was so profound that the post-war period became known as the "Era of Good Feelings." The interruption of international trade by the war had spurred the development of domestic manufacturing and an increase in commodity prices. At war's end, American consumers were eager to purchase goods long in short supply and British manufacturers were eager to unload accumulated stocks. Commodity prices now fell dramatically with the influx of low-cost imports. The economy began to boom, fueled by rapid credit and monetary expansion. American manufacturers, however, did not share in the general post-war prosperity of the nation, for they now faced stiff competition from foreign imports that were encouraged by favorable trade policies on both sides of the Atlantic. The trend toward industrial self-sufficiency promoted by the war began to reverse itself, as manufacturers with substantial capital investments found themselves hard-pressed merely to survive.

The saltpeter and gunpowder manufacturing industries of the west were among those that suffered most, collapsing virtually overnight. Saltpeter imported from Crown Colony British India was in a few years available to east coast powder factories at far less cost than that domestically produced from caves and shelters, but was expensive to transport overland to powder mills in the interior. Mine operators in Kentucky, already discouraged by the depleted resource and low prices offered by colluding buyers near the end of the war, had no incentive to continue mining. The saltpeter factories closed, leased bondsmen were returned to their masters, white workers put down their tools and walked away from operations large and small. Fortunes were lost as the saltpeter investment bubble exploded. No longer able to obtain saltpeter mined locally, and unable to compete with low-cost, high quality gunpowder imported from Britain or manufactured by eastern companies such as Du Pont, most of the powder mills of the west shut down forever.

The national economic boom lasted only a short while, ending with the nation's first real economic crisis, the Panic of 1819 (Anonymous). Tightening of over expanded credit led to the failure of many banks who had backed risky investments, particularly in real estate. Failed banks in turn pulled down still other banks, mortgages were foreclosed, and investments came to a halt. Factories were idled or closed, and unemployment mounted. In 1820, John C. Calhoun commented to John Quincy Adams (Adams, 1969, p.128): "There has been within these two years an immense revolution of fortunes in every part of the Union; enormous numbers of persons utterly ruined; multitudes in deep distress."

The Englishman, William Blane (1824, pp. 255-256), an astute observer, described the serious effects caused by the collapse of the saltpeter industry, the Panic of 1819, and the national economic depression that followed in the heartland of Kentucky. Passing through villages on his way to Mammoth Cave, he observed:

Most of these villages, throughout the greater part of the division of Kentucky, called the Green-river Country, are very much upon the decline, and will no doubt shortly cease to exist. They were founded during the late war with Great Britain, and owned their existence, not to any want of villages in these places, but to the unnatural state of things caused by a great war expenditure, by an immense issue of paper money, and by the efforts of speculators to enhance the value of their lands in the neighborhood. As soon as the war ceased, the great expenditure ceased also, as well as the demand for produce, &c, &c. The currency was also changed from paper to specie, and hence those who had easily borrowed money found it impossible to repay it. This occasioned the ruin of numbers of industrious people....

During boom times, Lexington merchants looked forward to mine shipments. Saltpetermen unloaded sacks or barrels of nitrate from their wagons and restocked them with fresh store-bought goods. Everybody prospered in the transaction. These were fat times and full purses. Very soon after the war, saltpeter shipments stopped coming to market centers. Merchants had to have been dismayed by the realization that a significant portion of their income and commerce had vanished. The Treaty of Ghent acted as the trigger for an economic domino effect cascading through commerce in general. It was similar to a storm moving through town, sweeping away all the customers – never to come back. The economic downturn started in the Midwest before the war and spread to east coast cities.

Despite the saturation of the market with saltpeter at war's end and the resumption of international trade, E. I du Pont was disturbed by rumors from the interior of the cessation of mining. Du Pont was the largest powder mill in the country, and the largest single consumer of saltpeter. Under the circumstances it was prudent to keep all options available. During the summer of 1815, du Pont sent his office manager and son-in-law Antoine Bidermann on a secret mission to the west, ostensibly as a land speculator, but in reality to investigate the conflicting reports about the saltpeter supply. Traveling through Tennessee and Kentucky, Bidermann interviewed powder makers, merchants and traders, posting a series of letters to keep his father-in-law apprised of his progress. One of his informants was General John Wilkins (Charles

Wilkins' brother) in Pittsburgh. Writing to du Pont, Bidermann (1815, p. 95) describes a, "conversation with Mr. Wilkins [in which] he told me himself that the Kentucky caves show signs of exhaustion; there must be some truth in the story since he says so himself although it hurts the value of his land." Bidermann concluded that saltpeter sites had been exhausted of their natural resources all over the Midwest largely because saltpeter makers had failed to recycle processed soils to allow for nitrate regeneration. A naturally renewable resource was, instead, wastefully discarded. Even Mammoth Cave was not exempt. George (1988, p. 17) summarized Bidermann's feelings on the subject.

> The inexhaustible nature of Kentucky saltpeter mining had become legend at this point in time. It was unthinkable that the "end" of saltpeter mining had passed un-noticed at the start of 1814. Yet there was this rationalization of optimism embodied that the hills were full of saltpeter and one need only to go and dig it out of numerous caves.

Mammoth Cave saltpeter works did not shut down entirely after the war ended. Archibald Miller, Sr., stayed on as caretaker and continued to supervised mining and refining well into 1816 (Anonymous). There was still some demand for saltpeter needed for local gunpowder production and as a preservative in the meat packing industry. Imported India saltpeter would not start to arrive in Louisville's port of entry until after 1819. Other large caves, especially Wyandotte Cave, Indiana, continued mining saltpeter and Epsom salts to 1818 (George, 2001b). The James M. Cannon Saltpeter Cave continued operations past 1820. "Free" Frank McWorter's successful saltpeter business prospered (1810 to May 1829) out of his Danville, Boyle County, saltpeter reprocessing facility, utilizing saltpeter mined from his Fishing Creek saltpeter cave in Pulaski County (Walker, 1983).

During the last years of the War of 1812, an interesting phenomenon developed that was to herald the future of Mammoth Cave. People began to visit the cave, not for business reasons associated with the mine operation, but for the pleasure of experiencing the cave as a natural wonder. The cave had been a destination for a few underground adventurers since the 1810 publication of *The Subterranean Voyage*. The cave received widespread national attention with the discovery and subsequent promotion of the mummy Fawn Hoof, and publication of Nahum Ward's 1816 account of Mammoth Cave. Ward's *Wonders of Nature* cave adventure included an amazing cave map (Figure 2-4). The map revealed the cave was huge, with over 11 miles known. One of the passages even crossed under the Green River. Purported discovery of the Indian mummy "in the far reaches" of the cave piqued imaginations on both sides of the Atlantic.

At first only a trickle of adventurers arrived at Mammoth Cave, and were accommodated as a courtesy. As the number of visitors increased, owner Gratz began to charge a fee. There was only one commercially operated tourist cave in the United States at this time, the Grand (Weyers) Caverns of Virginia, which had begun tours in 1806. By 1816, Mammoth Cave had become the second tourist cave attraction in America. Both caves have the distinction of being the two oldest continuously operated show caves in America. Mammoth Cave in the end truly proved a gold mine, but the wealth that was mined came not from cave soils but from the gold in tourist pockets. Mammoth Cave became a household name across the nation and Europe, and the trickle of visitors became a flood by the time of the Civil War. Today, more than million and a half people a year come to the Mammoth Cave National Park.

Long after the saltpeter boom had ended, Charles Wilkins returned to Mammoth Cave on many occasions in the company of his wife, Jane. These were not business trips, since Charles had long severed any connection, but excursions as a simple tourist, a way to escape the cares and travails of city life. One cannot help but wonder at what thoughts were in the mind of Charles Wilkins as he beheld those passageways from an entirely new perspective. Surely, over the guide's tourist patter, there was a vision of legions of workers toiling away with pick and shovel in the smoky atmosphere, shouts and curses echoing through the chambers and away through the distant and eternal dark. Truly, he must have thought, this was the greatest of all caves.

Figure 7-2. Projected giant shadow of Mat Bransford points the way to new discoveries and adventures in Mammoth Cave. *Every Saturday*, May 6, 1871.

NOTES

CHAPTER ONE NOTES

1. Calculation of relative worth in today dollars is based upon the gross domestic product of all goods sold in addition to normal consumer purchases (Williamson, 2004).

CHAPTER FIVE NOTES

1. It is perhaps ironic that calcium oxide, when heated with coke (carbon source), produces calcium carbide, the substance used by many cavers in carbide lamps.

REFERENCES

CHAPTER ONE REFERENCES

Adams, Benjamin, 1820, Account of a Great and Very Extraordinary Cave in Indiana. *Archaeologica Americana, Transactions and Collections of the Am. Antiquarian Soc.*, 1: 434-436.

Adams, Eric,1993, "Religion and Freedom: Artifacts indicate that African Culture persisted even in Slavery." *Omni*, 16 (2): 8.

Anonymous, 1810, "The Subterranean Voyage, or the Mammoth Cave, Partially Explored." *The Enquirer*, Richmond, Virginia, 6 (109), April 20, 1810.

Anonymous, 1816, "Account of the Mammoth Cave." *Hallowell Gazette*, Maine, 3: 1, September 4, 1816.

Anonymous, 1818, "The Living Mammoth." *Clarion & Tennessee State Gazette*, 10 (17): 2, May 5, 1818.

Anonymous, 1845, The Mammoth Cave. *The Boston Medical and Surgical Journal*, 31 (43): 43-45.

Anonymous, 1853, "The Mammoth Cave," *New-York Weekly Tribune*, 12 (623): 3.

Atherton, James H., 1831, Letters of 1831-32 About Kentucky. Edited by Samuel M. Wilson, 1942, *The Filson Club History Quarterly*, 16 (4).

Bird, Robert Montgomery, 1837, "The Mammoth Cave of Kentucky." *The Am. Monthly Magazine*, n.s., 2: 426-438, 525-546.

Blane, William N., 1824, *An Excursion Through the United States and Canada During the Years 1822-1824*. Baldwin, Cradock, and Joy, London.

Boles, John B., 1984, *Black Southerners 1619-1869*. The University of

Kentucky Press.

Brown, Samuel, 1809, A Description of a Cave on Crooked Creek, with Remarks and Observations on Nitre and Gun-Powder. *Trans Am. Philo. Soc.*, 6: 235-247.

Cobden, John C., 1859, *The White Slaves of England*. C. M. Saxon, New York.

De Paepe, Duane, 1986, *Gunpowder from Mammoth Cave*. Cave Pearl Press, Hays, Kansas.

Eskew, Garnett Laidlaw, 1948, *Salt the Fifth Element*. J. G. Ferguson and Associates, Chicago.

Farnham, John H., 1820, Extract of a letter from John H. Farnham, Esq. a Member of the American Antiquarian Society, describing the Mammoth Cave, in Kentucky. *Archaeologia Americana, Transactions and Collections of the American Antiquarian Society*, 1: 355-361.

George, Angelo I., 1994, *Mummies, Catacombs, and Mammoth Cave*. George Publishing Company.

George, Angelo I., 2001a, *The Saltpeter Empires of Great Saltpetre Cave and Mammoth Cave*. H.M.I. Press, Louisville, KY.

George, Angelo I., 2001b, *Outer Door to the Auger Hole ... and Beyond, the Exploration of Wyandotte Cave*. H.M.I. Press, Louisville, KY.

Groner, Alex, 1972, *American Business and Industry*. American Heritage Publishing Co., Inc., New York.

Hall, F., 1838, "Mammoth Cave." *National Gazette & Literary Register*, Philadelphia, Pa., July 24, 1838.

Hill, Carol A.; and Duane De Paepe, 1979, Saltpeter Mining in Kentucky Caves. *The Register of the Kentucky Historical Society*, 77 (4): 247-262.

Hovey, Horace C., 1882, *Celebrated American Caverns*. Robert Clarke & Co., Cincinnati, Ohio.

Joy, Charles A., 1877, "Forest Industries. The Manufacture of Charcoal." *Frank Leslie's Popular Monthly*, 3 (5): 633-638.

Kite, Thomas, 1847, Journal of a Trip Through Kentucky and Visit to Mammoth Cave, May and June, 1847. Unpublished type-written manuscript, Kentucky Library and Museum, Western Kentucky University.

Kurlansky, Mark, 2002, *Salt A World History*. Penguin Books.

Lee, Edmund F., 1835, *Notes on the Mammoth Cave, to Accompany a Map*. Printed by James & Gazlay, Cincinnati.

Maddox, D. T., 1813, Big Bone Cave. A description of the Big Bone Cave, in White county, Tennessee, by D. T. Maddox, esq. in a letter to a friend. *Niles, The Weekly Register, Supplement*, 5: 175-176.

Martin, Horace, 1851, *Pictorial Guide to the Mammoth Cave, Kentucky*. Stringer & Townsend, New York.

Meloy, Harold , 1985, The Bransfords Show Mammoth Cave. *Jour. Spelean Hist.*, 19 (1): 4-8.

Meloy, Harold, 1969, The Gatewoods at Mammoth Cave. *Jour. Spelean Hist.*, 2 (3): 51-62.

Meriam, Ebenezer, 1844, "Mammoth Cave." *New York Municipal Gazette*, 1 (17): 317-324, 328.

Mullin, Marsha, 1986, Mammoth Cave Saltpetre Works. Historic American Engineering Record, National Park Service. Type-written.

Royall, Anne N., 1826, *Sketches of History, Life, and Manners in the United States by a Travelor*. New Haven, Conn.

Shackleford, Oliver, n.d, An Account of the History of Mammoth Cave During the Middle Nineteenth Century by Oliver Shackleford, One of the Guides. Typewritten copy in Mammoth Cave Office Library.

Sloane, Eric, 1986a, *Eric Sloane's America*. Promontory Press.

Sloane, Eric, 1986b, *Eric Sloane's Sketches of American Past*. Promontory Press.

Stealey, John E., III, 1993, *The Antebellum Kanawha Salt Business and Western Markets*. The University Press of Kentucky.

Vigne, Godfrey T., 1833, *Six Months in America*. Thomas T. Ash, Philadelphia.

Walker, Juliet E. K., 1983, *Free Frank: A Black Pioneer on the Antebellum Frontier*. The University Press of Kentucky.

Ward, Nahum, 1816, "Kentucky Mammoth Cave." *Georgetown Patriot*, Georgetown, Kentucky, August 24, 1816, reprinted from the *National Intelligencer*, from a letter dated July 1816.

Wendt, Herbert, 1968, *Before the Deluge*. Doubleday & Company, Inc., New York.

Wilkins, Charles, 1809, Unpublished letter to E. I. du Pont, dated November 27, 1809. Longwood Manuscripts Group 5, Box 6, Hagley Museum and Library, Wilmington, Delaware.

Williamson, Samuel H., 2004, "What is the Relative Value?" Economic History Services, April 15, 2004, URL: http://www.eh.net/hmit/compare/.

Wood, John S., 1841, "Mammoth Cave of Kentucky." *The American Magazine and Repository of Useful Literature*, 1 (3): 86-90.

CHAPTER TWO REFERENCES

Bird, Robert Montgomery, 1837, "The Mammoth Cave of Kentucky." *The Am. Monthly Magazine*, n.s., 2: 426-438, 525-546.

Child, Lydia Maria, 1852, "The Underground Territories of the United States." *The International Monthly Magazine*, 5:17-28.

DePaepe, Duane, 1975, Economic Geography of the Mammoth Cave Regional Saltpetre Industry. *Cave Research Foundation Annual Report*, 67-69.

DePaepe, Duane, 1986, *Gunpowder from Mammoth Cave*. Cave Pearl Press, Hays, Kansas.

Drake, Daniel, n.d, Map of a saltpetre cave in Green River Kentucky. Draper manuscripts, 2O80, image No.WHi-32170.

Farnham, John H., 1820, Extract of a letter from John H. Farnham, Esq. a Member of the American Antiquarian Society, describing the Mammoth Cave, in Kentucky. *Archaeologia Americana, Transactions and Collections of the American Antiquarian Society*, 1: 355-361.

Faust, Burton, 1967, *Saltpetre Mining in Mammoth Cave, KY*. The Filson Club.

George, Angelo I., 1989, Rotunda V-Vat Complex, Mammoth Cave, Kentucky. *CRF Annual Report, 1988*, 74-76.

George, Angelo I., 1990, *Prehistoric Mummies from the Mammoth Cave Area: Foundations and Concepts*. George Publishing Company.

George, Angelo I., 1994, *Mummies, Catacombs, and Mammoth Cave*. George Publishing Company.

George, Angelo I., 2001, *The Saltpeter Empires of Great Saltpetre Cave and Mammoth Cave*. H.M.I. Press, Louisville, KY.

Hovey, Horace C., 1897, Our Saltpeter Caves in Time of War. *Sci. Am.*, 76 (19): 291.

Hunter, George, 1802, The Western Journal of Dr. George Hunter 1796 to 1805. Edited by J. F. McDermott, 1963, *Trans. Am. Philo. Soc.*, n.s. 53 (4).

Kronk, Gary W., 1984, *Comets A Descriptive Catalog*. Enslow Publishers, Inc., Hillside, NJ.

Meloy, Harold, 1968, Early maps of Mammoth Cave. *Jour. Spelean Hist.*, 1 (3): 49-57.

Meloy, Harold, 1969, The Gatewoods at Mammoth Cave. *Jour Spelean Hist.*, 2: 51-62.

Meloy, Harold, 1975, Historic maps of Mammoth Cave. *Jour. Spelean. Hist.*, 3 & 4: 26-31.

Meriam, Ebenezer, 1844, "Mammoth Cave." *New York Municipal Gazette*, 1 (17): 317-324, 328.

Mullin, Marsha, 1986, Mammoth Cave Saltpetre Works. Historic American Engineering Record, National Park Service. Typewritten.

Penick, James Lal Jr., 1981, *The New Madrid Earthquakes, Revised Edition*. University of Missouri Press, Columbia & London.

Ridgely, Frederick, 1811a, Unpublished letter and Eye-Draught Map of Mammoth Cave to Dr. Benjamin Rush, dated March 15, 1811. Library, American Philosophical Society.

Ridgely, Frederick, 1811b, Unpublished letter and Eye-Draught Map of Mammoth Cave to Archibald McCall, dated June 11, 1811. W4-5033, Hagley Museum and Library, Wilmington, Delaware.

Thomas, Samuel W., E. H. Conner and Harold Meloy, 1970, A History of Mammoth Cave, Emphasizing Tourist Development and Medical Experimentation Under Dr. John Croghan. *The Register of the Ky. Hist. Soc.*, 68 (4): 319-340.

Sagan, Carl and Ann Druyan, 1985, *Comet*. Random House, New York.

Ward, Nahum, 1816a, "Kentucky Mammoth Cave." *Georgetown Patriot*, Georgetown, Kentucky, August 24, 1816, reprinted from the *National Intelligencer*, from a letter dated July 1816.

Ward, Nahum, 1816b, "Description of the Great and Wonderful Cave in Warren County, Kentucky," and "Plan of the Great Cave in Warren County, Kentucky," *Worcester Spy*, in *The Monthly Magazine*, 41 (281): 286-288, April 1816.

White, Wayne R., 1967, Speleogeorgraphy of Great Saltpetre Cave. *NSS News*, 25 (9): 169-174.

White, Wayne R., n.d., The Speleogeography of Great Saltpetre Cave. Typewritten, 14 p.

Wood, John S., 1841, Mammoth Cave of Kentucky. *The American Magazine and Repository of Useful Literature*, 1 (3): 86-90.

CHAPTER THREE REFERENCES

Anonymous, 1812, *Wilson's Knoxville Gazette*, March 16, 1812. In: Street and Green, 1984. The Historical Seismicity of Central United States: 1811-1928. Typewritten, University of Kentucky, p. A71.

Anonymous, 1816, "Account of the Mammoth Cave." *Hallowell Gazette*, Maine, 3: 1, September 4, 1816.

Binkerd, A. D., 1869, *The Mammoth Cave and its Denizens: A Complete Descriptive Guide*. Robert Clarke & Co., Cincinnati.

Bird, Robert Montgomery, 1837, "The Mammoth Cave of Kentucky." *The Am. Monthly Magazine*, n.s., 2: 426-438, 525-546.

Borresen, Thor, 1942, Report on the Condition of the Leaching Vats, Saltpeter Works, Mammoth Cave National Park, Kentucky. Typewritten, January 14, 1942.

Brooks, Jared, 1818, Appendix. In: Henry McMurtrie, *Sketches of Louisville*. S. Penn Jr., Louisville, Kentucky.

Brumbaugh, David S., 1999, *Earthquakes Science and Society*. Prentice Hall, New Jersey.

De Boer, Jelle Zeilinga and Donald Theodore Sanders, 2005, *Earthquakes in Human History*. Princeton University Press.

Du Pont, Eleuthère Irénée, 1829, Unpublished letter to Colonel George Bomford, dated November 17, 1829. Hagley Museum and Library, Wilmington Delaware, O.S.O.R. Letter Book, 1829-1831, p. 36-44.

Farnham, John H., 1820, Extract of a letter from John H. Farnham, Esq. a Member of the American Antiquarian Society, describing the Mammoth Cave, in Kentucky. *Archaeologia Americana, Transactions and Collections of the American Antiquarian Society*, 1: 355-361.

Fuller, Myron L., 1912, The New Madrid Earthquake. *U. S. Geol. Sur.*, Bull. 494.

George, Angelo I., 1988, Pre-1815 Demise of the Domestic Saltpeter Industry Kentucky. *Jour. Spelean. Hist.*, 22 (2): 15-20.

George, Angelo I., 1989, Rotunda V-Vat Complex, Mammoth Cave, Kentucky. *CRF Annual Report, 1988*, 74-76.

George, Angelo I., 1990, Effects of the New Madrid Earthquake (1811-1812) Damage to the Mammoth Cave Saltpeter Works, Kentucky. *Jour. Spelean Hist.*, 24 (1): 10-12.

George, Angelo I., 2001a, *The Saltpeter Empires of Great Saltpetre Cave and Mammoth Cave*. H.M.I. Press, Louisville, KY.

George, Angelo I., 2001b, *Outer Door to the Auger Hole ... and Beyond, the Exploration of Wyandotte Cave*. H.M.I. Press, Louisville, KY.

George, Angelo I.; and Gary A. O'Dell, 1992, The Saltpeter Works at Mammoth Cave and the New Madrid Earthquakes. *The Filson Club History Quarterly*, 66 (1): 5-22.

Hamilton, Robert M; and Arch C. Johnston, editors, 1990, Tecumseh's Prophecy: Preparing for the Next New Madrid Earthquake. *U. S. Geol. Sur., Circ.* 1066.

Lee, Edmund F., 1835, *Notes on the Mammoth Cave, to Accompany a Map*. Printed by James & Gazlay, Cincinnati.

McCall, Archibald, 1812, Unpublished letter to E. I. du Pont, dated March 10, 1812. Longwood Manuscripts (LMSS), Group 5, Series A, Box 9, Hagley Museum and Library, Wilmington, Delaware.

Meriam, Ebenezer, 1844, "Mammoth Cave." *New York Municipal Gazette*, 1 (17): 317-324, 328.

Mullin, Marsha, 1986, Mammoth Cave Saltpetre Works. Historic American Engineering Record, National Park Service. Typewritten.

Olson, Colleen O'Connor, 2001, *Abs*. Nuclear Fallout Shelters in Mammoth Cave National Park. *Jour. Cave and Karst Studies*, 63 (3): 116.

Penick, James Lal Jr., 1981, *The New Madrid Earthquakes, Revised Edition*. University of Missouri Press.

Rauch, Alan F., 1997, EPOLLS: An Empirical Method for Predicting Surface Displacements Due to Liquefaction-Induced Lateral Spreading in Earthquakes. PhD Dissertation._http: // scholar. lib.vt.edu/theses/available/etd-219182249741411/.

Ridgely, Frederick, 1811, Unpublished letter and Eye-Draught Map of Mammoth Cave to Archibald McCall, dated June 11, 1811. W4-5033, Hagley Museum and Library, Wilmington, Delaware.

United States Geological Survey Staff, 1990, The Loma Prieta, California, Earthquake: An Anticipated Event. *Science*, 247: 286-293.

Ward, Nahum, 1816, "Kentucky Mammoth Cave." *Georgetown Patriot*, Georgetown, Kentucky, August 24, 1816, reprinted from the *National Intelligencer*, from a letter dated July 1816.

Wright, Charles W., 1860, *A Guide Manual to the Mammoth Cave*. Bradley & Gilbert, Louisville, Ky.

CHAPTER FOUR REFERENCES

Anonymous, 1847, "A Visit to the Mammoth Cave." *The American*

Eagle, 2 (3): 18-19.

Anonymous, 1853, "The Mammoth Cave," *New-York Weekly Tribune*, 12 (623): 3.

Anonymous, 1855, "Mammoth Cave, Kentucky." *Ballou's Pictorial Drawing Room Companion*, May 19, 1855, 309.

Anonymous, 1883, *Mammoth Cave America's Great Natural Wonder*. W. C. Comstock booklet.

Bailey, G. S., 1863, *The Great Caverns of Kentucky*. Church & Goodman, Chicago.

Binkerd, A. D., 1869, *The Mammoth Cave and its Denizens: A Complete Descriptive Guide*. Robert Clark & Co., Cincinnati.

Bird, Robert Montgomery, 1837, "The Mammoth Cave of Kentucky." *The Am. Monthly Magazine*, n.s., 2: 426-438, 525-546.

Borresen, Thor, 1942, Report on the Condition of the Leaching Vats, Saltpeter Works, Mammoth Cave National Park, Kentucky. Typewritten, January 14, 1942.

Brooks, Jared, 1818, Appendix. In: Henry McMurtrie, *Sketches of Louisville*. S. Penn Jr., Louisville, Kentucky.

Bullitt, Alexander, 1845, *Rambles in the Mammoth Cave*. Morton & Griswold, Louisville, KY.

Crothers, George M., 1996, Archaeological Testing of Houchins' Narrows, Rotunda, Broadway, and Audubon Ave. in Mammoth Cave, Kentucky. Typewritten report prepared for Mammoth Cave National Park. In Mammoth Cave office files.

De Paepe, Duane, 1986, *Gunpowder from Mammoth Cave*. Cave Pearl Press, Hays, Kansas.

Driscoll, Fletcher G., 1986, *Groundwater and Wells*. Johnson Division, St. Paul, Minnesota.

Eubanks, Bernard M., 1971, *This is a Story of the Pump and its Relatives*. Salem, Oregon.

Eubanks, Bernard M., 1972, A Pictorial History of the Hand Pump. *Water Well Jour.*, July, 44-47.

Farnham, John H., 1820, Extract of a letter from John H. Farnham, Esq. a Member of the American Antiquarian Society, describing the Mammoth Cave, in Kentucky. *Archaeologia Americana, Transactions and Collections of the American Antiquarian Society*, 1: 355-361.

Faust, Burton, 1967, *Saltpetre Mining in Mammoth Cave, Ky.* The Filson Club.

Ganter and Darnall, 1889a, Water Pipes of 1812. Photograph Card of Mammoth Cave.

Ganter and Darnall, 1889b, Salt Peter Vats of 1812. Photograph Card of Mammoth Cave.

George, Angelo I., 1989, Rotunda V-Vat Complex, Mammoth Cave, Kentucky. *CRF Annual Report, 1988*, 74-76.

George, Angelo I., 1990, Effects of the New Madrid Earthquake (1811-1812) Damage to the Mammoth Cave Saltpeter Works, Kentucky. *Jour. Spelean Hist.*, 24 (1): 10-12.

George, Angelo I., 2001a, *The Saltpeter Empires of Great Saltpetre Cave and Mammoth Cave.* H.M.I. Press, Louisville, KY.

George, Angelo I., 2001b, *Outer Door to the Auger Hole ... and Beyond, the Exploration of Wyandotte Cave.* H.M.I. Press, Louisville, KY.

George, Angelo I.; and Gary A. O'Dell, 1992, The Saltpeter Works at Mammoth Cave and the New Madrid Earthquakes. *The Filson Club History Quarterly*, 66 (1): 5-22.

Helweg, Otto J.; Verne H. Scott; and Joseph C. Scalmanini, 1983, *Improving Well and Pump Efficiency.* American Water Works Association.

Hill, Carol A.; and Duane De Paepe, 1979, Saltpeter Mining in Kentucky Caves. *The Register of the Kentucky Historical Society*, 77 (4): 247-262.

Hovey, Horace C., 1882, *Celebrated American Caverns.* Robert Clarke & Co., Cincinnati, Ohio.

Hovey, Horace C.; and Richard E. Call, 1897, *Mammoth Cave of Kentucky.* John P. Morton and Company, Louisville, Ky.

Kite, Thomas, 1847, Journal of a trip through Kentucky and visit to Mammoth Cave May and June, 1847. Unpublished typewritten manuscript, Kentucky Library and Museum, Western Kentucky University.

Leavy, William. A., 1943, A Memoir of Lexington and its Vicinity. *Register Kentucky Historical Soc.*, 41: (137): 310-346.

Lee, Edmund F., 1835, *Notes on the Mammoth Cave, to Accompany a Map*. Printed by James & Gazlay, Cincinnati.

McCall, Archibald, 1812, Unpublished letter to E. I. du Pont, dated March 10, 1812. Longwood Manuscripts (LMSS), Group 5, Series A, Box 9, Hagley Museum and Library, Wilmington, Delaware.

McCall, Archibald, 1813, Unpublished letter to E. I. du Pont, dated April 27, 1813. Longwood Manuscripts (LMSS), Group 5, Series A, Box 9, Hagley Museum and Library, Wilmington, Delaware.

Martin, Horace, 1851, *Pictorial Guide to the Mammoth Cave*. Stringer & Townsend, New York.

Marty, n.d., The History of Hoose, Hause, Hoase or Hose? http: // www. firefighterrealstories.com/hose.html.

Meriam, Ebenezer, 1844, "Mammoth Cave." *New York Municipal Gazette*, 1 (17): 317-324, 328.

Mullin, Marsha, 1986, Mammoth Cave Saltpetre Works. Historic American Engineering Record, National Park Service. Type-written.

Parker, Garald G., 1976, Early Stages of Hydrogeology in the United States. *Two-Hundred Years of Hydrogeology in the United States*. National Water Well Association, 6-29.

Pruse, Dorothy, 1973, A History of Pipe. *Water Well Journal*, October.

Sarton, George, 1959, *A History of Science*. Science Editions, John Wiley & Sons, Inc., New York.

Schmitzer, Jeanne C., 1993, The Sable Guides of Mammoth Cave. *The Filson Club History Quarterly*, 67 (2): 240-258.

Staples, Charles R., 1939, *The History of Pioneer Lexington (Kentucky) 1779-1806*. Lexington, Kentucky.

Thomas, Samuel W., E. H. Conner and Harold Meloy, 1970, A History of Mammoth Cave, Emphasizing Tourist Development and Medical Experimentation Under Dr. John Croghan. *The Register of the Ky. Hist. Soc.*, 68 (4): 319-340.

Usher, Abbott Payson, 1988, *A History of Mechanical Inventions*. Dover Publications, Inc., New York. Revised from 1954 edition.

Wood, John S., 1841, "Mammoth Cave of Kentucky." *The American Magazine and Repository of Useful Literature*, 1 (3): 86-90.

CHAPTER FIVE REFERENCES

Anonymous, 1812, "To Be Sold For One Half Its Value A Salt-Petre Cave." *American Statesman*, December 12, 1812.

Arnow, Harriette Simpson, 1984, *Flowering of the Cumberland*. The University Press of Kentucky.

Blane, William N., 1824, *An Excursion Through the United States and Canada During the Years 1822-1824*. Baldwin, Cradock, and Joy, London.

Brown, Samuel, 1809, A Description of a Cave on Crooked Creek, with Remarks and Observations on Nitre and Gun-Powder. *Trans Am. Philo. Soc.*, VI: 235-247.

Buffon, LeClerc de, 1798, *Histoire Naturelle Générale et Particuliére*. De L'Imprimerie de F. Dufart, Paris, 10.

Coy, Fred E.; Tom Fuller, Larry Meadows, Don Fig, Jim Rosene and Garland Dever, 1984, Samuel Brown on Saltpeter from Sandstone Cliffs in Eastern Kentucky. *Tennessee Anthropologist*, 9 (1): 48-65.

Craig, B. F., 1862, Report on Nitrification. *Ann. Rpt. Board of Regents Smithsonian Institution*, 305-318.

De Paepe, Duane, 1979, The Legend of the Mammoth-Dixon Cave Connection. *Cave Research Foundation 1979 Ann. Rpt.*, p. 61-62.

De Paepe, Duane, 1981, Saltpeter Mining Features and Techniques. *NSS Bulletin*, 43 (4): 103-105.

Des Jean, Tom, 1997, Niter Mining in the Area of the Big South Fork of the Cumberland River. *Tennessee Anthropologist*, 22 (2): 225-

239.

Diderot, Denis, 1790, Salpetrier. *Encyclopédie Methodique*, Chez Panckoucke. Libraire, Hotel de Thou, Paris, France.

Fig, Don; and Kary Knudsen, 1984, An Incipient Industry of the Red River Gorge, Kentucky. *Proc. of the Symposium on Ohio Valley Urban and Historic Archaeology*. 1: 667-673.

Ford, W. C., 1916, *Thomas Jefferson Correspondence, Printed from the originals in the Collection of William K. Bixby*, Boston.

George, Angelo I., 1985a, "Saltpeter Manufacturing at Breeding Saltpeter Cave, Adair County, Kentucky." *The Karst Window*, 21 (2): 10-11.

George, Angelo I., 1985b, "Saltpeter Caves of Cumberland County, Kentucky." *The Karst Window*, 21 (3): 4-6.

George, Angelo I., 1985c, "Edmonson County Saltpeter Sites." *The Karst Window*, 21 (5): 6-7.

George, Angelo I., 1985d, "Hatcher Saltpeter Cave, Hart County, Kentucky." *The Karst Window*, 21 (3): 16-17.

George, Angelo I., 1986a, Saltpeter and Gunpowder Manufacturing in Kentucky. *The Filson Club History Quarterly*, 60 (2): 189-217.

George, Angelo I., 1986b, Saltpeter Rock Mining Activity in Dixon Cave, Edmonson County, Kentucky. *Jour. Spelean Hist.*, 20 (4): 92-103.

George, Angelo I., 2001, *Outer Door to the Auger Hole ... and Beyond, the Exploration of Wyandotte Cave*. H.M.I. Press, Louisville, KY.

Graham, Thomas, 1827, An Account of M. Longchamp's *Theory of Nitrification*; with an Extension of it. *The Philosophical Magazine or Annals of Chemistry, Mathematics, Astronomy, Natural History, and General Science*, 1: 172-180.

Hill, Carol A., 1981a, Origin of Cave Saltpeter. *NSS Bulletin*, 43 (4): 110-126.

Hill, Carol A., 1981b, Origin of Cave Saltpeter. *Jour. Geol.*, 89: 252-259.

Hill, Carol A., 1984, Origin of Cave Nitrates. *The Cave Research Foun-*

dation 1974-1978 (Richard A. Watson, editor), p 171-172. Cave Books, St. Louis (originally published in *1976 CRF Annual Report*, p. 26-27.

Hill, Carol A.; and Duane De Paepe, 1979, Saltpeter Mining in Kentucky Caves. *The Register of the Kentucky Historical Society*, 77 (4): 247-262.

Hill, Carol A.; and Paolo Forti, 1986, *Cave Minerals of the World*. National Speleological Society, Huntsville, Alabama

Hoss, Elijah E., 1916, *David Morton: A Biography*. Board of Church Extension of the Methodist Episcopal Church, South, Louisville, Ky.

Hovey, Horace C., 1882, *Celebrated American Caverns*. Robert Clarke & Co., Cincinnati, Ohio.

Hovey, Horace C., 1897, Our Saltpeter Caves in Time of War. *Sci. Am.*, 76 (19): 291.

Hovey, Horace C., 1899, Saltpeter Caves of Kentucky. *Kentucky History and Genealogical Magazine*, 1 (1): 49-51.

Hovey, Horace C.; and Richard E. Call, 1897, *Mammoth Cave of Kentucky*. John P. Morton and Company, Louisville, Ky.

Jefferson, Thomas, 1813, Letter to Abel Morgan, dated January 11, 1813. In: W. C. Ford, editor, *Thomas Jefferson Correspondence, Printed from the originals in the Collection of William K. Bixby*, Boston, 1916.

Longchamp, M., 1826, Theorie Nouvelle de la Nitrification. *Annals de Chimie et de Physique*, 32: 5-29.

Maddox, D. T., 1813, Big Bone Cave. A description of the Big Bone Cave, in White county, Tennessee, by D. T. Maddox, esq. in a letter to a friend. *Niles, The Weekly Register, Supplement*, 5: 175-176.

Meriam, Ebenezer, 1844, "Mammoth Cave." *New York Municipal Gazette*, 1 (17): 317-324, 328.

Mitchell, Samuel, 1805, Caverns in Virginia, Kentucky and Tennessee Which Afford an In exhaustible Supply of Salt-Petre. *Medical Repository*, 9: 86.

Morgan, Abel, 1812, Letter to Thomas Jefferson, dated December 5, 1812. In: W. C. Ford, editor, *Thomas Jefferson Correspondence, Printed from the originals in the Collection of William K. Bixby*, Boston, 1916.

Palmer, Arthur N., 1975, A Guide to the Limestone Formations in Mammoth Cave National Park. Typewritten, Cave Research Foundation, Yellow Springs, Ohio.

Palmer, Arthur N., 1981, *A Geological Guide to Mammoth Cave National Park*. Zephyrus Press, Teaneck, NJ.

Pettijohn, F. J., 1957, *Sedimentary Rocks*. Harper & Row, Publishers.

Thomas, Samuel W., E. H. Conner and Harold Meloy, 1970, A History of Mammoth Cave, Emphasizing Tourist Development and Medical Experimentation Under Dr. John Croghan. *The Register of the Ky. Hist. Soc.*, 68 (4): 319-340.

Troost, G., 1835, On the Localities in Tennessee in Which Bones of the Gigantic Mastodon and Megalonyx Jeffersonii are Found. *Trans. Geol. Soc. Pennsylvania*, 1: 236-243.

Ward, Nahum, 1816, "Kentucky Mammoth Cave." *Georgetown Patriot*, Georgetown, Kentucky, August 24, 1816, reprinted from the *National Intelligencer*, from a letter dated July 1816.

Wilkins, Charles, 1820, Letter to Samuel M. Burnside. *Trans. Am. Antiquarian Soc.*, (1): 361-364.

CHAPTER SIX REFERENCES

Adams, C. F., 1969, *Memoirs of John Quincy Adams*. 5 : 128.

Anonymous, n.d., http:// www. mises.org/rothbard/panic1819.pdf.

Ashe, Thomas, 1808, *Travels in America Performed in 1806*. Reprinted for Wm. Sawyer & Co. by E. M. Blunt, State Street, Newburyport, London.

Betham-Edwards, 1900, *Arthur Young's Travels in France During the Years 1787, 1788, 1789*. George Bell and Sons, London.

Buffon, Georges LeClerc, 1798, *Histoire Naturelle, Générale et Particuliére*. De L'Imprimerie de F. Dufart, Paris 10.

Burke, Monte, 2005, "Mavericks: Cave Woman." *Forbes*, 175: 7: 64-66.

Diderot, Denis, 1790, Salpetrier. *Encyclopédie Methodique*. Chez Panckoucke. Libraire, Hotel de Thou, Paris, France.

Duc de La Rochefoucauld, 1786, Mémoire sur la Génération du Salpêtre Dans la Craie. *Recueil de Mémoires et de Pièces sur la fabrication du Salpêtre*; Savants Étrangers, 2: 610-624.

Duc de La Rochefoucauld; and Clouet, 1786, Mémoire sur des Terres Naturellement Salpêtrées Existant en France. *Recueil de Mémoires et de Pièces sur la fabrication du Salpêtre*; Savants Étrangers, 2.

Faust, Burton, 1967, *Saltpetre Mining in Mammoth Cave, KY*. The Filson Club.

Ford, Derek; and Paul Williams, 1989, *Karst Geomorphology and Hydrology*. Unwin Hyman, London.

Ford, Paul Leicester editor, 1892-1899, *The Writings of Thomas Jefferson*. Putnam's, New York, 3.

Freeze, R. Allen; and John A. Cherry, 1979, *Groundwater*. Prentice-Hall, Inc., New Jersey.

George, Angelo I., 1988, Pre-1815 Demise of the Domestic Saltpeter Industry, Kentucky. *Jour. Spelean Hist.*, 22 (2): 15-20.

George, Angelo I., 1994, *Mummies, Catacombs, and Mammoth Cave*. George Publishing Company.

George, Angelo I., 2001, *The Saltpeter Empires of Great Saltpetre Cave and Mammoth Cave*. H.M.I. Press, Louisville, KY.

Gale, Hoyt S., 1912, Nitrate Deposits. *U.S. Geol. Sur., Bull.* 523.

Gillispie, Charles Coulston, 1980, *Science and Polity in France at the End of the Old Regime*. Princeton University Press, Princeton, New Jersey.

Graham, Thomas, 1827, An Account of M. Longchamp's *Theory of Nitrification*; with an Extension of it. *The Philosophical Magazine or Annals of Chemistry, Mathematics, Astronomy, Natural History, and General Science*, 1: 172-180.

Hamlin, L. Belle, 1910, Peyton Short. *Quarterly Publication of the Historical and Philosophical Society of Ohio*, 5 (1): 3-20.

Hersh, Charles K., 1968, Nitrogen. In: *The Encyclopedia of the Chemi-*

cal Elements, edited by Clifford A. Hampel, Reinhold Book Corp., 454-459.

Hess, W. H., 1900, The Origin of Nitrates in Caverns Earths. *Jour. Geol.*, 8: 129-134.

Horsman, Reginald, 1962, *The Causes of the War of 1812*. University of Pennsylvania Press, Philadelphia.

Leavy, William. A., 1942, A Memoir of Lexington and its Vicinity. *Register Kentucky Historical Soc.*, 40: (131): 107-267.

Lewis, Warren C., 1989, Some Historical Speculations on the Origin of Saltpeter. *The NSS Bull*, 51: 66-70.

Meriam, Ebenezer, 1844, "Mammoth Cave." *New York Municipal Gazette*, 1 (17): 317-324, 328.

Nichols, H. W., 1901, Nitrates in Cave Earths. *Jour. Geol.*, 9: 236-243.

Northup, Diana E.; and Kathleen H. Lavoie, 2004, Microorganisms in Cave. In: *Encyclopedia of Caves and Karst Science*, edited by John Gunn; Fitzroy Dearborn, New York, London, 506-509.

O'Dell, Gary A., 1995, Saltpeter Manufacturing and Marketing and its Relation to the Gunpowder Industry in Kentucky During the Nineteenth Century. In: *Historical Archaeology in Kentucky*. Edited by Kim A. McBride, W. Stephen McBride, and David Pollack. Kentucky Heritage Council, Frankfort, 67-105.

Owen, David Dale, 1856, *Report of the Geological Survey in Kentucky*. A. G. Hodges, State Printer.

Phillips, William, 1823, *An Elementary Introduction to the Knowledge of Mineralogy*; 3d edition.

Rice, Howard C. Jr., 1976, *Thomas Jefferson's Paris*. Princeton University Press, Princeton, New Jersey.

Rice, James H., undated letter, in the Draper Manuscripts 2 O 30 ff, Wisconsin Historical Society, Madison, Wisconsin.

Ridgely, Frederick, 1811, Unpublished letter and Eye-Draught Map of Mammoth Cave to Archibald McCall, dated June 11, 1811. W4-5033, Hagley Museum and Library, Wilmington, Delaware.

Shackleford, George Green, 1993, *Jefferson's Adoptive Son – The Life of William Short 1759-1848*, The University Press of Kentucky.

Short, C. W.; and Mary Churchill Richardson, 1879, *A Chronological Record of the Families of Charles Wilkins Short and Mary Henry Churchill*. Typewritten copy, Louisville Free Public Library.

Sneed, Joel M., 1986, "Investigations Short Cave Kentucky." *NSS News*, 44 (2): 33-36.

Wainscott, B., 1974, "Short Cave." *Kentucky Underground*, 3 (3): 44-45.

Ward, Nahum, 1816, "Wonders of Nature." *Kentucky Gazette*, September 9, 1816, n.s., 2 (37): 2.

Ward, Samuel, 1937, William Short. *Tyler's Quarterly Historical and Genealogical Magazine*, 18 (3): 132-140.

White, William B., 1976, Cave Minerals and Speleothems. In: *The Science of Speleology*, edited by T. D. Ford and C. H. D. Cullingford, Academic Press.

Wilkins, Charles, 1820, Letter dated October 2, 1817 to Samuel Burnside. *Trans. and Collections of Am. Antiquarian Soc.*; 1: 363-364.

CHAPTER SEVEN REFERENCES

Anonymous, 1810, "The Subterranean Voyage, or the Mammoth Cave, Partially Explored." *The Enquirer*, Richmond, Virginia, 6 (109), April 20, 1810.

Anonymous, 1812, "To Be Sold For One Half Its Value A Salt-Petre Cave." *American Statesman*, December 12, 1812.

Anonymous, 1816, "Account of the Mammoth Cave." *Hallowell Gazette*, Maine, 3: 1, September 4, 1816.

Bidermann, Anthony, 1815, Letter to E. I. du Pont, dated Pittsburgh, June 16, 1815. In: B. G. du Pont, 1923. *Life of Eleuthère Irénée du Pont from Contemporary Correspondences*. University of Delaware Press.

Bird, Robert Montgomery, 1837, "The Mammoth Cave of Kentucky." *The Am. Monthly Magazine*, n.s., 2: 426-438, 525-546.

Blane, William N., 1824, *An Excursion Through the United States and*

Canada During the Years 1822-1824. Baldwin, Cradock, and Joy, London.

Dutton, William S., 1942, *Du Pont One Hundred and Forty Years*. Charles Scribner's Sons, New York.

George, Angelo I., 1988, Pre-1815 Demise of the Domestic Saltpeter Industry Kentucky. *Jour. Spelean. Hist.*, 22 (2): 15-20.

George, Angelo I., 1994, *Mummies, Catacombs, and Mammoth Cave*. George Publishing Company.

George, Angelo I., 2001a, *The Saltpeter Empires of Great Saltpetre Cave and Mammoth Cave*. H.M.I. Press, Louisville, KY.

George, Angelo I., 2001b, *Outer Door to the Auger Hole ... and Beyond, the Exploration of Wyandotte Cave*. H.M.I. Press, Louisville, KY.

George, Angelo I.; and Gary A. O'Dell, 1992, The Saltpeter Works at Mammoth Cave and the New Madrid Earthquakes. *The Filson Club History Quarterly*, 66 (1): 5-22.

Gray, Laman, Sr., 1987, *The Life & Times of Ephraim McDowell*. R. V. Reed and Sons, Printers, Louisville, Kentucky.

Horsman, Reginald, 1962, *The Causes of the War of 1812*. University of Pennsylvania Press, Philadelphia.

Leavy, William. A., 1942, A Memoir of Lexington and its Vicinity. *Register Kentucky Historical Soc.*, 40 (133): 353-375.

McCall, Archibald, 1806, Unpublished letter to E. I du Pont, dated July 26, 1806. Accession 500, Series 1, Part 1, Box 249, Hagley Museum and Library, Wilmington, Delaware.

McCall, Archibald, 1808, Unpublished letter to E. I du Pont, dated November 14, 1808. Accession 500, Series 1, Part 1, Box 249, Hagley Museum and Library, Wilmington, Delaware.

O'Dell, Gary A., 1989, Bluegrass Powdermen: A Sketch of the Industry. *Register of the Kentucky Historical Society*, 87 (2): 99-117.

O'Dell, Gary A., 1990, The Trotter Family, Gunpowder, and Early Kentucky Entrepreneurship, 1784-1833. *Register of the Kentucky Historical Society*, 88 (4): 394-430.

O'Dell, Gary A., 1995, Saltpeter Manufacturing and Marketing and its Relation to the Gunpowder Industry in Kentucky During the Nineteenth Century. In: *Historical Archaeology in Kentucky*, edited by Kim A. McBride, W. Stephen McBride, and David Pollack. Kentucky Heritage Council, Frankfort, 67-105.

Peter, Robert, 1882, *History of Fayette County, Kentucky, Blue Grass Region*. O. L. Baskin & Co., Historical Publishers, Chicago.

Rice & Sterrett vs Perkins & Perkins, 1814, Barren County (Kentucky) Circuit Court, Equity Judgment No. 45, 1814.

Short, C. W.; and Mary Churchill Richardson, 1879, *A Chronological Record of the Families of Charles Wilkins Short and Mary Henry Churchill*. Typewritten copy, Louisville Free Public Library.

Staples, Charles R., 1939, *The History of Pioneer Lexington (Kentucky) 1779-1806*. Lexington, Kentucky.

Walker, Juliet E. K., 1983, *Free Frank: A Black Pioneer on the Antebellum Frontier*. The University Press of Kentucky.

Ward, Nahum, 1816, "Wonders of Nature." *Kentucky Gazette*, Lexington, Kentucky, n.s., 2 (37), 2, September 9, 1816.

Wilkins, Charles, 1809, Unpublished letter to E. I. du Pont, dated November 27, 1809. Longwood Manuscripts Group 5, Box 6, Hagley Museum and Library, Wilmington, Delaware.

Wilkins, Charles, 1820, Letter from Charles Wilkins, Esq. A Member of the American Antiquarian Society, to Samuel M. Burnside, Esq, letter dated October 2, 1817, *Archaeologia Americana, Transactions and Collections of the American Antiquarian Society*, 1: 361-364.

Imbricate half round log filter system in Hopper No 2, Rotunda, Mammoth Cave. Diana Emerson George, photograph.

Giant size imbricate half round log filter system in a hopper located in the entrance vestibule, Beckner Saltpeter Cave. Diana Emerson George photograph.

The author contemplates a cairn in Blue Spring Branch of Mammoth Cave. Diana Emerson George photograph.